# The Advanced Programmer's Guide to AIX 3.x

## Titles in the IBM McGraw-Hill Series

Details of these titles in the series are available from:

The Product Manager, Professional Books
McGraw-Hill Book Company Europe
Shoppenhangers Road, Maidenhead, Berkshire, SL6 2QL
Telephone: 0628 23432 Fax: 0628 770224

Phil Colledge

# The Advanced Programmer's Guide to AIX 3.x

McGRAW-HILL BOOK COMPANY

**London** · New York · St Louis · San Francisco · Auckland
Bogotá · Caracas · Lisbon · Madrid · Mexico · Milan
Montreal · New Delhi · Panama · Paris · San Juan · São Paulo
Singapore · Sydney · Tokyo · Toronto

Published by
McGRAW-HILL Book Company Europe
Shoppenhangers Road, Maidenhead, Berkshire, SL6 2QL, England
Tel 0628 23432; Fax 0628 770224

---

**British Library Cataloguing in Publication Data**

Colledge, Phil
   Advanced Programmer's Guide to AIX 3.x.—
   (IBM McGraw-Hill Series)
   I. Title   II. Series
   005.4

ISBN  0-07-707663-x

**Library of Congress Cataloging in Publication Data**

Colledge, Phil
   The advanced programmer's guide to AIX 3.x / Phil Colledge.
      p.   cm. — (The IBM McGraw-Hill series)
   Includes bibliographical references and index.
   ISBN  0-07-707663-X
1. Operating systems (Computers)   2. AIX (Computer file)   3. IBM RS/6000
Workstation—Programming.   I. Title.   II. Series.
QA76.76.O63C647   1944
005.4'469—dc20                                                    93-29674
                                                                      CIP

1234 CUP 97645

Typeset by Paston Press Ltd, Loddon, Norfolk
and printed and bound in Great Britain at the University Press, Cambridge

# Contents

# Foreword

## The IBM McGraw-Hill Series

IBM UK and McGraw-Hill Europe have worked together to publish this series of books about information technology and its use in business, industry and the public sector.

The series provides an up-to-date and authoritative insight into the wide range of products and services available, and offers strategic business advice. Some of the books have a technical bias, others are written from a broader business perspective. What they have in common is that their authors — some from IBM, some independent consultants — are experts in their field.

Apart from assisting where possible with the accuracy of the writing, IBM UK has not sought to inhibit the editorial freedom of the series, and therefore the views expressed in the books are those of the authors, and not necessarily those of IBM.

Where IBM has lent its expertise is in assisting McGraw-Hill to identify potential titles whose publication would help advance knowledge and increase awareness of computing topics. Hopefully these titles will also serve to widen the debate about the important information technology issues of today and of the future — such as open systems, networking and the use of technology to give companies a competitive edge in their market.

IBM UK is pleased to be associated with McGraw-Hill in this series.

Sir Anthony Cleaver
Chairman
IBM United Kingdom Limited

# Trademarks

**AIX, AIXwindows, PHIGS+, graPHIGS, POWER, SNA** are trademarks of International Business Machines Corporation.

**IEEE, POSIX** are trademarks of the Institute of Electrical and Electronics Engineers.

**ISO** is a trademark of International Organization for Standardization.

**Motif** is a trademark of Open Software Foundation.

**NCS** is a trademark of Apollo Computer Inc.

**NFS, Sun Microsystems** are trademarks of Sun Microsystems Inc.

**OSF, OSF/1, OSF/MOTIF** are trademarks of Open Software Foundation Inc.

**System V** is a trademark of UNIX Systems Laboratories Inc.

**UNIX, UNIX SVID** standards are trademarks of AT&T Corporation Inc.

**X Window System** is a trademark of Massachusetts Institute of Technology.

**X/Open** is a trademark of X/Open Company Ltd.

# Conventions

This book contains many examples of the use of commands and facilities of AIX version 3 and IBM RISC System/6000. The following table outlines the conventions that govern the use of such things as commands in relation to the examples and the use of a terminal attached to IBM RISC System/6000:

| Convention | Meaning |
| --- | --- |
| <F1> | Press the key within the angle brackets. In this case the *F1* function key. |
| <Ctrl-P> | Press the two keys within the angle brackets simultaneously, in this case the *Ctrl* and the *P* keys. |
| command<object> | Provide an instance of the object requested. For example, `ls-1<filename>` means that you should provide a filename when using the command. |
| $ 1s<br>alpha | Text printed in this font represents output from AIX version 3 or input to it. |

*To my grandfather Tom, who died before this book was published but will live in spirit, for ever within its pages*

# Preface

Before writing this book I had often wondered why all the books I ever read had very similar subject matter in the preface, usually with dedications and thanks to the author's spouse and family.

Until now, I had no idea how difficult it was to write an original preface.

During the course of writing this book, I often felt that I would never finish it; the task ahead of me seemed impossible. During these times I was reassured by the words of Archimedes:

> 'Give me a platform on which to place my fulcrum and I will move the world with my lever.'

Phil Colledge

# 1
# Introduction: IBM and open systems

The IBM Corporation has for many years been known for its mainframe computer technology, together with its proprietary operating system environments. Over the past 20 years it would be true to say that the mainframe and latterly the PC markets have been the lifeblood of the Corporation.

With this in mind, many people find it difficult to believe IBM's commitment to a concept known as 'Open systems', the aim of which is to produce an operating system environment on which applications may run totally independently of the hardware platform used. The reasons behind IBM's decision not only to take part in the project to create the world's first totally open system, but also to become a founder member of the Open Systems Foundation (OSF) are, in the author's opinion, open to speculation. The real reasons are known only to IBM itself. However, one thing is clear: IBM has contributed significantly to the development of the concept of open systems.

In 1986 IBM introduced its first commercial RISC (Reduced Instruction Set Computer), the IBM 6150 or RT as it was affectionately known within the corporation. This computer was revolutionary for its time. Not only was the processor radically different from anything IBM or anyone else had ever produced before, but the choice of operating system was an innovation for IBM. They chose to position the RT as a technical workstation, and in order to gain acceptance in the largest market for workstations at that time, namely the universities, the machine had to have an operating system which was compatible with the ever-popular UNIX. IBM, together with an initial source licence to UNIX System V, developed AIX 1.0, later to be revised to AIX 2.1. AIX (which stands for Advanced Interactive Executive) was even then a greatly enhanced version of UNIX, providing additional functionality that standard UNIX System V.x still does not provide today.

Sadly, the RT was not a blistering success for IBM. The reason for this is unclear; perhaps at the time the market did not believe IBM was really interested in an operating system like UNIX or even its own version, AIX. It is interesting to note, however, that the project that would eventually give the world the RISC System/6000 began in the same year as the announcement of the IBM 6150. At least inside IBM there was confidence in the future, with the corporation as a leader in the open systems market.

I remember a lecture given in London in the summer of 1988 by Art Goldburg, a senior IBM executive from the USA. He hinted at the possibility of a processor that could dispatch multiple instructions in one clock cycle. Two years later IBM announced the RISC System/6000 with its POWER architecture, which was capable of dispatching more than one instruction per clock cycle. Not content with this bombshell to its competitors, IBM announced AIX 3.1, its new version of UNIX to run on the RISC System/6000, with even more advanced features than ever before.

Despite their development of a new processor, a new machine architecture and a new enhanced operating system, there are still sceptical people who doubt IBM's commitment to open systems. AIX 3.x has been accepted as one of the base software technologies used by the Open Systems Foundation to develop its open operating system OSF/1. This I believe is proof, if more proof were required, of the commitment of IBM to 'open systems'.

## 1.1    AIX 3.x: the design philosophy

Back in 1986, when the development of AIX 3.x and the RISC System/6000 began, it was obvious at least to the marketing and technical experts within IBM that an operating system like UNIX would become the *de facto* standard within the mini and super-mini marketplace.

Although UNIX was at that time increasing in popularity not only within its traditional academic stronghold, but in business applications as well, IBM recognized that UNIX in its native state had few if any desirable characteristics. An operating system ought to be extendible, manageable, and able to take full advantage of the hardware on which it runs.

For IBM, the development of AIX 3.x had three major goals:

- To provide a UNIX-based operating system including the latest systems software technologies which will provide an operating system base for computing in the 1990s.
- To produce an operating system that can take advantage of the new RISC/ System 6000 architecture and hardware.
- To ensure that the system design allows the system to be portable to other architectures, such as the Intel 80386 and the IBM System/370-XA.

Finding the balance between the second and the third objectives was not easy. Balancing trade-offs must have been made between optimization of AIX 3.x to use the RISC System/6000 hardware efficiently and the need for hardware independence. Eventually good modular design of the operating system led to the hardware dependent components being isolated and kept to the minimum.

Early work used in the development of AIX 2.x on the IBM 6150 or RT was not wasted. In order to achieve the stated objectives, major changes had to be made to the UNIX operating system at the structural and kernel level. However, these changes had to be made in a way that did not compromise the semantics and interfaces of the operating system.

AIX 2.x also had major structural changes, but most of these changes were made outside the UNIX kernel itself and were placed in a lower operating system layer called the VRM (Virtual Resource Manager). The VRM was an operating system in its own right, which allowed a virtual machine environment to be created similar to that of the mainframe operating system VM. AIX 2.x was effectively a guest operating system on top of the VRM operating layer. This allowed for UNIX devices to be dynamically modified, and also allowed certain real-time functionality.

The base technology of the VRM system was used in the construction of the AIX 3.x kernel, but it is collapsed into a single operating system kernel.

AIX 3.x also incorporated other software technologies in order to meet the objectives stated including:

- Berkeley Software Distribution (BSD) 4.3
- X-Windows system (X11) from MIT
- Network computing system (NCS) from Apollo Inc.
- Network Filesystem (NFS) from SUN Microsystems
- UNIX System V.3 SVID standards

The final result of three years' work has been to produce an operating system which is truly revolutionary, enhancing UNIX and open systems but providing a standard base on which to build open applications.

## 1.2    AIX 3.x: the software technology

As a software engineering exercise, the development of AIX 3.x must rank among the most successful ever. However, such success does not come from chance and luck, but as a result of careful planning and well-defined goals. In order for IBM to achieve the objectives of AIX 3.x, a set of technical objectives was defined. These objectives form the basis for many of the revolutionary new features of AIX 3.x and its comparative openness as a UNIX variant.

### 1.2.1    *Adherence to standards within the UNIX environment*

It is quite plain that if you are intending to develop a UNIX-based operating system for the 1990s it must look a little like UNIX. UNIX has many faults, and even more standards or pseudo-standards which have become so widely accepted that not to include them in any new version of UNIX would be commercial suicide.

A commitment was made to provide compatibility with the main UNIX standards:

- IEEE POSIX standards
- AT&T System V interface standard (SVID)
- Berkeley Software Distribution standards (BSD 4.x)
- ANSI
- X/OPEN

It was often a difficult task to maintain compatibility with all the above standards within a single function definition, but wherever possible functions were combined to provide the functionality with a common system interface. AIX 3.x was designed to adhere to POSIX 1003.1, ANSI and X/OPEN standards, but including merged functionality for System V.x, AIX 2.x and BSD 4.3. AIX 3.x also gives a defined priority to the standards. In order to resolve any possible direct conflicts between them, the priority is that AIX 3.x will adhere first to the POSIX 1003.1 standard, followed by X/OPEN and ANSI, then System V.x SVID and BSD 4.x standards.

Most of the initial work on AIX 3.x was complete before the POSIX 1003.1 standard was available, but IBM personnel participating in the deliberations of the POSIX committees were thus in a position to anticipate the final state of the standard. However, where the eventual standard was somewhat different from the way AIX 3.x was designed, then IBM's commitment to conformity with POSIX will ensure that later versions of AIX 3.x are fully compliant.

### 1.2.2  Enhanced UNIX kernel

The standard UNIX kernel is small and inherently simple in design, which leads to several shortcomings. AIX 3.x has a kernel which is far from small and certainly not simple in design, but it provides additional features which would be impossible using the standard design.

The AIX 3.x kernel is the combination of the old VRM (Virtual Resource Manager) of AIX 2.x and a greatly enhanced UNIX kernel. These combine to provide the following additional features:

- Execution control, support for preemption and real-time support.
- Extended VMM (Virtual Memory Manager) with pageable kernel.
- Support for between 1 and 10 000 processes and the hardware configurations required to support that number of processes.

### 1.2.3  Enhanced reliability and availability

The requirement for systems to be more reliable and available, with a degree of fault tolerance, led to the inclusion of the LVM (Logical Volume Manager) and the concept of the JFS (Journalled File System).

The LVM was an extension of the earlier minidisk concept found in AIX 2.x, but this system was to allow dynamic reconfiguration of disk partitions and mirroring of disk data.

The JFS was a new concept; standard UNIX is inherently poor at system recovery after a system crash. Under standard UNIX the filesystems in any system that undergoes a sudden crash are very likely to be left in an internally inconsistent state. This situation is often corrected by the utility fsck, but this utility is rather limited in its abilities to recover partially damaged files or filesystems. Users often have to revert to backups. The JFS treats all critical changes made to the filesystem as a relational database system would treat data written to a database; each change is journalled so that a consistent state may be restored automatically during system start-up after a crash. This system is much more effective at recovering from system crashes than standard UNIX filesystems.

### 1.2.4 Enhanced system management, ease of use and security

In standard UNIX, there is no real standard for system management. Each manufacturer or vendor of UNIX provides their own tools to enable administration of the UNIX operating system. The real UNIX professional, however, often prefers the tried and trusted method of editing numerous flat files to achieve the same result. With AIX 3.x IBM introduced the concept of an Object Data Manager (ODM) and an Object Data Library (ODL). The ODM manages the complex relationships between objects within the system in an object orientated way. However, for the real die-hards, the flat files are still maintained. This enabled the development of the System Management Interface Tool (SMIT), which provides a common user interface to both the ODL and the standard UNIX flat files for administration.

Significant improvements were made to the structure of the AIX 3.x system to allow very easy installation, configuration and system management. All of these changes combine to make AIX 3.x an administrator's dream; tasks that would take hours under standard UNIX, can take a matter of minutes.

AIX 3.x also included some changes to comply with US Department of Defense security standards, providing Access Control Lists (ACL) to enhance the standard features of UNIX security. Trusted Computing Environment via the secure attention key was provided to ensure that secure communications are established between user and computer system.

### 1.2.5 Enhanced program development environment

For the programmer, AIX 3.x provides a greatly enhanced environment in which to develop applications. There is a set of common compilers and development tools which provide interlanguage calling, including the ability to detect interface mismatches between modules written in different languages. Often in the UNIX environment C compilers have a problem in achieving this objective, even when all of the modules are written in the same language.

IBM's compiler technology is widely accepted to be among the best in the world, if not the best. With the RISC System/6000 and AIX 3.x the compilers provide a level of optimization that allows the programmer to gain all of the benefits of the machine architecture without programming at the assembly level.

Other advanced program management facilities are provided in the form of:

- **Shared library support**   This allows application code to share a single copy of a reentrant shared library and its code, significantly reducing the requirement for chip memory used by applications that take advantage of this technique.
- **Run-time and load-time linking**   This allows program and operating system code to be dynamically linked at load-time or run-time, thus providing a significant improvement in the overall management of program development. It is this feature, coupled with extensions to the kernel, which allow AIX 3.x to dynamically load device drivers and sub-systems. The AIX kernel itself is linked at load-time using these features.
- **Page-mapped loading of files**   This allows files or programs to be page-mapped and loaded by the memory management system when required. This provides AIX 3.x with the ability to load very large programs with relatively small chip memory capacity.

An added advantage with most of these new facilities is that there is no requirement to alter program code to take advantage of these features. It often requires only compiler and linker directives to enable the functionality.

## 1.2.6   Support for powerful sub-systems

The term 'sub-system' is typical of IBM, and probably originates in the mainframe computing arena. However, AIX 3.x does provide very powerful sub-systems.

For AIX 3.x, a sub-system is any logical unit of code, which may be dynamically configured and controlled outside the kernel, but in itself may act as a kernel extension. This is a relatively new concept to UNIX, but I suspect an old one for IBM. AIX 3.x provides sub-system type management of the following operating system features:

- **Communications sub-systems**   These sub-systems provide support for a wide range of communications protocols, including Transmission Control Protocol/Internet Protocol (TCP/IP), System Network Architecture (SNA), Open Systems Interconnection (OSI), X.25 and a host of others. There is little change from AIX 2.x, but the features have been greatly enhanced and are considerably more powerful and functional. These sub-systems allow the RISC System/6000 with AIX 3.x to be one of the most communicative UNIX minis in the world.

- **Graphics sub-system** This system is built around a generic display sub-system, which enables AIX 3.x to accommodate almost any presentation system. AIX 3.x supports a wide variety of display systems, including X-Windows (from MIT) as AIX-Windows. With this environment AIX provides OSF/Motif display systems. Also supported is the graPHIGS product which has been enhanced to a greater degree than the PHIGS+ system, and is fully integrated within the X-Windows facilities.
- **Relational database and transaction processing sub-system** The AIX environment provides the facilities for the development of a relational database sub-system. Often these systems are externally developed outside IBM by large software corporations such as Oracle, Ingress and Informix. However, there may be moves from IBM to release its own relational database system under AIX 3.x, running as a true sub-system within the AIX 3.x environment.

### 1.2.7 Transparent distributed computing

AIX 3.x goes a long way towards providing transparent distributed computing, a stated goal of open systems, with the support of systems like Network File System (NFS) from SUN Microsystems, Network Computing System (NCS) from Apollo and finally the X-Windows display environment. With these tools the developer can certainly provide a truly distributed environment with transparent interfaces between application in a heterogeneous computing environment. However, IBM's commitment to OSF and its development of OSF/1 will eventually provide the true distributed platform for UNIX-based applications. AIX 3.x and its successors will undoubtedly have a major role to play in the formation and development of the open operating system standards.

In summary, AIX 3.x is to UNIX what C++ is to C. It provides an environment in which applications may be written and ported with the minimum of effort from either a UNIX System V.x environment, a BSD 4.x environment or an AIX 2.x environment. The additional features added to AIX only alter its functionality and not its interface semantics, so AIX is most certainly not 'IBM's first open/proprietary system' as one cynic has been quoted as saying.

## 1.3    How to use this book

This book is written for the UNIX professional who wants to learn about AIX 3.x and how it resembles or differs from UNIX system V.x and BSD 4.x, as well as its unique features.

How one should use a book is largely a matter of personal preference. Before writing this book I spent many hours considering how I learn. I came quickly to the conclusion that endless hours of reading about theory are not helpful. I hope this book is balanced, introducing a little theory, then some practical implementation details with examples. Some exercises and questions are given in the Appendix. The book is not meant to be read from cover to cover without touching a keyboard, it is intended as a 'read and try it out' book.

I wish the potential readers of this book good luck on their adventure in the land of AIX 3.x. I hope they will find it as interesting and rewarding as I have.

# Part One
# The shell

# 2
# Shell programming

## 2.1   The shell: an introduction

Many AIX and UNIX users perceive the familiar dollar prompt of the Bourne or Korn shell to be 'the UNIX command prompt'. Like many other popular perceptions in the AIX and UNIX world, this is technically incorrect. The shell is for all practical purposes a convenient (or not so convenient) user interface to the real part of AIX, namely the 'kernel'.

There are many different shells that a user of AIX may wish to use on the RISC System/6000, but the three major shells provided are the Bourne shell, the Korn shell and, last but not least, the C shell. The default shell for the AIX 3.x user on the RISC System/6000 is the Korn shell. However, which shell a user should use is largely down to personal preference and to the degree of functionality required. In general terms, all three shells provide their users with the same generic set of services.

## 2.2   The command line

The shell takes a sequence of 'words' from the command line, each word separated from the previous word and the next by one or more delimiter characters. The shell interprets the first word it reads to be the name of the AIX command that the user requires to initiate, and all subsequent words as command line options to that command. Words are usually defined as being one or more characters from a set of characters that does not include delimiter characters.

The general syntax of a generic shell command line is outlined in Fig. 2.1. The syntax used here is as general as possible, to be applicable to all of the shells currently available. Now let us look at a few simple examples of AIX command lines. In the examples below, the delimiter characters are denoted by a space character.

```
$ ls -l -i fred.c
```

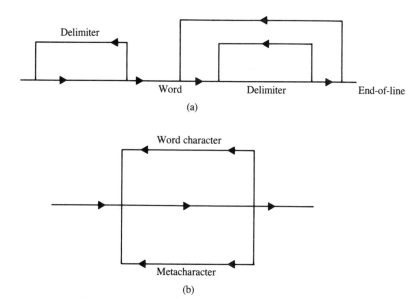

Figure 2.1(a–b). Generic shell syntax diagram. (*Continues*)
    (a) command line syntax.
    (b) command word syntax.

In the above example the first word is ls and the subsequent words are -l, -i and fred.c. As mentioned above, the shell by convention considers the first word on the command line to be the name of the command to initiate, in this case the AIX command ls, and all subsequent words as parameters to this command.

## 2.3    Metacharacters

Apart from blindly passing the command line options to the utility or command that the user has specified, the shell may if requested perform some translation or expansion of one or more of the command line options. As you can see from the syntax diagram in Fig. 2.1 a 'word' may contain zero, one or more metacharacters. These metacharacters have a special meaning for the shell, and are expanded by the shell before the word or words are passed as parameters to the utility.

    In order to expand metacharacters the shell will try to match any file(s) present in the specified directory path and expand the word containing the metacharacter into one or more filename(s) that satisfy the metacharacter sequence. If the shell cannot expand words containing metacharacters with filenames present in the specified directory path, the word containing the metacharacter(s) will be passed to the utility unchanged.

    The two most common metacharacters are * and ?. These are the 'wild card' metacharacters and will be expanded by the shell. The * metacharacter is taken to

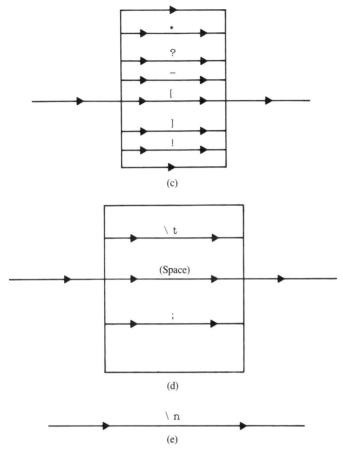

Figure 2.1(c–e). Generic shell syntax diagram. (*Concluded*)
(c) metacharacter syntax.
(d) delimiter syntax.
(e) line terminator syntax.

mean 'zero or more characters' and the ? metacharacter to be 'exactly one character'.

For example, assume we are currently at the Korn shell prompt in a directory containing the following files:

```
fred.c
jim.o
jim.c
jim
fred.o
fred
```

and at the command line we type

```
$ ls *.c
```

The shell would search the current directory (as no directory path was given) and expand `*.c` into two words, `fred.c` and `jim.c`. The command line would then become equivalent to

```
$ ls fred.c jim.c
```

The shell will effectively expand `*.c` to any filename that ends in `.c` with zero or more characters before it. We could of course have specified a directory path for the expansion, as follows:

```
$ ls /usr/bin/*.c
```

The shell would then (if possible) expand the `*.c` word from the directory `/usr/bin`.

The ? metacharacter is expanded by the shell in the same way as * but its criteria for expansion are different. The ? metacharacter requires any single character to be present in the position in the word where it is specified. For example,

```
$ ls f?e*
```

from the above directory would be expanded to

```
$ ls fred.c fred.o fred
```

In this instance the first character of the expanded word must be an f, followed by any unspecified character, then an e; the rest of the word is zero or more characters, specified by the *.

There are other metacharacters, apart from the * and ?. The most common are [, ], – and !. These four metacharacters are used in conjunction with each other to enable the shell user to specify a set of characters, any one of which may match a character at a specified position. This metacharacter sequence is similar to the ? metacharacter, but only a limited set of characters may match. For example, consider the command line

```
$ ls [fj]*.c
```

Here the sequence [fj] means 'a single character which must be "f" or "j"', so this command line is expanded to

```
$ ls fred.c jim.c
```

and the command line

```
$ ls [fj]*.[co]
```

is interpreted as any word starting with f or j with zero or more characters before a . followed by c or o. It is therefore expanded to

```
$ ls fred.c jim.c fred.o jim.o
```

In fact the metacharacter sequence [xy....z] can be used to limit the number of characters that match a single positional metacharacter substitution, and may be considered as a special case of the metacharacter ?.

Within the metacharacter sequence [xy....z] there are two further metacharacters which may be applied, the ! and the —. The ! metacharacter is functional only if it appears as the first character after the [ metacharacter, and it has the affect of logically negating the result of the set expression evaluation. For example,

```
$ ls [!fj]*.c
```

Here the shell would try to expand the word to any filename that did *not* begin with f or j and had zero or more characters before a .c sequence, and in our example above no matches would be found. Compare this example with the first example given of this type, and note the significant difference.

The final metacharacter which may be used within the [ ] sequence is —. This is used to signify a sequence of characters without being totally explicit. For example, you may wish to allow only words that begin with a letter to be matched. You can achieve this by using

```
$ ls [abcdefghijklmnopqrstuvwxyz]*
```

or

```
$ ls [a-z]*
```

The — will be substituted for all characters between ASCII code a and ASCII code z, in ascending order.

Metacharacters and their expansion by the shell can be a very powerful tool when used by the experienced programmer, but in the wrong hands they may result in disaster.

## 2.4    Quoting metacharacters

The shell will always expand metacharacters in words before passing any word as a parameter to a utility or command. This feature of the shell can at times be potentially dangerous. There is a mechanism by which the significance of any metacharacter can be 'switched off' so that the shell treats the metacharacter as if it were a normal character. This mechanism is known as 'quoting'. Metacharacters are said to be 'quoted' if they will not be expanded by the shell.

For example, consider the unfortunate user who has accidentally created a word-processor file with the name *.doc. This could easily happen because most commercial word processors in the AIX and UNIX world do not check for such a potentially dangerous choice of name.

Assume that this user has a directory where he or she keeps these files, and the contents of the directory are as follows:

```
letter.doc
accs.doc
mail.doc
*.doc
```

The user, now recognizing his or her mistake, may wish to use the AIX command rm (remove file) to remove the file *.doc from the directory. At the shell prompt the user may type

```
$ rm *.doc
```

At first sight this seems like the correct thing to do; after all, the command rm does just require the filename of any file you wish to remove, and *.doc is the filename. However, the shell will expand the word *.doc with the metacharacter * embedded in it to all filenames ending in the string .doc, so the command line is equivalent to

```
$ rm letter.doc accs.doc mail.doc *.doc
```

Because * in a filename is a valid character, the file *.doc will also match the metacharacter sequence *.doc. This will of course give our user a big shock when he or she finds that all of the files with names that end in the string .doc have been removed.

The solution to our user's problem is of course to instruct the shell not to interpret the * character in the sequence *.doc as a metacharacter, but to treat it as a literal *. There are three ways in which this can be achieved within the shell. The simplest way is to prefix any metacharacter with a \ character. This character instructs the shell to ignore the significance of the following character if it is a metacharacter, so the command line

```
$ rm \*.doc
```

would remove only the file *.doc because the significance of the * is negated by the \ character directly preceding it. The \ character only negates the significance of a single metacharacter, and must be repeated if more than one metacharacter is to be negated. For example, to remove a file with the name *C?.doc the following sequence would be required:

```
$ rm \*C\?.doc
```

with one \ for the * and one for the ?.

Another example of a potentially dangerous file, or at least one which is inconvenient to remove, is one with the name \*.doc. You may be tempted to try to remove it with the command

```
$ rm \*.doc
```

However, this will try to remove a file with the literal name *.doc and not \*.doc, the \ character serving only to negate the significance of the * metacharacter. In order to place a literal \ character next to a metacharacter we need to double the \ character, so the correct way to delete such a file is

```
$ rm \\*.doc
```

As you can see, using the \ character to 'quote' metacharacters can be a little confusing at times, so the shell provides two other ways of doing it. The first way is to surround the word or words containing metacharacters with ' (a forward single quote character, ASCII 39). Any metacharacter(s) between the first ' character and the next will be treated as literal characters and not metacharacters. An alternative way to remove the \*.doc file is thus

```
$ rm '\*.doc'
```

In this case, because of the single quotes the word \*.doc will not be expanded. The file \*.doc will be removed, but not the file *.doc.

The second method of quoting whole words is similar. Certain metacharacters are still expanded within the quoted word, but *, ?, [ ], ! and − are not expanded. This method requires the word(s) to be surrounded by " (double quotes, ASCII 34) and between one double quote and the next only selected metacharacters are expanded. Then we could have removed the file \*.doc with the command

```
$ rm "\*.doc"
```

## 2.5    Environment variables

For each process AIX creates an environment which consists of one or more environment variables. These variables are used to pass information to the process that it may require. The shell, like any other process, has a set of environment variables initiated for it before it is executed by its parent process. Environment variables can have any name you choose, and there are few restrictions on their length, but a good guide is always to start the name with a letter and to restrict its length to less than 80 characters. By convention these names are usually given in upper case. Some common shell environment variables are

```
PATH
PS1
PS2
CDPATH
LOGNAME
```

In order to assign a value to an environment variable, the variable name is used on the left-hand side of an expression with an = sign between it and the value to be assigned on the right-hand side. For example to assign the word hello > to the PS1 environment variable we simply type

```
$ PS1="hello >"
```

Note that in this case the double quotes are necessary, so that a word may contain a space character. For example, the command

```
$ PS1=hello >
```

would assign only hello to PS1 and the shell would complain about the > character because unless it is quoted it too is a metacharacter.

The shell is often very sensitive about spaces when it comes to assigning shell variables. No space is permitted between the variable name and the = sign, or between the = sign and the value of the expression to be assigned. For example, most shells will complain about the command:

```
$ PS1 = "hello >"
```

In order to create a new shell environment variable you simply use its name in an expression, and from then on it is known to the shell. For example, to create a variable called TODAY you could use the command

```
$ TODAY="Wednesday"
```

This would create the shell variable TODAY and assign it a value of Wednesday. This shell variable may then be reassigned with different values as many times as you wish, simply by using it in an expression.

Accessing the current value of a shell variable requires the use of yet another shell metacharacter, the dollar sign $. Whenever the shell sees a $ directly in front of a shell variable name it will expand the word to be 'the current value of' that shell variable name. The only exception to this is when this word appears between single forward quotes, and then no expansion is done. Within double quotes the value is expanded as normal.

Thus using the echo command, which displays a string to the STDOUT file, and with the command

```
$ echo $TODAY
```

the result would be

```
Wednesday
$
```

printed to the screen, whereas the command

```
$ echo '$TODAY'
```

would result in

```
$TODAY
$
```

being printed to the screen. This is obviously a significant difference in behaviour from the shell, and one that often mystifies many beginners to shell programming.

The values of shell variables may also be assigned to other shell variables in the way you may expect, for example

```
$ PS1=$TODAY
```

This will assign the value of the shell environment variable TODAY to the shell environment variable PS1.

## 2.6 Exported or not exported: that is the question

The shell inherited its standard set of environment variables from its parent process. However, these environment variables are nothing more than a copy of the set of environment variables that the parent either inherited from its own parent (i.e. the grandparent of the shell), or created itself. The important word here is 'copy': this is true of all parent/child relationships within the AIX and UNIX process world.

Does this have some implications for the child and the parent, you may ask. Are all environment variables known to the parent automatically copied to the children? The answer is no. Unless the environment variable is in AIX terminology 'exported', then a copy of it will not be given to any child process.

Assume we have a shell prompt and we arrange for the environment variable EDITOR to be set to a value of vi. We can do this with the command

```
$ EDITOR="vi"
```

Then using the shell we initiate another command which will attempt to access the value of this environment variable and print it to the screen. If this command is called showenv, then we can just type

```
$ showenv
```

and showenv may respond with

```
The value of EDITOR=
$
```

It may or may not surprise us to find that showenv believes that the EDITOR environment variable has no value, when if we use the shell echo command to echo the value of EDITOR we see

```
$ echo $EDITOR
vi
$
```

The reason for this is quite simply that the command showenv is running as a child of the shell. Because the environment variable EDITOR was not exported, it was therefore undefined for the command showenv. We can solve this problem quite simply by exporting our environment variable with the following command

```
$ export EDITOR
```

From then on the environment variable EDITOR will be exported to all sub-processes of the parent shell, their children and their children's children and so on. Thus after the above export command using the environment variable EDITOR, running the command showenv would result in

```
$ showenv
The value of EDITOR=vi
$
```

Another property of environment variables is that any changes made to a common environment variable in a sub-process will not be reflected in the parent processes environment, but will be reflected in the environment of any sub-process initiated by the process that made the change. Consider the following example. At the shell prompt we set an environment variable called NAME to have a value of fred, and export it with the commands

```
$ NAME="fred"
$ export NAME
$
```

Then from the shell prompt we initiate a copy of the shell:

```
$ /bin/sh
$
```

Now although we have our $ prompt back, in this case it is the prompt of the new shell running as a child to the old shell. If we now examine the contents of the environment variable NAME within the sub-shell, we see

```
$ echo $NAME
fred
$
```

as we would expect. If we now reassign our copy of the environment variable to have a value of jim and initiate yet another copy of the shell as a sub-shell of our sub-shell,

```
$ NAME="jim"
$ /bin/sh
$
```

again the $ prompt reappears, but this is the prompt of the grandchild of our original shell. If we examine the contents of its copy of the environment variable NAME,

```
$ echo $NAME
jim
$
```

as we would have expected the shell has a copy of its parent's environment at the instant *it* was initiated, together with any changes made to it. Thus NAME does not have a value of fred because this was changed by its parent to jim before the child process was initiated. If we were to return to the original shell from the grandchild shell, what would we see happen to the value of the environment variable NAME? To terminate a shell you could simply type

```
$ exit          /* at grandchild shell, exit and */
$               /* return to parent             */
$               /* at child shell               */
$ echo $NAME    /* check value of NAME, it still */
jim             /* has a value of "jim"          */
$
$ exit          /* exit to original shell        */
$
$ echo $NAME    /* check value of environment variable NAME */
fred            /* its original value of "fred"             */
$
```

The moral of this story is that it is pointless to make changes to environment variables in sub-processes and expect the changes to be reflected in the parent's environment.

## 2.7    Standard input, output and error files

Up to now we have assumed that all output from the shell and other AIX commands and utilities is directed to the user's terminal. This may or may not be so. Every time AIX initiates a command or utility, the shell itself may be included as an AIX utility; it opens three files for that process. These files have special names and special significance. The first file opened is assigned the 'file number' 0 and is called STDIN (standard input file). This file is attached by default to the user's input device, usually a terminal, and is the file from which the command expects to receive user input. The second file opened is assigned to the 'file number' 1, and is called STDOUT (standard output file). This file too is attached by default to the user's output device, again usually the terminal, and it is where the command will send all output for interaction with the user. The third file opened is called STDERR (standard error file) and is assigned to 'file number' 2. This file has the same default assignment as STDOUT, but is used only for sending specific error messages to the user from the command or utility. The primary reason for having a STDERR file is that error messages may be sent to a different output device from STDOUT, so as not to confuse users by mixing normal output with error messages.

Diagrammatically this can be represented as in Fig. 2.2.

## 2.8    Command substitution

The term 'command substitution' in AIX terminology means literally substituting the word or command between the command substitution characters with any output sent to STDOUT (the standard output file) by the command. In some shells the metacharacters used for command substitution are ' (backward single quote, ASCII 96) characters, and any word surrounded by these characters will be substituted. For example, the AIX pwd command prints to STDOUT the name of the current directory in which the shell is working, so if we type the command

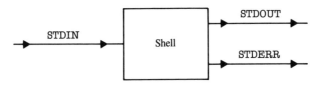

Figure 2.2.  STDOUT and STDERR.

```
$ pwd
/usr/bin
$
```

we may expect to see the directory /usr/bin printed on the screen if we are currently working in that directory. We could use command substitution to capture this printed value in an environment variable for later use perhaps. This could be done with the command

```
$ CURDIR=`pwd`
$
```

The result of this would be to run the command pwd but instead of its output going to STDOUT it would be substituted for the word 'pwd' and assigned to the environment variable CURDIR. If we happen to be currently working in the directory /usr/bin then the command

```
$ echo $CURDIR
/usr/bin
$
```

would print the current contents of the environment variable CURDIR, after the command substitution. In fact we can substitute any valid AIX command or command sequence within the command substitution characters, and the standard output will be returned. This is a very useful and powerful technique.

## 2.9    Input/output redirection

Whenever AIX initiates a command or utility it automatically opens the STDIN, STDOUT and STDERR files for that process and attaches them to their default devices. The shell has two further metacharacters that enable the user to reassign the STDOUT, STDIN or STDERR to any file or device the user wishes, without the command or utility being aware that its output or input device files has changed.

These metacharacters are > and <. When redirection of an output file is required then > is used, and when the redirection of an input file is required < is used.

Consider some examples. STDOUT is assigned the file number 1 by AIX, so if we wish to redirect STDOUT for the command ls to a file in our current directory called fred, we can type

```
$ ls 1> fred
$
```

This tells the shell to attach file number 1 for the process ls to a file called fred in the current directory, and not to its normal default, the user's terminal. The file fred will be created if it does not already exist. In this example the shell on recognizing the metacharacter > will assume the user wishes to redirect the STDOUT file by default, so in this case it is not necessary to specify the file number. For example, the command

```
$ ls > fred
$
```

will also redirect STDOUT to a file called fred. A word of warning is in order here: all shells are sensitive about spaces. For example with the command

```
$ ls 1 > fred
$
```

all the shells will simply send nothing to the file fred and report to STDERR that the file 1 is not found, because of the space between the number and the > metacharacter.

We could have redirected STDERR, which is file number 2, with this command, but in this case the file number is mandatory to instruct the shell to redirect STDERR and not STDOUT by default. The command

```
$ ls 2> errors
$
```

will send all output sent to STDERR by ls to a file called errors. When the metacharacter > is used to redirect the output of a command or utility to a file, the file will automatically be created or recreated, thus making its size zero when the redirection begins. This may not be desirable if you wish to redirect the outputs of several commands to the same file and accumulate the output results, so if the file exits you may use the following to append the redirected output to the end of the file:

```
$ ls >> fred
$
```

Again note the spaces; the two > characters must *not* be separated.

The STDIN file may also be redirected from any file or device, simply by using the < metacharacter. For example, the command

```
$ /bin/sh < commands
$
```

will initiate a new shell /bin/sh and redirect its STDIN file from a file in the current directory called commands. In this example the shell will not become interactive with the user, it will simply read the lines of text from the file commands and execute them (if possible). One important point to make is that when the shell finds the end-of-file (EOF) it will terminate, just as it would if the user typed ⟨CTRL-D⟩, or the internal command `exit`.

Any of the standard files STDERR, STDOUT and STDIN may also be redirected to each other. For example, the command

```
$ ls -l 2>&1
$
```

redirects the STDERR file (file number 2) to the STDOUT file (file number 1). Note the & symbol before the 1; this serves the purpose of instructing the shell that you wish to redirect to a file *numbered* 1 as opposed to a file *called* 1. The command

```
$ ls -l 2>1
$
```

will redirect STDERR to a file in the current directory called 1, not to STDOUT as was intended. You may even redirect STDOUT to STDIN, but why would you want to? Consider the following silly example:

```
$ pg 1>&0
$
```

This would result in a rather unproductive pg command. The command instructs the shell to redirect pg STDOUT to its STDIN, and as it takes its input from STDIN and sends its output to STDOUT this is a 'catch 22' situation.

## 2.10 Interprocess pipes

As we have seen above all of the standard input/output files may be redirected, but the redirection is usually to another file or device. There is a mechanism for redirecting the standard files STDIN and STDOUT of one process to the STDOUT and STDIN of another process. This mechanism is called 'interprocess pipes', or 'pipe' for short. An interprocess pipe is a notional file which has FIFO (first-in first-out) properties. The shell using the metacharacter | or ^ will attach the STDOUT file of the process on the left-hand side of the pipe symbol to the STDIN of the process on the right-hand side of the symbol, via this notional file called a pipe. For example, we may use the AIX command pg (pager) to paginate long outputs to the screen. The command

```
$ ls -Rl / * | pg
```

will send the standard output (STDOUT) of the command ls through a pipe to the

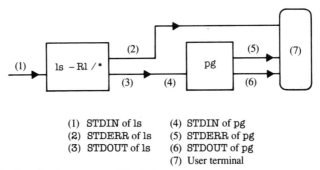

(1) STDIN of ls     (4) STDIN of pg
(2) STDERR of ls    (5) STDERR of pg
(3) STDOUT of ls    (6) STDOUT of pg
                                 (7) User terminal

Figure 2.3. Simple pipe standard file behaviour.

standard input (STDIN) of the command pg. Thus the full filesystem listing of the command ls -Rl / * will be paged one page at a time to the user's terminal.

This is represented diagrammatically in Fig. 2.3.

You will notice that the STDERR of the ls command is not redirected through the pipe; only the STDOUT is redirected. Thus because the commands in the AIX environment run asynchronously, both commands may send messages to the user's terminal through their STDERR files. It is also important to notice that the STDIN file of the ls command is still attached to the user's input device, but the STDIN to the pg command is attached to the STDOUT of the ls command. The implication of this is that only the ls command will respond to user interaction, i.e. an interrupt key. If the interrupt key is pressed the ls will respond and die, leaving our pg command at the other end of the pipe with no possibility of any input arriving and unable to accept an interrupt key from the user because its STDIN is redirected. AIX solves this problem by using a simple rule which states that if either process that is connected to another process via a pipe dies, then the other process will also be killed by AIX. Thus the interrupt signal received by ls will also indirectly cause pg to die.

There are few real restrictions on the number of processes that may take part in a pipe sequence, but these are system restrictions on the maximum number of processes a user session can initiate and these will of course limit the number of processes that may be placed in a pipe sequence. This restriction is often more than 30 processes, so it is not exceeded very often by most users!

For example, consider the command

```
$ ls -Rl / * | grep "fred" | pg
$
```

In this case the output of ls is piped to the input of grep, which searches the input for the string fred and sends any lines containing the string fred via its STDOUT to the input of pg.

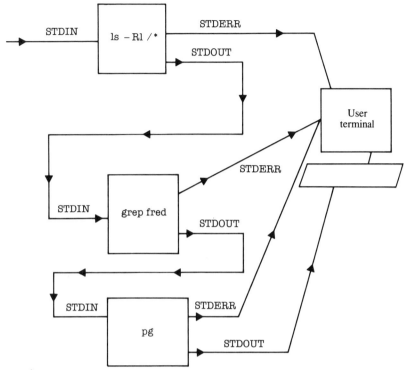

Figure 2.4. Multiple command pipe standard file behaviour.

This is shown diagrammatically in Fig. 2.4.

Notice again that the STDERR files of all the commands remain attached to the user's terminal and are not redirected. However, you may use redirection to combine STDERR and STDOUT together so that they are both redirected through the pipe.

## 2.11 Command groups

The shell also has two further metacharacters, ( and ). They are used to form what are known as command groups. A command group is one or more AIX commands or utilities which should be treated by the shell as if they form one single command. A command group begins with the ( character and ends with the ) character.

For example, consider a common problem. A user wishes to redirect the output of two commands to the same file. He or she may do so like this:

```
$ date > file
$ ls -l >> file
$
```

In this case both commands are initiated separately and output redirection is applied to send the output to the file called `file`. However, the user may wish to use a single redirection statement and redirect all of the output of both commands. Using the semicolon as a command separator, he or she may try to do so like this:

```
$ date ; ls -l > file
$
```

Although this command looks reasonable at first sight, the user would be

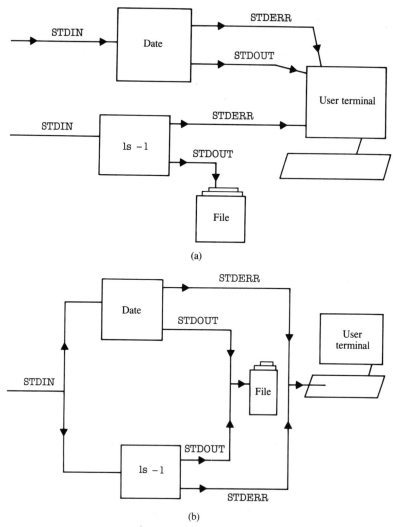

(a)

(b)

Figure 2.5.  Standard file redirection.
         (a)  multiple commands.
         (b)  command groups.

disappointed to find that the output from the command date would be sent to the user's terminal and the output of the command ls -l to the file called file. This is not what the user intended. The mistake is due to the shell's interpretation of the metacharacter >. The shell will only redirect the output of a single command immediately to the left of the >, and because the command date is a separate command its output will not be redirected.

Using command groups we may instruct the shell to consider one or more commands as one single command, i.e. combine their individual STDOUT, STDIN and STDERR files into single collective STDOUT, STDIN and STDERR files. For example,

```
$ (date ; ls -l) > file
$
```

will output both the output of date and ls -l to the file called file because it will treat the sequence date; ls -l as one single command.

This is shown diagrammatically in Fig. 2.5. The command

```
$ date ; ls -l > file
```

is shown in Fig. 2.5(a), and the command

```
$ (date ; ls -l) > file
$
```

is shown in Fig. 2.5(b).

# 3
# The Bourne shell

The Bourne shell was the first standard shell released by AT&T with the early versions of UNIX. It is called after its author Steven Bourne, of AT&T's Bell Laboratories. The Bourne shell has become the *de facto* standard within the UNIX industry, and is often the first shell many UNIX newcomers encounter.

- **Bourne shell functionality**   /bin/bsh   Standard Bourne shell
- **Command line options**   /bin/bsh [-acefhiknrstuvx] [args]

## 3.1   Command line options and their function

*Option*                                                         *Function*

-a

Mark variables which are modified or created for export.

-c string

Read commands from string.

-e

Exit shell immediately if a command exits with a non-zero exit status.

-f

Disable filename generation.

-h

Locate and remember function commands as functions are defined.

-i

If flag is present the shell is interactive and TERMINATE, INTERRUPT and QUIT signals are ignored.

-k

All keyword arguments are placed in the environment for a command, not just those that precede the command name.

-n

Read commands but do not execute them.

`-r`

> The present shell is a restricted shell.

`-s`

> Read commands from STDIN.

`-t`

> Exit shell after reading and executing one command.

`-u`

> Treat unset variables as an error when substituting.

`-v`

> Print shell input lines as they are read.

`-x`

> Print commands and their arguments as they are executed.

## 3.2     Usage of command line options

### 3.2.1   /bin/bsh -a

The -a option causes all environment variables defined or modified within the current shell to be automatically exported. Consider the following example at the shell command line:

```
$ NFS="/usr/bin"
$ /bin/bsh
$ echo $NFS
/usr/bin
```

Within the child shell the environment variable NFS is defined because of the -a option on the command line of the parent. Without the -a option the value of the environment variable NFS would be unknown to the child shell unless it was explicitly exported.

### 3.2.2   /bin/bsh -c string

The -c option causes the shell to read its commands from the string specified and to terminate after all of the commands within the string are executed. Multiple commands may be given within the string, separated by command delimiters.
For example, consider

```
$ /bin/bsh -c "echo directory listing\\n ; ls -l ; echo \\ndone"
Directory listing
total 2
-rw-r--r-- 1 fred   staff     96 Sep 13  10:04  fred.c
-rw-r--r-- 2 fred   staff   1296 Sep 13  10:14  jim.c
done
$
```

In this example all three commands are executed, and then the shell terminates. Notice the use of the ; as a command delimiter and the requirement to double the \ character in order to insert a single literal \ in the string after command line parsing by the parent shell.

### 3.2.3   /bin/bsh −e

The −e option causes the shell to exit immediately when the return status of any command is non-zero. For example, the return status of a command that is not found is non-zero, so the shell will terminate with

```
$ lss -l
```

because the command lss is not found.

### 3.2.4   /bin/bsh −f

The −f option disables filename generation from any string containing metacharacters; the strings will be passed to the command unchanged.
   For example, with

```
$ echo *[abcd]*
*[abcd]*
$
```

no attempt will be made to satisfy the metacharacter sequence with filename(s) existing in the current directory.

### 3.2.5   /bin/bsh −k

The −k option instructs the shell to place all keyword arguments in the environment, not just those that are present before the command. For example, consider

```
  $ phil="hello"
$ echo fred=$phil bye
bye
$ echo $fred "---> " $phil
hello ---> hello
```

In this case the expression fred=$phil is evaluated and the assignment made to fred. However, without the −k option we would get

```
  $ phil="hello"
$ echo fred=$phil bye
fred=hello bye
$ echo $fred "---> " $phil
----> hello
  $
```

with the value of fred being undefined, because no assignment takes place without the -k option.

### 3.2.6  /bin/bsh −n

The -n option causes the shell to read commands but not execute them; this applies to external and internal commands alike. For example, with

```
  $ ls -l
$ echo hello
$
```

The only command the shell will execute in this mode is the terminate command via the end-of-file character. The exit command is also disabled.

### 3.2.7  /bin/bsh −r

The -r option causes the shell to be initiated in a restricted mode. The actions of the shell are identical to /bin/bsh alone, except that:

- changing directory via the cd command is restricted
- setting of the environment variable PATH is restricted
- specifying any command names containing /
- redirection of output (> and >>)

The above restrictions are applied after the .profile script has been interpreted. When a restricted shell, usually denoted by /bin/rsh executes a shell script /bin/rsh will invoke a full /bin/bsh to run the script. It is therefore possible to provide the end user with a limited shell but with shell procedures and scripts that can use the full power of the shell.

### 3.2.8  /bin/bsh −t

The -t option causes the shell to execute only one command then to exit. For example,

```
$ ls -l
total 2
-rw-r--r-- 1 fred   staff   96 Sep 13 10:04 fred.c
-rw-r--r-- 2 fred   staff 1296 Sep 13 10:14 jim.c
```

After executing the command ls -l the shell exits.

### 3.2.9 /bin/bsh −u

The -u option causes the shell to treat any substitution of an undefined environment variable as an error, instead of expanding it to a NULL string as is the case without the -u option. For example,

```
$ echo hello $phil
sh: unset variable phil
$
```

Whereas without the -u option

```
$ echo hello $phil
hello
$
```

### 3.2.10 /bin/bsh −v

The -v option causes the shell to print all lines input as they are read. For example,

```
$ ls -l
ls -l
total 2
-rw-r--r-- 1 fred   staff   96 Sep 13 10:04 fred.c
-rw-r--r-- 2 fred   staff 1296 Sep 13 10:14 jim.c
$
```

Notice the input line ls -l is printed before it is executed by the shell.

### 3.2.11 /bin/bsh −x

The -x option causes the shell to print the commands and their expanded arguments as they are executed. For example,

```
$ ls -l f*.c
+ ls -l fred.c
total 1
-rw-r--r-- 1 fred staff   96 Sep 13 10:04 fred.c
$
```

Notice that the fully expanded command line is printed with a + symbol in front of it.

## 3.3    Initialization scripts

If the shell is invoked through an exec() system call and the first character of the argument zero is a -, commands are initially read from /etc/profile and then from the file $HOME/.profile, if such files exist. Thereafter the commands are read from STDIN as is the case if the shell is invoked by /bin/bsh.

## 3.4    Quoting of metacharacters

Metacharacters within the Bourne shell are quoted in the manner described in the previous chapter.

## 3.5    Shell commands

### 3.5.1    *Simple commands*

A simple command is a sequence of words separated by command separator characters (see IFS environment variable, Section 2.4). The first word specifies the command to be executed and subsequent words are passed as arguments to the command, the command name being passed as argument zero. The exit status of a command, if it terminates normally, is returned to the calling process as the value of the simple command.If the command exits abnormally then the exit status returned to the shell is (octal) 200+status where status is the exit error status of the command. See Fig. 3.1.

```
$   ls -l fred.c
```

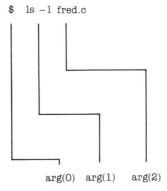

arg(0)   arg(1)     arg(2)

Figure 3.1.  Relationship between the command line arguments and the C variable.

### 3.5.2  *Pipeline*

A pipeline, or pipe for short, is a sequence of one or more commands separated by
a | (pipe character) or for historical compatibility by a ˆ character. The STDOUT
file of each command but the last is connected via a pipe to the STDIN of the next
command. Each command in a pipe sequence runs as a separate process, and the
calling shell waits for the last command to terminate before returning its exit status
as the exit status of the pipeline:

```
$ ls | grep fred.c | pg
```

### 3.5.3  *Command list*

A command list is one or more pipelines or simple commands separated by 'new-
line characters', ;, &, && or || and optionally terminated by ;, 'new-line
characters' or &. The symbols ; and & alone have equal operator precedence which
is lower than the operator precedence of && and ||. The symbols && and || have
equal operator precedence.

   Commands separated by ; will be executed sequentially from left to right, but
commands separated by & will execute the preceding command or pipeline
asynchronously—the shell does not wait for the command or pipeline to terminate
before continuing its operations.

   Consider the following examples:

- Commands are executed sequentially and the shell waits for the last command
  to terminate:

  ```
  $ ls ; df
  ```

- Commands are executed asynchronously and the shell does not wait for the
  last command to terminate:

  ```
  $ ls & df &
  ```

The symbol && causes the list of commands following it to be executed only if the
preceding pipeline or command returns a (zero) exit status. The symbol || causes
the list of commands following it to be executed only if the preceding pipeline or
command returns a (non-zero) exit status. For example, the && symbol may be
used as in

```
$ ls -l fred.c > /dev/null 2>/dev/null && echo "Found fred.c"
```

or the || symbol may be used as in

```
$ grep 'ˆFred' /etc/passwd || echo "No user Fred known to the system"
```

### 3.5.4 *Internal shell commands*

A command is either a simple command or an internal shell command, and unless stated otherwise the exit status of these internal shell commands is the exit status returned by the last simple command executed within that command. The internal shell commands are described in this section, with examples of their usage.

for *command*

```
for arg [ in word....]
   do
       list
   done
```

Each time a for command is executed, the environment variable, arg is set to the next word taken from the in word ... clause. The for command then executes the list between the do and the done, and this process is repeated until there are no more words in the in word list. If the in word list is omitted then the for command is executed once for each positional parameter that is set. (This is known as set positional parameter substitution.)

case *command*

```
case word in

[ pattern [ | pattern ] .. ) ... list ;;   ] ... esac
```

The case command executes the list associated with the first pattern that matches the word. The patterns may be any regular expression containing metacharacters.

if/else/elif *command*

```
if list
  then
        list [ elif list then list ] ...
                [ else list] fi
```

The list following the if is executed and the exit status examined. If the exit status is zero then the list following the first then is executed, otherwise the list following the elif is executed. If the exit status of this list is zero the list following the next then is executed, failing that the else is executed. If no elif term is present then the else, if present, will be executed. The exit status of the if command is the exit status of the last list executed, but, if no then or else list is executed then the exit status will be zero.

while *command*

```
while list
  do
        list
  done
```

The list of commands between the do and the done is repeatedly executed, while the exist status of the list of commands following the while is zero. If no commands are executed between do and the done then the exit status of the while command is zero, otherwise its exit status is the exit status of the last command executed within this list.

(list) *command*

This command executes the list in a sub-shell.

{ list ; } *command*

This command executes the list in the current shell.

*Shell functions*

```
name ()
  {
       list ;
  }
```

The above defines a shell function referenced by name. The body of the function is defined as a list of commands between the { (open curly bracket) and the } (close curly bracket).

*Shell comments*

Any word beginning with # will cause the word and all subsequent words up to a new-line character to be ignored.

*Command substitution*

The standard output (STDOUT) from the command enclosed inside a pair of ` (backward single quotes) may be used as part or all of a word. Any new-line characters in the STDOUT stream are removed.

*Parameter substitution*

The dollar sign ($) is used to introduce substitutable parameters. There are two types of parameters, positional and keyword. If the parameter is a digit, it is a positional parameter e.g. $0,$1...$9.

- *Positional parameters* may be assigned with the `set` command.
- *Keyword parameters*, also known as *environment variables* may be assigned by writing

```
name=value
```

There cannot be a function and an environment variable of the same name.

*Sequence*                 *Result after substitution*

`${parameter}`
> The value, if any, of the parameter is substituted. The { and } characters are required only if the parameter is followed by a non-white-space character, which should not be interpreted as part of the parameter's name.

`${parameter:-word}`
> If the parameter is set and is not null, its value is substituted for that of the expression, otherwise the value of the word provided is substituted.

`${parameter:=word}`
> If the parameter is not set or is null then the value of the parameter is set to the word provided, and then the value of the parameter is substituted. Positional parameters may not be assigned in this way.

`${parameter:?word}`
> If the parameter is set and not null then the parameter's value is substituted, otherwise the word provided is printed and the shell is exited. If no word is provided then the message `Parameter null or not set` is printed.

`${parameter:+word}`
> If the parameter is set and is not null then the word provided is substituted, otherwise nothing is substituted.

In the above parameter substitutions the value of the word is not evaluated unless it is to be used in the substitution. For example, in

```
echo ${HOME:-`pwd`}
```

the `pwd` command is executed only if the value of the variable `HOME` is not set or is set to NULL.

Several parameters are automatically set by the shell, and these are as follows:

*Sequence*                 *Result after substitution*

`${*}`
> Substitutes for all of the positional parameters separated by spaces, i.e. `$1 $2 ... $n`

*Sequence*                          *Result after substitution*

`${@}`

Also substitutes for all of the positional parameters separated by spaces, but each parameter is separately quoted, i.e. $1, $2, ... , $n

`${#}`

Substitutes for the number of positional parameters. It is returned in decimal notation.

`${-}`

Substitutes for the flags given to the shell on invocation or via the set command.

`${?}`

Substitutes for the returned value from the last synchronously executed command.

`${$}`

Substitutes for the process ID number of this shell.

`${!}`

Substitutes for the process ID number of the last asynchronously executed command invoked.

Certain keyword parameters or environment variables are set and used by the shell. The most common ones are:

*Variable/parameter*                *Function in the shell*

`HOME`

Default argument (the home directory) for the cd command.

`PATH`

Default search path for locating commands.

`CDPATH`

Search path for the cd command, to resolve relative path names.

`MAIL`

The parameter which is set to the name of the mail file. If the MAILPATH is not set then the shell informs the user of the arrival of mail in this file.

`MAILCHECK`

Specifies the interval (in seconds) for the shell to check that mail has arrived in the files specified by either MAIL or MAILPATH. The default is 600 (10 minutes), but if set to zero the shell will check before each prompt.

`MAILPATH`

A list of filenames separated by colons (:). If this parameter is set the shell informs the user of the arrival of mail in any of the specified files. Each filename may optionally be followed by a % and a string message that will be printed by the shell when the modification time of the file changes. The default message is you have mail.

PS1

> Primary prompt string used by the shell. The default is $.

PS2

> Secondary prompt string used by the shell. The default is a >.

*Blank interpretation*

The command separator characters are defined in the environment variable IFS. Its default values are ' ' (a space character), \t (a tab character) and \n, a new-line character. The value of this variable may be changed to enable the shell to interpret different characters as command separators.

## 3.6    Input/output redirection

The STDIN, STDOUT and STDERR of any command may be redirected before the shell initiates any command. This is achieved using a special notation which is interpreted by the shell. The following special character sequences may appear before or after any command. They are not passed to the command itself but serve only as instructions to the initiating shell.

*Command*                                    *Function*

`< word`

> The file called `word` is used as the standard input (STDIN) for the command.

`> word`

> The file called `word` is used as the standard output (STDOUT) for the command. If the file `word` does not exist, it will be created, but if the file already exists it will be truncated

`>> word`

> The file called `word` is used as the standard output (STDOUT) for the command. If the file `word` exists, then the output is appended to the end of the file, otherwise the file is created.

`<<[-] word`

> The shell input is read up to a line that is the same as word, or the end-of-file (EOF). If any character of the word is quoted then no interpretation is placed upon the character within the input stream. Otherwise, parameter and command substitution occurs. Un-escaped new-line characters are ignored, and the \ character must be used to quote the characters \, $, ` and '. If the – is appended to the << then all leading tabs are stripped from the word and the input stream.

`<&digit`

> The file associated with file number `digit` is used as the standard input (STDIN).

*Command*                                    *Function*

`>&digit`

     The file associated with file number `digit` is used as standard output (STDOUT).

`<&—`

     The standard input (STDIN) file is closed.

`>&—`

     The standard output (STDOUT) file is closed.

If any of the above is preceded by a digit, then the file descriptor that is associated with that digit will be used in the redirection instead of the usual defaults of file descriptor 0 and 1. For example,

```
2>&1
```

associates file descriptor 2 with the file currently associated with file descriptor 1. This type of input/output redirection is necessary if you want to synchronously connect STDOUT and STDERR to the same file.

The order in which redirections are made is important; the shell evaluates redirections from left to right. For example, in

```
$ ls 1> temp 2>&1
```

the STDOUT of the command `ls` is redirected to the file `temp`, and subsequently the STDERR is redirected to the file associated with file number 1, i.e. STDOUT. At the time of redirection file number 1 was redirected to the file `temp`, thus the STDERR is also redirected to the file `temp`. If the order of redirection was

```
$ ls 2>&1 1>temp
```

then STDERR would have been attached to the terminal, that is STDOUT's default file, and subsequently STDOUT alone would have been redirected to the file `temp`.

## 3.7    Special commands

The commands listed below are executed as internal commands to the shell; that is, they are executed within the shell process.

*Command*                                    *Function*

`:`

     Does nothing, but has a zero exit status.

. file

> Read and execute the commands from the file file. These commands are executed within the current shell, i.e. no new shell process is spawned. This command differs from the execution of a shell script command.

break [n]

> Exit from enclosing for or while loop, if any. If n is specified then the break command breaks n levels of nesting.

continue [n]

> Resume the next iteration of the enclosing for or while loop. If n is specified, resume at the nth enclosing loop.

cd [arg]

> Change the current directory to arg. The shell variable HOME contains the default value of arg. The shell parameter CDPATH contains the search path for the directory containing arg.

echo arg

> Echo arguments to STDOUT.

eval arg

> The arguments are read as input to the current shell, and the resulting command(s) executed.

exec [arg]

> Causes the current shell to execute the command specified by arg in place of itself. No new process is created.

exit [ n ]

> Causes the shell to exit with the exit status n. If n is omitted then the exit status of the last command is returned.

export [ name ..]

> The name(s) given as arguments are marked for automatic export to subsequently executed commands. If no name is given then a list of all exported shell variable names will be printed.

pwd

> Print the current work directory to STDOUT.

read [ name ..]

> Read one line from STDIN file, and assign the first word to the first name, second word to the next and so on. Any remaining words will be assigned to the last name. Unless end-of-file is encountered, read returns zero as an exit status.

readonly [ name ..]

> The names of shell environment variables given as arguments are marked readonly and may not be changed by subsequent assignments. If no name is given a list of all the variables that are marked readonly is produced.

*Command*                                      *Function*

`return [ n ]`

Causes a shell function to return n as its return result. If n is omitted then the exit status of the last command executed is returned.

`set [ -arg(s) ]`

Set shell characteristics (see command line options, Section 3.1). If + is used instead of -, then the `arg` is turned off. If no `arg` is given, a list of all of the environment variable names and values is printed.

`shift [ n ]`

The positional parameters from $n+1 .. are renamed $1 .... If n is omitted 1 is the default.

`test [ expr ]`

Evaluate the expression `expr` and return the Boolean result to the shell. [`expr`] in an `if` statement is interpreted as `test expr`, but there must be spaces before and after the brackets.

`trap [ arg ] [ n ]`

The command `arg` is a command to be read and executed when the shell receives the signal n. If n is zero the command `arg` is executed on exit from the shell. The trap command with a null value for `arg` causes the signal to be ignored. The trap command with no value of `arg` causes the signal to be restored to its default action within the shell. The trap command with no arguments prints all signals trapped together with their command lists.

`type [ name .. ]`

For each name, indicate how it would be interpreted if it were used as a command name.

`ulimit [ n ]`

Set the maximum size of a file in blocks that may be created or extended by a child process. If no value of n is given the current `ulimit` is printed.

`umask [ n ]`

Set the current file creation mask. If n is not given then the current value of `umask` is printed.

`unset [ name .. ]`

For each name specified remove the name from the current environment. Note that the environment variables `PATH`, `PS1`, `PS2`, `MAILCHECK` and `IFS` cannot be removed.

`wait [ n ]`

Wait for the child process having process number n to terminate and report its termination status. If no value of n is provided then wait for all currently active children to terminate, exit status in this case is zero.

# 4
# The Korn shell

The Korn shell was written by David Korn at AT&T's Bell laboratories to provide the extra functionality not found in the Bourne shell. It was intended to supersede the Bourne shell and provide a superset of its functionality combining all of the best features of both the Bourne shell and the BDS C shell as well as providing some unique features of its own. The Korn shell is the default user shell provided with the RISC System/6000 under AIX 3.x.

- **Korn shell functionality**  `/bin/ksh`  standard Korn shell
- **Command line options**

```
/bin/ksh    [ -aefhikmnoprstuvx ] [ -o option ]
                                  [ -c string ] [ arg ]
```

## 4.1    Command line options and their function

*Option*                                   *Function*

`-a`

Mark variables which are modified or created for export.

`-c string`

Read commands from `string`.

`-e`

Exit shell immediately if a command exits with a non-zero exit status.

`-f`

Disable filename generation.

`-h`

Locate and remember function commands as functions are defined.

`-i`

If present the shell is interactive and TERMINATE, INTERRUPT and QUIT signals are ignored.

*Option*                                    *Function*
-k

All keyword arguments are placed in the environment for a command,
not just those that precede the command name.

-m

Background jobs will be run in a separate process group and a line will be
printed when the job is completed. The exit status of the background job
is reported in the completion message.

-n

Read commands but do not execute them.

-o [ option]

The option following the -o will be one of the following:

allexport

Same as -a option.

errexit

Same as -e option.

bgnice

Background jobs will run with a low nice priority.

emacs

Selects emacs style editor for command line entry.

ignoreeof

The shell will not exit on end-of-file. The exit command must be
used.

keyword

Same as -k option.

markdirs

All directory names resulting from filename generation will have
a trailing / appended to them.

monitor

Same as -m option.

noexec

Same as -n option.

noglob

Same as -f option.

nounset

Same as -u option.

protected

Same as -p option.

verbose

Same as -v option.

trackall

Same as -h option.

vi
> Selects vi style editor for command line. Entry is allowed until
> ⟨ESC⟩ (ASCII 033) is typed which will place the user in command
> mode, where editing of the command line can be achieved. A
> return sends the line.

viraw
> Each character is processed as it is typed in, in vi mode.

xtrace
> Same as -x.

If no option is supplied then the current option setting is printed to
STDOUT.

-p

Resets the PATH environment variable to its default value. Disables
the processing of $HOME/.profile file and uses the file
/etc/suid_profile instead of the ENV file. This mode is automatically
enabled when the effective uid and/or gid is not equal to the real uid or
gid.

-r

The present shell is a restricted shell.

-s

Sort positional parameters.

-t

Exit shell after reading and executing one command.

-u

Treat unset variables as an error when substituting.

-v

Print shell input lines as they are read.

-x

Print commands and their arguments as they are executed.

—

Turns off -x and -v flags and stops examining arguments for flags.

## 4.2    Usage of command line options

Many of the options in Section 4.1 have the same functionality as the options in the
Bourne shell. Only the options not present in the Bourne shell are discussed here,
and reference should be made to Chapter 3 for common options.

### 4.2.1    /bin/ksh —m

The -m option causes all background jobs to be run as a separate process group.
These background processes will therefore not be killed by the kernel when their

parent dies, as they are in the default case. Thus with this option background
processes may be run after the user logs out.

## 4.2.2   /bin/ksh –o [ option ]

This interface to the Korn shell provides several additional shell functions not
found in the Bourne shell. These are listed below.

/bin/ksh -o bgnice
: Causes the shell to use the nice() system call to ensure that background
processes run at lower priority than the shell itself.

/bin/ksh -o [ emacs ] [ vi ]
: Allows the line editor style to be nominated for the entry of command
lines within the shell.

/bin/ksh -o ignoreeof
: Causes the shell to ignore the traditional end-of-file to terminate, and
requires the exit command to be used. For example, consider the
following simple shell script called dir.sh:

```
# dir.sh version 1.0
ls -1       # output vertical listing of directory
```

Running the shell script with a shell invoked in this way may produce the
following results:

```
$ /bin/ksh < dir.sh
fred.c
jim.c
jack.c
xx.c
jack
jim
```

Notice that the dollar prompt of the parent shell does not reappear after
the ls command has completed; the sub-shell reading the end-of-file in
the shell script file dir.sh does not cause it to terminate. The addition of
the exit command into the shell script dir.sh would be required to force
the sub-shell to terminate.

/bin/ksh -o markdirs
: Causes the shell to append the / character to the end of any directory
names resulting from filename generation. For example, consider the
following echo command:

```
$ echo /bi*
/bin/
$
```

The / character has been appended to the end after the filename generation of /bin.

### 4.2.3 /bin/ksh –p

In this protected mode, when the shell detects that the effective user ID (euid) or effective group ID (egid) is not the same as the real user ID (uid) or real group ID (gid), it disables processing of $HOME/.profile for that user and processes the file /etc/suid_profile instead. This allows the administrator to control the values of key environment variables such as PATH for users using the AIX su command or running setuid programs. This security is of course violated if the directory /etc or the file suid_profile are writable to all users.

### 4.2.4 /bin/ksh –s

This option shorts the positional parameters, i.e. $1 to $9.

## 4.3 Initialization scripts

These are primarily the same as in the Bourne shell, with the addition of the /etc/suid_profile for users using the su command or setuid programs, together with the shell option -p.

## 4.4 Quoting of metacharacters

Metacharacters within the Korn shell are quoted in the manner described in Chapter 2.

## 4.5 Shell commands

### 4.5.1 *Simple commands*

These are primarily the same as in the Bourne shell.

### 4.5.2 *Pipelines*

These are primarily the same as in the Bourne shell.

### 4.5.3 *Command lists*

A command list is a sequence of one or more simple commands or pipelines separated by any of the characters ; , &, && or || and optionally terminated by ; , &, or |&. Of these five symbols ; , &, and |& have equal precedence. The symbols ; , &,

&&, || have the same meaning in the Korn shell as they do in the Bourne shell, but the symbol |& is interpreted differently. The symbol |& causes the preceding command or pipeline to be executed asynchronously with the parent shell. A two-way pipe is established between this process and the parent shell. The standard input STDIN and the standard output STDOUT of the co-process may be written to or read from using the -p options of both the read and the print commands. Only one such process may be active at any one time.

A command is either a simple command or one of the internal shell commands listed below, and unless stated otherwise the exit status of these internal shell commands is the exit status returned by the last simple command executed within that command.

### 4.5.4   Internal shell commands

for *command*

Identical to the Bourne shell command of the same name.

select *command*

```
select arg [in words]
        do
                list
        done
```

The select command prints words on the standard error (STDERR), each preceded by a number. If the words are omitted then the positional parameters are used. Then the PS3 prompt is printed, and a line is read from standard input (STDIN). If the line read matches the number of one of the listed words, the value of the variable arg is set to the word. If the line is empty then the selection list is printed again. If the line does not match any of the numbers listed then the variable arg is set to null. The line read from STDIN is stored in the variable REPLY. The commands in list are executed for each selection until either a break or an end-of-file is encountered.

case *command*

Identical to the Bourne shell command of the same name.

if/else/elif *command*

Identical to the Bourne shell command of the same name.

```
while command
```

Identical to the Bourne shell command of the same name.

```
(list) command
```

Identical to the Bourne shell command of the same name.

```
{ list ;} command
```

Identical to the Bourne shell command of the same name.

*Shell functions*

```
function identifier { list ; }
identifier () { list ; }
```

The above declarations declare shell functions to the Korn shell. Notice the additional keyword `function` as an alternative way of defining functions in the Korn shell. The shell functions in the Korn shell have the same functionality as the functions in the Bourne shell.

```
TIME command
```

```
time pipeline
```

The pipeline is executed and the elapsed time as well as the user and system time are printed to `STDERR`.

*Shell comments*

This command is identical to the Bourne shell command of the same name.

*Command substitution*

This command is identical to the Bourne shell command of the same name. In addition to the standard ` (backward single quote) characters used as the delimit command substitution commands, the Korn shell allows a dollar sign directly associated with () (open and close brackets): for example `$(cat file)` instead of `` `cat file` ``. The command `$(cat file)` may also be further reduced to `$(<file)`.

*Aliasing*

This provides a facility to create aliases for all command except the keywords defined above. The general form of an `alias` command is as follows:

- To set an alias `newname` for the command `ls –1`:

```
    $ alias newname "ls —1"
$
```

- To show the resolved form of an alias called `newname`:

```
    $ alias newname
ls —1
$
```

- To remove an alias from the alias list, thus making the alias `newname` undefined after being defined by the `alias` command:

```
    $ unalias newname
$
```

An alias is resolved by the shell by replacing the first word of the command which contains an alias with the value of the alias as defined above. After this substitution has taken place, the resulting command is not tested for further alias substitution. For example, consider

```
    $ alias dir="ls —1"
$ dir *.c                /* becomes ls —1 *.c after substitution */
fred.c
jim.c
$
```

However, look what happens if we try

```
    $ alias xdir="ls -li"
$ alias dir="xdir"
$ dir *.c                /* becomes xdir *.c after substitution */
ksh: xdir not found      /* no further substitution takes place */
$                        /* so xdir is not resolved as may be   */
$                        /* expected                            */
```

If the last character of the alias command is a space or a tab character, then the next word in the command is also checked for aliasing. For example,

```
$ alias dir="ls "
$ alias opts="-li"
$ dir opts *.c         /* becomes ls -li *.c after substitution */
$
```

But this does not work with the command

```
$ alias dir="ls"
$ alias opts="-li"
$ dir opts *.c         /* becomes ls opts *.c after substitution */
$
```

Aliasing is performed when scripts are read, not while they are executing. Therefore, for an alias to take effect the alias command must be executed before the command which references the alias is read. Exported aliases remain in effect for sub-shells, but must be re-initialized for separate invocations of the shell.

Aliases are frequently used as a shorthand for the full pathnames. An option to the aliasing facility allows the value of the alias to be automatically set to the full pathname of the corresponding command. These aliases are called *tracked aliases*. The value of a tracked alias is defined the first time the corresponding command is looked up and becomes undefined each time the PATH variable is reset. These aliases remain tracked so that the next subsequent reference will redefine the value. There are several tracked aliases compiled into the shell, and the set option –h makes each alias a tracked alias.

The following are all exported aliases and are compiled into the Korn shell. They can, however, be unset with unalias or redefined:

```
  false='let 0'
function='typeset -f'
 history='fc -l'
 integer='typeset -i'
   nohup='nohup '
       r='fc -e -'
    true=':'
    type='whence -v'
    hash='alias -t'
```

*Tilde substitution*

After alias substitution is performed each word is examined to see if it begins with an unquoted ~ (a tilde). If it does, then the word up to a / is checked to see if it matches a user name in the /etc/passwd file. If a match is found, the ~ and the matched login name are replaced by the user's home directory. If no match is found, the text is left unchanged. A ~ by itself or in front of a / is replaced by the value of the HOME variable. A ~ followed by a + or a – is replaced by the value of the parameter PWD and OLDPWD respectively. For example, if the user fred is known to the system, and his home directory is /usr2/data/fred, then

```
$ directory=~fred/tmp
$ echo $directory
/usr2/data/fred/tmp
$
```

If PWD and OLDPWD are /usr2 and /tmp respectively, then

```
$ now=~+/tmp
$ before=~-/tmp
$ echo $now
/usr2/tmp
$ echo $before
/tmp/tmp
$
```

If the value of the HOME variable is /usr2/fred, then

```
$ echo ~/tmp
/usr2/fred/tmp
$
```

### Process substitution

This feature of the Korn shell is available only on versions of UNIX operating systems that support the /dev/fd directory for naming open files. Each command argument of the form (list), <(list) or >(list) will run a list process asynchronously connected to some file in the /dev/fd directory. The name of this file will become the argument to the command. If the form with > is selected then writing on this file will provide input for the list. If < is used, then the passed argument will contain the input of the list process. For example,

```
paste ( cut -f1 file1 ) ( cut -f3 file2 ) | tee
          >( process1) >(process2)
```

This command cuts fields 1 and 3 from files file1 and file2 respectively, pastes the results together, and sends this output to the processes process1 and process2, as well as to STDOUT. Note that the file that is passed as an argument to the command is a UNIX pipe, so programs that expect to use the system call lseek() on the file will fail.

### Parameter substitution

A parameter is an identifier with one or more digits, or any of the characters *, @, #, ?, -, $, or !. A keyword parameter (a parameter denoted by an identifier) has a value and zero or more attributes. Keyword parameters can be assigned values and attributes using the typeset special command. Exported parameters pass their values and attributes to sub-shells, but only values to the environment.

The Korn shell supports a limited single-dimensional array facility. An element of an array parameter is referenced by a subscript. A subscript is denoted by a [, followed by an arithmetic expression, followed by a ]. For example, the value of the ninth element of the array sum could be accessed like this:

```
$ echo $sum[9]
```

The value of all subscripts must be in the range 0 . . . 511. Arrays need not be declared, and any reference to any legal subscript will cause the array to be created. Reference to an array without a subscript is equivalent to referencing the first element.

- The value of a *keyword parameter* may also be assigned by

  ```
  $ name=value
  ```

  If the integer attribute is set for name, then the value is subject to arithmetic evaluation.
- *Positional parameters*, i.e. parameters denoted by a number, may be assigned values with the set special command.

*Sequence*                                 *Result after substitution*

${parameter}
> The value, if any, of the parameter is substituted. The { and } characters are required only if the parameter is followed by a non-white-space character, which should not be interpreted as part of the parameter's name.

${#parameter}
> If the parameter is * or @ then the number of positional parameters is substituted, otherwise, the length of the value of the parameter is substituted.

${#identifier[*]}
> The number of elements in the array identifier is substituted.

${parameter:-word}
> If the parameter is set and is not null, then its value is substituted for that of the expression, otherwise the value of the word provided is substituted.
> ${parameter:=word}
> If the parameter is not set or is null then the value of the parameter is set to the word provided, and the value of the parameter is then substituted. Positional parameters may not be assigned in this way.

*Sequence*                          *Result after substitution*

`${parameter:?word}`

>    If the parameter is set and not null then the parameter's value is
>    substituted, otherwise the word provided is printed and the shell is exited.
>    If no word is provided then `Parameter null or not set` is printed.

`${parameter:+word}`

>    If the parameter is set and is not null then the word provided is
>    substituted, otherwise nothing is substituted.

`${parameter#pattern}`

`${parameter##pattern}`

>    If the shell pattern matches the beginning of the value of the parameter,
>    then the value of this substitution is the value of the parameter with the
>    matched portion deleted, otherwise the value of the parameter is substi-
>    tuted. In the first form the smallest matching pattern is deleted and in the
>    second form the largest.

`${parameter%pattern}`

`${parameter%%pattern}`

>    Same as above.

The following parameters are automatically set by the shell.

*Sequence*                          *Result after substitution*

`${#}`

>    The number of positional parameters set by the shell.

`${-}`

>    The flags supplied to the shell on invocation or by the set command.

`${$}`

>    The exit status of the last command executed by the shell.

`${_}`

>    The last argument of the previous command. This parameter is not set for
>    commands which are asynchronous. This parameter is also used to hold
>    the name of the matching `MAIL` file when checking for mail. Finally, the
>    value of this parameter is set to the full pathname of each program the
>    shell invokes and is passed in the environment.

`${!}`

>    The process ID of the last background command invoked.

   There are certain keyword parameters or environment variables that are set
and used by the shell. The most common ones are listed below.

*Variable/parameter*                *Function in the shell*

`PPID`

>    The process ID of the parent of the shell.

PWD
> The present working directory set by the cd command.

OLDPWD
> The previous working directory set by the cd command.

RANDOM
> Each time this parameter is referenced, a random integer is generated. The sequence of random numbers can be initialized by assigning a numeric value to RANDOM.

REPLY
> This parameter is set by the select command and by the read special command when no arguments are supplied.

SECONDS
> Each time this parameter is referenced, the number of seconds since the shell was invoked is returned. If this value is assigned a value then the value returned on next reference will be that value plus the number of seconds which have elapsed.

CDPATH
> This is the search path for cd command, to resolve relative pathnames.

COLUMNS
> If this variable is set, the value is used to define the width of the edit window for the shell edit modes and for printing select lists.

EDITOR
> If the value is set and ends in emacs, gmacs or vi and the VISUAL variable is not set, then the corresponding option for the shell line editor will be switched on.

ENV
> If this parameter is set, then parameter substitution is performed on the value to generate the pathname of the script that will be executed when the shell is invoked.

FCEDIT
> The default editor name for the fc command.

IFS
> Same as in the Bourne shell

HISTFILE
> If this parameter is set when the shell is invoked, then the value is the pathname of the file that will be used to store command history. The default value is $HOME/.sh_history.

HISTSIZE
> If this parameter is set when the shell is invoked, then the value defines the number of previously entered commands that are accessible by this shell (which will be less than or equal to this number). The default is 128.

HOME
> The default argument (the home directory) for the cd command.

*Variable/parameter*                    *Function in the shell*

LINES

> If this variable is set, the value is used to determine the column length for printing select lists. Select lists will print vertically until about two-thirds of LINES lines are filled.

MAIL

> The parameter which is set to the name of the mail file. If the MAILPATH is not set then the shell informs the user of the arrival of mail in this file.

MAILCHECK

> Specifies the interval (in seconds) for the shell to check that mail has arrived in the files specified by either MAIL or MAILPATH. The default is 600 (10 minutes) but if set to zero the shell will check before each prompt.

MAILPATH

> A list of filenames separated by colons (:). If this parameter is set the shell informs the user of the arrival of mail in any of the specified files. Each filename may optionally be followed by a % and a string message that will be printed by the shell, when the modification time of the file changes. The default message is you have mail.

PATH

> Same as in the Bourne shell.

PS1

> Same as in the Bourne shell, except that a ! in the value of this parameter is expanded to the current command number.

PS2

> This is the secondary prompt string used by the shell, the default is >.

PS3

> Selection prompt string, used within a select loop, by default #?.

SHELL

> The pathname of the shell is kept in the environment. At invocation, if the value of this variable contains an r in the basename, then the shell becomes a restricted shell.

TMOUT

> If set to a value greater than zero, the shell will terminate if a command is not entered within the prescribed number of seconds after issuing the PS1 prompt.

VISUAL

> If the value of this variable ends in emacs, gmacs or vi then the corresponding option for the line editor is set.

*Blank interpretation*

The Korn shell uses the environment variable IFS in the same way as the Bourne shell.

*Input/output redirection*

The Korn shell has identical functionality to the Bourne shell, allowing all of the Bourne shell's input/output redirection mechanisms.

*Arithmetic evaluation*

The ability of the Korn shell to perform arithmetic is provided via the special command `let`. Evaluations are performed using long arithmetic. Constants are of the form `[base#]n`, where `base` is a decimal number between 2 and 36, representing the arithmetic base, and n is a number in that base. If `base` is omitted then base 10 is used.

An internal integer representation of a keyword parameter can be specified with the `-i` option using the `typeset special` command. When this attribute is selected, the first assignment to the parameter determines the arithmetic base to be used when parameter substitution occurs.

Since many of the arithmetic operators require quoting, an alternative form of the `let` command is provided. For any command which begins with a `((`, all the characters until a matching `))` is reached are treated as a quoted expression: i.e. `(( ... ))` is equivalent to ....

*Jobs*

If the monitor option of the `set` command is turned on, an interactive shell associates a job with an individual pipeline. It keeps a table of current jobs, printed by the `jobs` command, and assigns each of them a small integer job number. When a job is started asynchronously with &, the shell prints a line which looks like

```
[1] 1234
 |    |
 |    └────── process id of command
 |
 └────── job number of job
```

Certain job control features are provided by the shell. These features, listed below, may not be available on all versions of UNIX, but are available under AIX 3.x

*Command*                         *Function within the shell*
`Ctrl-Z`
      If this character is typed while running a foreground task, the task will be suspended. This character may be redefined using the `stty` command.

*Command*                              *Function within the shell*

bg [%job] [%string]

   Places the job that is associated with the job number job or that begins
   with string into the background.

fg [%job] [%string]

   Places the job associated with the job number job or that begins with
   string into the foreground.

kill %job

   Kills the job associated with job number job.

The shell maintains a notion of the current and previous jobs. In the output
produced by the jobs command, the current jobs is marked with a + symbol, and
the previous job is marked with a – symbol. The job numbers %+ and %– are the
current job and the previous job respectively. The symbol %% is also a synonym for
the current job.

When you try to leave the shell while jobs are running or stopped, you will be
warned that You have stopped(running) jobs. If you try to exit the shell a
second time the shell will not warn you, and any stopped jobs will be terminated.

## 4.6     Command reentry

The shell variables HISTSIZE and HISTFILE are used to determine the number of
commands entered from the terminal that are saved in the history file, and the
name of the history file itself. The default size is 128 commands and the default
history filename is $HOME/.sh_history.

### 4.6.1   emacs *and* gmacs *editing mode*

This mode is initiated via the set option -o followed by either emacs or gmacs.
   For example at the shell you could type:

```
   $ set -o emacs
$
```

or

```
   $ set -o gmacs
$
```

The only difference between these two modes is the way they handle the ⟨CTRL-
T⟩. To edit, the user moves the cursor to the point needing correction and then
inserts or deletes characters or words as required. In the command lists given
below for the emacs or gmacs editor modes, the following conventions apply:

- control characters are denoted by ˆ (caret symbol) before the character
- escape sequences or metasequences are denoted by M- before the charac-
  ter(s).

- To obtain a control character, the control key and the character are depressed together. An escape sequence is obtained by pressing ⟨ESC⟩ (ASCII 033) followed by the character(s) required. For the ⟨DEL⟩ key the symbol used is ^?.

| *Command* | *Function* |
|---|---|

^F

Move cursor forward (right) one character.

M-f

Move cursor forward (right) one word.

^B

Move cursor backwards (left) one character.

M-b

Move cursor backwards (left) one word.

^A

Move cursor to start of line.

^E

Move cursor to end of line.

^]char

Move cursor to character char on current line.

^X^X

Interchange cursor and mark.

erase

User-defined erase character as defined by the stty command. Usually ^H or #, it deletes the previous character.

^D

Delete current character at cursor position.

M-d

Delete current word at cursor position.

M-^H

Delete previous word at cursor position.

M-h

Delete previous word at cursor position.

M-^?

Delete previous word (if your interrupt character is ^? then this will not work).

^T

Transpose current character with next character in emacs mode. Transpose two previous characters in gmacs mode.

^C

Capitalize current character.

M-c

Capitalize current word.

*Command*                                    *Function*

M-l

Change current word to lower case.

^K

Kill all characters from cursor position to the end of line. If given a parameter of zero then the kill begins from the start of the line to the current cursor position.

^W

Kill from cursor position to mark.

M-p

Push the region from the cursor to the mark on to the stack.

kill

User-defined kill character usually defined by the stty command. Usually set to ^G or @. Its function is to kill the current line. If two kill characters are entered in succession, then all kill characters from then on cause a line feed.

^Y

Restore last item removed from line.

^L

Line feed and print current line.

^@

(Null character) to set mark.

M-

(Metaspace) to set mark.

^J

(New line) Execute the current line.

^M

(Return) Execute the current line.

eof

User defined character for end-of-file, normally ^D. This will terminate the shell if the current line is null.

^P

Fetch previous command. Each time ^P is entered the previous command back in time is accessed.

M-<

Fetch least recent (oldest) history line.

M->

Fetch most recent (youngest) history line.

^N

Fetch next command. Each time ^N is entered the next command forward in time is accessed.

^Rstring

Reverse search history for a previous command line that contains string. If a parameter of zero is given, the search is forward. The string is terminated by a return or a new-line character. If the string is omitted, then the most recent string used is used in the search.

ˆO

Operate—execute the current line and fetch the next line relative to the current one from the history file.

M-digits

(⟨ESC⟩). Define numeric parameter. The digits are taken as a parameter to the next command.

M-letter

(Soft key). Your alias list is searched for an alias letter. If an alias of this name is defined, its value is inserted on the input queue. The letter must not be one of the above metafunctions.

M-.

The last word of the previous command is inserted on the current line. If the command is preceded by a numeric parameter, then the value of this parameter determines which word is inserted rather than the last.

M-*

Attempt filename generation of the current word. An asterisk is appended to the word if it does not contain any special pattern characters.

M-=

List files matching current word pattern if an asterisk were appended.

ˆU

Multiply parameter of next command by 4.

\

Escape next character. Editing characters (the user's erase, kill and interrupt characters) may be entered in a command provided that they are prefixed with \.

ˆV

Display the version number of the shell.

### 4.6.2 vi *line-editing mode*

This line-editing mode is initiated by the following option to the set special command:

```
$ set -o vi
$
```

There are two modes within the vi editing mode. Initially, when you enter a command you are in *input mode*. To edit, the user enters *control mode* by typing ⟨ESC⟩ (ASCII 033), moves the cursor to the point needing correction and then inserts or deletes characters or words as required. Most control commands accept an optional repeat count prior to the command.

    In vi editing mode on most systems, canonical processing is initially enabled and the command will be echoed again if the line speed is 1200 baud or greater and it contains any control characters, or if less than one second has elapsed since the prompt was printed. The ⟨ESC⟩ character terminates canonical processing for the remainder of the command and the user can then modify the command line. This scheme has the advantages of canonical processing with the type-ahead echoing of raw mode.

    If the option viraw is also set, the terminal will always have canonical processing disabled. This mode is implicit for systems that do not support the two alternate end-of-line delimiters.

    In the following list of commands for vi editing mode, control characters are denoted by the ^ character, which implies depressing ⟨CTRL⟩ and the letter together.

| *Command* | *Function* |
|---|---|
| ESC | Toggle from input mode to control mode. |
| erase | User-defined erase character as defined by stty, usually defined as ^H or #. Its function is to delete previous characters. |
| ^W | Delete the previous blank-separated word. |
| ^D | Terminate the shell. |
| ^V | Escape next character, so that editing characters, such as the user's erase character or kill characters, may be entered in a command line. |
| \ | Same as ^V. |

The following commands move the cursor. If count is omitted, the 1 is assumed.

| *Command* | *Function* |
|---|---|
| [count]l | Move cursor forward (right), count characters. |
| [count]w | Move cursor forward (right), count words. |
| [count]W | Move cursor to the beginning of the count word that follows a blank. |

[count]e
> Move cursor to the end of the count word.

[count]E
> Move cursor to the end of the count word delimited by blanks.

[count]h
> Move cursor backward (left) count characters.

[count]b
> Move cursor backward (left) count words.

[count]B
> Move cursor to preceding blank separated word.

[count]fchar
> Find the next character char in the current line.

[count]Fchar
> Find the previous character char in the current line.

[count]tchar
> Equivalent to f followed by h.

[count]Tchar
> Equivalent to F followed by l.

;

> Repeat the last single-character find command.

,

> Reverse the last single-character find command.

0

> Move cursor to start of line.

^

> Move cursor to first non-blank character in the current line.

$

> Move cursor to end-of-line.

The following are search and edit commands.

| *Command* | *Function* |
|---|---|

[count]k
> Fetch previous command. Each time k is entered the previous command back in time is accessed.

[count]-
> Same as k.

[count]j
> Fetch next command. Each time j is entered the next command forward in time is accessed.

[count]+
> Same as j.

*Command*                                         *Function*

[count]G

  The command number count is fetched. The default is the last command,
  i.e. count = 1.

/string

  Search backwards through history for a previous command containing
  the string string. If the string is null the previous string will be reused.

?string

  Same as /string except that search will be in the forward direction.

n

  Search to the next match to the last pattern string used in either the
  ?string or the /string commands.

N

  Same as n but in the reverse direction.


The following commands are for text modification and editing.


*Command*                                         *Function*

a

  Enter input mode and enter text after the current character.

A

  Append text to the end of the line.

[count]cmotion

  Delete current character through to the character that the motion would
  move the cursor to, and then enter input mode. When motion is c, then
  the complete line is deleted.

c[count]motion

  Same as above.

C

  Delete the current character up to end-of-line, and enter input mode.

S

  Equivalent to cc command.

D

  Delete the current character through to the end-of-line.

[count]dmotion

  Same as [count]cmotion except that input mode is not entered.

d[count]motion

  Same as above.

i

  Enter input mode and insert text before current cursor position.

I

  Enter input mode and insert text before the beginning of the current line.

[count]P
> Place the previous text modifications before the cursor.

[count]p
> Place the previous text modification after the cursor.

R
> Enter input mode and replace characters on the screen with characters typed in an overlay fashion.

rchar
> Replace the current character with char.

[count]x
> Delete current character.

[count]X
> Delete preceding character.

[count].
> Repeat previous text modification command.

~
> Invert the case of the current character and advance the cursor.

[count]_
> Causes the count word of the previous command to be appended and input mode entered. If no count is given, then the last word is used.

*
> Causes * to be appended to the current word and filename generation attempted. If no match is found, it rings the bell, otherwise the word is replaced by the matching pattern and input mode is entered.

The following commands provide other editing functions:

| *Command* | *Function* |
| --- | --- |

[count]ymotion
> Yank current character through to the character that motion would move the cursor to and put them in the delete buffer. Text and cursor are unchanged.

y[count]motion
> Same as [count]ymotion command.

Y
> Yanks from current position to end-of-line.

u
> Undo the last text-modifying command.

U
> Undo all of the text-modifying commands performed on the line.

[count]v
> Returns the result of the command fc -e ${VISUAL:-${EDITOR:-vi}}.

| *Command* | *Function* |
|---|---|

`count` in the input buffer. If `count` is omitted, then the current line is assumed.

`ˆL`

Line feed and print the current line. Effective only in control mode.

`ˆJ`

(New line) Execute current line regardless of mode.

`ˆM`

(Return) Same as `ˆJ`.

`#`

Sends line after inserting a # in front of the line and after each new-line character. This is useful for inserting commands into the history without executing them.

`=`

List filenames that would match the current word if an asterisk were appended to it.

`@letter`

The alias list is searched for an alias by the name of `letter`. If an alias of this name is found, its value will be inserted in the input queue for processing.

## 4.7   Special commands

| *Command* | *Function* |
|---|---|

`:`

Does nothing, but has a zero exit status.

`. file`

Read and execute the commands from the file `file`. These commands are executed within the current shell, i.e. there is no spawning of a new shell process. This command differs from the execution of a shell script command.

`alias [ -tx ]`

`[ name[=value]]`

With no arguments `alias` prints the list of aliases in the form `name=value` to the `STDOUT` file. An alias is defined for each name for which a value is given. A trailing space in the value causes the next word to be checked for an alias also. The flag `-t` is used to set and list tracked aliases. The `-x` flag is used to set or print exported aliases. The `alias` command returns `true` unless a name is given for which no alias exists.

`bg [ %job ]`

Puts the specified job into background. The current job is put into background if no job is specified.

`break [ n ]`
> Exit from enclosing `for` or `while` loop, if any. If n is specified then the break command breaks n levels of nesting.

`continue [ n ]`
> Resume the next iteration of the enclosing `for` or `while` loop. If n is specified resume at the nth enclosing loop.

`cd [ arg ]`
`cd old new`
> In the first form this command behaves as it does in the Bourne shell. In the second form `cd` substitutes the string `new` for the string `old` in the current directory name, `PWD`, and tries to change to this new directory.

`echo arg`
> Echo arguments to `STDOUT`.

`eval arg`
> The arguments are read as input to the current shell, and the resulting command(s) executed.

`exec [arg]`
> Causes the current shell to execute the command specified by `arg` in place of itself. No new process is created.

`exit [ n ]`
> Causes the shell to exit with the exit status n. If n is omitted then the exit status of the last command is returned.

`export [ name ..]`
> The name(s) given as arguments are marked for automatic export to subsequently executed commands. If no `name` is given then a list of all exported shell variable names will be printed.

`fc [ -e ename ]`
`   [ -nlr ]`
`   [ first ]`
`   [ last ]`
`fc -e - [ old=new ]`
`[ command ]`
> In the first form, a range of commands from `first` to `last` are selected from the last `HISTFILE` commands that were typed at the terminal. The first and last arguments may be given as a num! ɔr or a string. If the flag `-l` is selected then the commands are listed on `STDOUT`, otherwise the editor program ename is invoked on a file containing these keyboard commands. If ename is not supplied, the value of `FCEDIT` is used. When editing is complete the edited command(s) are executed. If last is omitted then its value will be assumed to be that of first. If first is omitted then its value is the previous command. The `-r` flag reverses the order of the commands and the `-n` flag suppresses command numbers when listing. In the second

*Command*                                    *Function*

form of the command the command command is re-executed after the substitution old=new is performed.

fg [ %job ]

If job is specified it brings it to the foreground. Otherwise, the current job is brought to the foreground.

jobs [ -l ]

Lists the active jobs. Given the -l options, it lists process IDs in addition to the normal information.

kill [ -sig]
   process ...

Sends either the TERM (signal) or the specified signal to the specified process. The argument process can be either a process ID or a %job number.

let arg ..

Each arg is an arithmetic expression to be evaluated. Expressions consist of constants, named parameters, and operators. The valid operators are listed in decreasing order of precedence.

—

Unary minus.

!

Logical negation.

* / %

Multiplication, division, modulus.

+ —

Addition, subtraction.

<= >= < >

Comparison (Boolean).

== !=

Equality, inequality.

=

Arithmetic assignment. The use of ( and ) to enclose expressions that should be evaluated first functions in the normal way. Evaluation is normally from left to right, within the operator precedence groups. A parameter name must be a valid identifier. When a parameter name is encountered, the value associated with it is substituted and the expression evaluation resumes. Up to nine levels of recursion are permitted. The return code is 0 if the value of the last expression is non-zero, and 1 otherwise.

newgrp [ arg ..]

Equivalent to exec newgrp arg.

```
print [ -Rnprsu[n] ]
```
```
      [ arg .. ]
```
The shell's output mechanism. With no flags or with flag -, the arguments are printed to STDOUT file as described by echo. Options are as follows:

    -R

        echo escape conventions are not used. Anything that follows is processed except -n as an argument, even if it begins with a -.

    -n

        No trailing new line is added to the output.

    -p

        All arguments are redirected to a co-process started by the |& command.

    -r

        Same as -R.

    -s

        All arguments are redirected to the history file.

    -u n

        Redirects output to the file which has descriptor n. Without n, file descriptor 1 (STDOUT is assumed).

    pwd

        Equivalent to printing -r - $PWD. Prints current working directory to STDOUT.

```
read [ -prsu[n] ]
```
```
     [ name?prompt ]
```
```
     [ name ]
```
The shell input mechanism. One line is read and is broken up into words using the characters in IFS as separators. The default variable to which input is placed is the variable REPLY, i.e. when name is omitted. If the option name?prompt is used and this is an interactive shell, the value of the prompt will be output to STDERR and any value read assigned to name.

    The options are as follows:

    -p

        Read input from co-process. This will disconnect any co-process when either an error occurs or end-of-file is met.

    -r

        Do not append a new line on input text.

    -s

        Save input in history file.

    -u n

        Read from file descriptor n. The default file descriptor is 0. Read returns a zero exit status unless an end-of-file is encountered.

*Command*                                  *Function*

`readonly [ name ..]`

> The names of shell environment variables given as arguments are marked `readonly` and may not be changed by subsequent assignments. If no name is given then a list of all the variables that are marked `readonly` is produced.

`return [ n ]`

> Causes a shell function to return n as its return result. If n is omitted then the exit status of the last command executed is returned.

`set [ -aefhkmnostuvx ]`

> See command line options, Section 4.1.
>
> `shift [ n ]`
>
> The positional parameters from $n+1 .. are renamed $1 .... If n is omitted, then 1 is the default.

`test [ expr ]`

> As in the Bourne shell, with the addition of the following primitive expressions:
>
> `-L file`
>> True if file is a symbolic link.
>
> `file1 -nt file2`
>> True if `file1` is newer than `file2`.
>
> `file1 -ot file2`
>> True if `file1` is older than `file2`.
>
> `file1 -ef file2`
>> True if `file1` has the same device and i-node number as `file2`.

`times`

> Prints the accumulated user and system times for the shell and for processes run from the shell.

`trap [ arg ] [ n ]`

> The command `arg` is a command to be read and executed when the shell receives the signal n. If n is zero the command `arg` is executed on exit from the shell. The `trap` command with a null value for `arg` causes the signal to be ignored. The `trap` command with no value of `arg` causes the signal to be restored to its default action within the shell. The `trap` command with no arguments prints all signals trapped together with their command lists.

`typeset [ -HLRZfilprtux [n]`
`        [ name[ =value] ]]`

> Set attributes for shell variables and functions. The options are as follows:

-H

Provides an AIX-to-host name file mapping on non-AIX machines.

-L

Left-justify and remove leading blanks from value. If n is non-zero it defines the width of the field. Otherwise the field width is determined during the first assignment. Leading zeros are removed if the -Z flag is also set, and the -R flag is turned off.

-R

Right justify and fill with leading blanks. If the n parameter is present, it defines the field width. Otherwise it is determined during the first assignment. The -L flag is turned off.

-Z

Right justify and fill with zeros. Otherwise same as -R.

-f

Defines an identifier as a function. Other valid options are -t, which turns on execution tracing for this function, and -x which allows a function to remain in effect across shell procedures executed in the same process environment.

-i

Defines a parameter as an integer. If n is defined it determines the output base; if n is not defined the first assignment determines the output base.

-l

All upper-case characters are converted to lower-case characters and the -u flag is turned off.

-p

The output of this command, if any, is written on to a two-way pipe.

-r

The given names are marked readonly.

-t

Tags the name parameters. Tags are user-definable and have no special meaning to the shell.

-u

All lower-case characters are converted to upper-case characters and the -l option is turned off.

-x

The given names are marked for auto export. Using + rather than - causes these flags to be turned off.

*Command*                                         *Function*

```
ulimit [ -acdfmpst ]
          [n]
```
Sets and displays current resource limits. The options are as follows:

```
-a
```
Lists all of the current limits (BSD only).

```
-c
```
Imposes a size limit of n 512 byte blocks on the size of core dumps (BSD only).

```
-d
```
Imposes a size limit of n kilobytes on the size of the data area (BSD only).

```
-f
```
Imposes a size limit of n 512 byte blocks on files written by child processes (file of any size may be read).

```
-m
```
Imposes a soft limit of n kilobytes on the size of physical memory (BSD only).

```
-p
```
Changes the pipe size to n (UNIX/RT only).

```
-s
```
Imposes a size limit of n kilobytes on the size of the stack area (BSD only).

```
-t
```
Imposes a time of n seconds to be used by each process (BSD only). If no option is given -f is assumed, and if no value of n is given then the current value is printed.

```
umask [ nnn ]
```
The user's file creation mask is set to nnn. If nnn is omitted, the current value of the mask is printed.

```
unalias name ..
```
The parameters given by the list of names are removed from the alias list.

```
unset [ -f ] name ..
```
The parameters given in the list of names are unassigned. Variables with readonly attributes cannot be unset.

```
wait [ n ]
```
Wait for the child process having process number n to terminate and report its termination status. If no value of n is provided then wait for all currently active children to terminate; exit status in this case is zero.

```
whence [ -v ] name ..
```
As in the Bourne shell type command.

# 5
# The C shell

---

The C shell was developed by the University of California at Berkeley (BSD). It has its own unique programming language, and is often the preferred choice in the academic world.

- **C shell functionality**   /bin/csh   Standard C shell.
- **Command line options**   /bin/csh [ -cefinstvxTVX ] [ command file ]
  
  [ args ].

## 5.1   Command line options and their function

| Option | Function |

*Option*                                  *Function*

-c

The shell's commands are read from the single following argument, which must be present. Any remaining arguments are placed in the variable argv.

-e

Exit the shell if any command exists with a non-zero exit status.

-f

Suppress execution of the .cshrc file in the user's home directory.

-i

Causes csh to respond interactively when called from a device other than a user's terminal. csh will normally not respond interactively in such a case. However, if csh is called from a terminal it will always respond interactively irrespective of the options used.

-n

Causes commands to be read but not executed. This may be used to check syntax of shell scripts, as all substitutions are performed.

-s

Command line input is read from STDIN file.

*Option*                                    *Function*

-t

A single line of text is read and executed, and the shell will then terminate.

-v

Causes the shell to enter verbose mode, which causes commands to be echoed to the STDOUT device after history substitutions are made. Also sets the verbose shell variable.

-x

Causes the shell to enter echo mode and to echo all commands to STDOUT before they are executed.

-T

Enables tenex features.

-V

Causes the shell to enter verbose mode before the .cshrc is executed, in contrast to -v which enters verbose mode after .cshrc is executed. This command also sets the verbose shell variable.

-X

Causes the shell to enter echo mode before .cshrc is set, unlike the -x option.

If any arguments remain in the argument list after processing the command options, and the options -c, -i, -s, or -t were not specified, the first remaining argument is taken as the name of the file of commands to be executed.

## 5.2    Usage of command line options

Some of the options present in the C shell are also present in the Bourne shell or the Korn shell. Only options unique to the C shell are presented here, and for the other options reference should be made to the Bourne shell and Korn shell chapters (Chapters 3 and 4).

### 5.2.1    /bin/csh −T

This option enables the tenex features of the C shell, in which ⟨ESCAPE⟩ is used for command/file name completion and ⟨CTRL-D⟩ for listing available files.

### 5.2.2    /bin/csh −V

This is the same as −v except that the commands in .cshrc are also affected by the option.

### 5.2.3  /bin/csh -X

This is the same as -x except that the commands in .cshrc are also affected by the option.

## 5.3    Initialization scripts

Before the C shell searches the user's home directory for any initialization files, the file /etc/csh.login is executed, if present. Then the C shell searches the user's home directory for the file .cshrc which it will run, if present. After executing the .cshrc file the shell will examine the user's home directory for the file .login, and if this file is present it will also be executed. After both .cshrc and .login are executed, the shell will pass control to the user. When the user types either the internal commands exit or logout, or an end-of-file character (《CTRL-D》) is read, the shell will examine the user's home directory for the file .logout and if present will execute it.

## 5.4    Quoting metacharacters

Metacharacters are quoted in the C shell as described in the introduction to this part of the book—see Section 2.4.

## 5.5    Shell commands

### 5.5.1  *Simple commands*

The C shell simple commands are the same as for both the Bourne and Korn shells, except that the environment variable IFS is not used for blank interpretation. Blanks are always interpreted as space characters, tabs, new lines or ; characters.

### 5.5.2  *Pipelines*

The C shell pipelines are the same as in the Korn shell.

### 5.5.3  *Command lists*

The C shell is the same as the Korn shell in this respect. A command is either a simple command or one of the following internal commands, and unless stated otherwise the exit status of these internal shell commands is the exit status returned by the last simple command executed within that command.

### 5.5.4   *Internal shell commands*

case *command*

This is analogous to the case command in the Korn and Bourne shells, but its syntax is slightly different:

```
switch ( string )
  case str1:
                list
            [ breaksw ]
  case str2:
                list
            [ breaksw ]
  [ default ]  :
                list
            [ breaksw ]
  endws
```

The string after the switch statement is compared against each of the patterns str1, str2...strn found after the case statement, and if a match is found the command list up to the breaksw command is executed. If no match is found then the list following the default command, if present, is executed. If no default command is present the execution will continue at the command after the endsw. The breaksw command causes execution to continue to the command after the endsw command. This statement is directly analogous to the C programming language switch command of the same name. If the optional breaksw commands are not present then the command execution will continue from one case list to the following case list in sequence.

if/then/else *command*

This command is analogous to the if/else/elif command in the Korn and Bourne shells, but its syntax is slightly different:

```
if (expression1) then
      list
[ else if  ( expression2 ) then ]
      list
[ else ]
      list
endif
```

If the specified expression expression1 is true, i.e. non-zero, the commands to the first else are executed, otherwise the commands after the first else are executed. If expression1 is true and expression2 is true, then commands up to the second else are executed. Any number of else-if pairs may be nested, but only one `endif` at the end is necessary. The `else` and the `else if` clauses are optional.

### `foreach` *command*

This command is analogous to the `for` command in the Korn and Bourne shells, except that its syntax is slightly different.

```
foreach name ( wordlist )
    list
  end
```

For each of the words in the `wordlist` the variable name is assigned to each of them in turn, and the list of commands between the `foreach` and the `end` statement executed. The loop may be terminated by the `break` command, or prematurely reiterated by the `continue` command.

### `repeat` *command*

This command is unique to the C shell. It repeats the given command `count` a number of times:

```
repeat count command
```

### `while` *command*

This command is analogous to the `while` command in the Korn and Bourne shells, but its syntax is slightly different:

```
while ( expression)
      list
end
```

If the expression is true, i.e. not zero, then the commands between the `while` and the `end` are executed. Again the `break` and `continue` commands may be used to alter the loop's standard behaviour as in the Bourne and Korn shells.

### `goto` *command*

This command is unique to the C shell and allows unconditional jumps to a label point within the shell script source:

```
goto word
```

The shell expands the `word` given to a label of the form `label:`, the shell will rewind its input as far as possible, and will initiate a search for the string of the form label:. If one is found, execution will continue with the command after this label. The use of goto in scripts is potentially dangerous, as the shell's behaviour may not be consistent with backward goto requests.

### ( list ) *command*

Any command list executed as

( list )

will be executed in a subshell, as in the Korn and Bourne shells.

### TIME *command*

With no arguments, a summary of the time used by this shell and its children is printed. If an argument is given, the time taken to execute the simple command is given after the command completes. This command is similar to the Korn shell command time.

time [ command ]

### Command substitution

This is the same as in the Bourne shell.

### Shell comments

This is the same as in the Bourne shell.

### Aliasing

This is similar to the Korn shell command of the same name, but there are some differences. As in the Korn shell an alias may be created or destroyed using the commands alias and unalias. After the command line is scanned, it is parsed into distinct commands. The first word of each command, left to right, is checked to see if it contains an alias. If it does, the text which is the alias is substituted for its alias value. This is done by rereading the history file and replacing the aliased words in the command list. Thus, if the alias for ls is ls -l, the command ls /usr will result in ls -l /usr, leaving the argument list undisturbed. If an alias is found, the word substitution takes place and the resulting line is re-examined for aliases. This is very different from the Korn shell `alias` command. Looping is prevented by a check for recursive aliases.

### Tilde substitution

This is similar to the Korn shell in that whenever the ~ character is found next to a / character it is expanded to the value of the environment variable `home`.

### Parameter substitution

`csh` maintains a set of variables, each of which has a value equal to zero or more strings or words. Variables may have names up to 20 characters in length. The value of a variable may be displayed and changed using the `set` and `unset` commands.

Some variables are Boolean, in other words the shell considers set variables as true and unset variables as false. Other variables may be numerically evaluated using the @ command. This command in front of a word causes it to be evaluated numerically, and any other words on the line are ignored. The following parameters are set by the shell, and except where noted it is an error to reference any variable that is not set.

| *Sequence* | *Result after substitution* |

`${parameter}`

> The value, if any, of the parameter is substituted. The { and } characters are required only if the parameter is followed by a non-white-space character, which should not be interpreted as part of the parameter's name.

`$parameter[n]`
`${parameter[n]}`

> Allows modification of the nth word in the parameter. The value of n is subject to variable substitution and may consist of any single number or two numbers separated by a dash. The first word of the parameter is numbered 1. The first number defaults to 1, and the last number if omitted defaults to the total number of words in the parameter. A * character selects all words.

`$#parameter`
`{#parameter}`

> Gives the number of words in the parameter, useful in the option above.

`$0`

> The name of the file from which the current commands are being read, and error occurs if this is not known.

| *Sequence* | *Result after substitution* |
|---|---|

`$number`
`${number}`

Similar to the Korn and Bourne shells' $1 .. $9 parameters. Another way of indexing the variable `argv`, equivalent to `$argv[number]`.

`$*`

The same as the Korn and Bourne shells' `$*`. In the C shell this is equivalent to the number of words in the variable `argv` or `$argv[*]`.

In the above examples certain modifiers can be applied using the notation `:letter` where letter is the modifier, directly after the parameter name. If curly brackets (`{ }`) are used, the modifier must be placed inside the brackets.

The following substitutions do not allow any modifiers:

| *Sequence* | *Result after substitution* |
|---|---|

`$?parameter`
`${?parameter}`

The string 1 is returned if parameter is set, 0 if it is not set.

`$?0`

The string 1 is returned if the current input file is known, 0 if not.

`$$`

Returns the decimal process ID of the parent shell.

`$<`

Substitutes for a line of input from STDIN, can be used to read a line of input from the STDIN in shell scripts.

The C shell also has some defined keyword parameters that may be set and used by the shell. The following are the most common:

| *Sequence* | *Function in the shell* |
|---|---|

`argv`

Set to the arguments of the shell command line, and it is from this that positional parameters are substituted. For example $1 .. $9, which may be replaced by `$argv[1]` .. `$argv[9]`, etc.

`CDPATH`

The search path for the `cd` command, to resolve relative pathnames.

`cwd`

Contains the path of the current working directory, and is changed by the `cd` command. It has the same function as the Korn shell `PWD` variable.

`echo`

The variable set by the `-x` command line option.

`history`

The variable used to create a command history buffer, and is set to its size. If this variable is not set then there is no command history and the command history commands will not work. Very large values of history may cause the shell to run out of memory. Values of 10 to 20 are normal.

home

The default argument (the home directory) for the cd command.

ignoreeof

Same as the Korn shell -o option ignoreeof.

mail

Contains the lists of files that csh checks for mail. csh checks periodically (default 10 minutes) for new mail arriving. If mail has arrived in one of the files specified then the shell prints You have mail.

If the first word of the value of mail is numeric, this specifies the mail check time interval in seconds.

If multiple mail files are specified, the shell will print New mail in file, where file is the filename of the mail file containing the mail.

noclobber

If set, this places restrictions on output redirection to ensure that files are not accidentally destroyed, i.e. commands using the >> directive for files that already exist.

noglob

If set, filename expansion is inhibited.

nomatch

If set, it is no longer an error for a filename expansion not to match any existing files. If there is no match then the original pattern is returned.

notify

If set, csh will notify the user immediately through the STDOUT device file when a background process terminates. In the default case when the variable is unset the shell will notify the user just before printing the shell prompt.

path

The default search path for locating commands.

prompt

The same as the Korn shell PS1 prompt, but the default prompt is a % for users and a # for the superuser.

shell

Contains the name of the csh shell executable file, as in the Korn shell. However, no rcsh exists.

status

Contains the return status of the last executed command, similar to Bourne and Korn shell $? variable.

time

A numeric value which controls the automatic timing of commands. If it is set, for any command that takes more than the specified number of CPU

*Sequence*                          *Function in the shell*

    seconds, csh prints a line of information to STDOUT, giving the user the system, users and percentage utilization of the CPU of that process. The percentage utilization is the ratio of user plus system times to real time. The message is printed after the command finishes execution.

verbose

    Set by the −v command line option; see above.

autologout

    Has a numeric value, and is set to the number of seconds' inactivity allowed before the shell automatically logs the user out.

### *Blank interpretation*

The C shell separates words using a fixed set of characters. It does not use an environment variable to configure these characters, as the Bourne and Korn shells do.

### *Input/output redirection*

The STDOUT and STDIN device files may be redirected in a similar way to the Bourne and Korn shells.

*Command*                          *Function*

< word

    Use the file called word as the standard input (STDIN) for the command.

> word

    Use the file called word as the standard output (STDOUT) for the command. If the file word does not exist, it will be created. If the file does already exist, it will be truncated.

<< word

    The same as in the Bourne and Korn shells.

>! word

    If the variable noclobber is set then certain restrictions are placed on redirection of STDOUT and STDERR to files that already exist, except special files for device files such as /dev/null. The ! will force the shell to ignore these restrictions.

>& word

    Redirects STDOUT and STDERR together to the file word.

>&! word

    Redirects STDOUT and STDERR together to the file word, ignoring the noclobber restrictions.

```
>> word
```
The same as in the Bourne and Korn shells.
```
>>& word
```
Appends both STDOUT and STDERR to the file word.
```
>>! word
```
Same as >> word, but ignores the noclobber restrictions.
```
>>&! word
```
Same as >>& word, but ignores the noclobber restrictions.
```
|&
```
Provides diagnostic output for pipes as the output or input is sent to STDOUT as well as through the pipe. This command may be used instead of |. This is very different to the Korn shell use of the symbol.

*Expression evaluation*

A number of the special commands take expressions in which the operators are similar to those found in the C programming language. The following operators are valid. The groups are listed in decreasing order of precedence:

```
*  /  %
+  -
>>  <<
<=  >=  <  >
==  !=  =~-  !~
```

The operators ==, !=, =~ and !~ compare their arguments as strings: all the other operators operate on numeric arguments. The operators =~ and !~ are like != and == except that the right-hand side is a pattern containing * or ? and instances of [..] against which the left-hand side is matched. This reduces the need for a switch statement in shell scripts when all that is required is a pattern match.

Any strings beginning with 0 are considered to be octal numbers, and null or missing arguments are considered to be 0. The results of all expressions are strings, which may represent decimal numbers.

It is important to note that no two operators may be part of the same word, and operators should be separated by white-space characters from all other significant characters of the command line.

Also available in expressions as operands are command executions enclosed in curly braces ({ }) and file enquiries of the form

```
-option filename
```

where -option is one of the following:

```
-r    read access
-w    write access
-x    execute access
-e    existence
```

-o       ownership
-z       zero size
-f       ordinary file
-d       directory

The specified filename is expanded and then tested to see if it has the relationship specified to the real user ID (uid). If the filename does not exist then the returned value of any enquiry will be false. The expression will return true if the command exits with a status of true, otherwise it will be false. The variable status is set to the returned value of all expressions.

### *Filename substitutions*

Each command line word is processed as a pattern for filename substitution. Any pattern found will be replaced with a sorted list of filenames which match the pattern. The form of the pattern may be any regular expression as seen in the Bourne and Korn shells, with the following exceptions:

- Non-matching list in bracket expressions are not supported.
- In a list of words specifying filename substitution it is an error for no pattern to match an existing filename, but it is not required for each pattern to match.
- The metanotation a{b,c,d}e is a shorthand for abe ace ade. The left-to-right order is preserved, with results of matches being sorted separately at a low level to preserve this order. This construct may be nested, so for example

```
% ~fred/data/{this, is}.c
```

expands to

```
  /usr/fred/data/this.c
/usr/fred/data/ls.c
```

whether or not these files exist, without any chance of an error if the home directory for fred is /usr/fred. Similarly,

```
../{zed, *jim}
```

might expand to

```
../zed ../jim ../xjim
```

Note that zed was not sorted with the results of the matching *jim. As a special case {, } and { } are passed unchanged.

*Jobs*

The shell controls jobs in the same way as the Korn shell

*Command line reentry*

History substitution enables the user to use words from previous commands as portions of new commands, repeat commands, or repeat arguments of previous commands in the current command.

History substitutions begin with a ! character. Substitutions may begin anywhere in the input stream, but may not be nested. The ! character can be quoted using a \ character to negate its special meaning. The ! character is passed unchanged when it is followed by any white-space character, i.e. blank, tab, new line, equal sign, or left parenthesis. Any input line which contains history substitutions is echoed to the STDOUT device file before it is executed for verification.

Commands as they are input from the terminal are stored in the history list. These commands are numbered from 1, and the number of commands which may be stored is controlled by the environment variable history.

The user may refer to commands in the history file using any of the following methods:

!command_number
>    The user may issue the command !10, for example, to return the tenth command line in the history file.
!-offset
>    The user may issue the command !-3, for example, to return the third previous command line in the history file.
!pattern
>    Any regular expression may be used to search the history file for command line matching. For example, !f returns the first command in the history file that has an initial character of f and !?fred? searches the history file for any line containing the characters fred.
!!
>    A special case of the ! special character; it simply repeats the last command.

The forms given above simply reintroduce the words of the previous commands to the input stream separated by a single space.

To select words from a previous command the user follows any of the above commands with a : (colon) and a designator for the desired words. The words in any input line are numbered from zero. The base designators are now listed:

| *Command designator* | *Function* |
|---|---|
| 0 | |
| | Selects the first word, i.e. the command name itself. For example, the command !!:0 would select the command name of the last command. |
| n | |
| | Selects the nth word. |
| ^ | |
| | Selects the first argument. This is equivalent to 1. |
| $ | |
| | Selects the last word on the command line. |
| m-n | |
| | Selects words in the numeric range m through to n. The special cases are -n which select all words up to word n from word zero, and m- which selects all words from word m up to but not including the last word on the line. |
| * | |
| | This is a symbol used to mean 1-$, i.e. the penultimate word. This includes all of the arguments. |
| % | |
| | Used with a search sequence to substitute the immediately preceding matching word. |

The colon character (:) separating the command specification from the word specification can be omitted if the word specification begins with ^, $, - or %.

After each word specification the user may place a sequence of modifiers, each preceded by a : character. The following modifiers are defined.

| *Word designator* | *Function* |
|---|---|
| h | |
| | Use only the first components of the pathname by removing all following components. |
| r | |
| | Use the root filename, by removing any suffix (.xxx). |
| e | |
| | Use the filename's trailing suffix (.xxx) by removing the root name. |
| s/l/r/ | |
| | Substitute the value of r for the value of l in the indicated command. |
| t | |
| | Use only the final filename part of the pathname by removing all leading pathname components. |
| & | |
| | Repeat previous substitution. |
| p | |
| | Print new command but do not execute it. |

q

> Quote substituted words, preventing further substitutions.

x

> Like q, but breaks words at blanks, tabs or new-line characters.

g

> Use a global command as a prefix to another modifier to cause the specified changes to be made to all words. All words in the command line are changed, one change per word, and each string enclosed in either ' (single quotes) or " (double quotes) is considered as a word.

Unless preceded by a g modifier, the modification is applied only to the first word which is modifiable. The shell will cause an error if a substitution is attempted and cannot be completed.

The value of l in the modifier s/l/r is not a regular expression in the AIX editor sense, but a string. Any character may be used as a delimiter in place of the / character, and a \ quotes the delimiter character in either l or r. The & character in the r string is replaced with the text from the l string, and a \ also quotes this character. A null l string will cause substitution to use the previous string either from an l string or from a context scan string in the form !?string?. The trailing delimiter in the substitution may be omitted if a new line follows immediately, as may the trailing ? in a context string scan.

A history reference may be given without any command specification, e.g !$. In this case the reference is to the previous command unless a previous history reference occurred on the same line, in which case this form repeats the previous reference to the same command line. For example, the command

```
% !?ls?^ !$
```

select the first word that matches ls and the last word of the same command line.

A special abbreviation of a history reference occurs when the first non-blank character of an input line is ^ (caret character). Thus the command ^ is equivalent to !:s^, providing a convenient method of substitution on the text of the previous line. For example, the command

```
% ^lb^lib
```

changes the string lb to lib in the previous line, because this command is equivalent to !:s^lb^lib.

A history substitution may be surrounded with curly braces ({ }) if necessary to insulate it from the characters which follow. For example, after the command

```
% ls -ld al
```

the command

```
% !{l}ways
```

will produce

```
% ls -ld always
```

It should be noted that the command !lways would look for any string starting with lways, as required.


## 5.6　　Special commands

*Command*　　　　　　　　　　　　　*Function*

```
alias [ name ]
      [ wordlist]
```
Same as in the Korn shell.

```
bg [%job] [%string]
```
Places the job either associated with the job number job or beginning with string into background.

```
break
```
Similar to the Bourne and Korn shells, except no optional parameter is allowed. However, breaks found on the same input line provide a method of emulating the multi-level break found in the Korn shell.

```
cd [ name ]
chdir [ name ]
```
Same as in the Bourne shell.

```
dirs
```
Prints the directory stack. The top of the stack is at the left, and the first directory in the stack is the current directory.

```
echo arg
```
Echo arguments to STDOUT.

```
eval arg
```
The arguments are read as input to the current shell, and the resulting command(s) executed.

```
exec [arg]
```
Causes the current shell to execute the command specified by arg in place of itself. No new process is created.

```
exit [ n ]
```
Causes the shell to exit with the exit status n. If n is omitted, then the exit status of the last command is returned.

`fg [%job] [%string]`
　　Places the job either associated with the job number `job` or that begins
　　with `string` into foreground.

`glob wordlist`
　　Like `echo`, but recognition of \ escapes is not supported.

`history [ -h ]`
　　　　　　`[ -r ]`
　　　　　　`[ n ]`
　　Displays the command history list. If n is given, only the nth most recent
　　commands are printed. The `-r` option reverses the order in which the
　　commands are printed, i.e. the most recent command is printed first and
　　the oldest command printed last. The `-h` option prints the history list
　　without leading numbers.

`jobs [ -l ]`
　　Same as the Korn shell command

`kill [ % job ]`
　　　　`[ -sig %job]`
　　　　`[ pid ]`
　　　　`[ -sig pid ]`
　　Same as in the Korn shell.

`login`
　　Terminates the current login shell, and returns user to the standard login
　　program, i.e. `/bin/login`.

`logout`
　　Same as exit, or end-of-file character.

`newgrp`
　　Similar to the Korn shell command of the same name.

`nice [ +n ]`
　　　　`[ command ]`
　　Without parameters, sets the current shell `nice` priority to the default. If
　　`+n` option is specified the priority of the following command will be
　　lowered by the value of n. If the `+n` is omitted then the command runs
　　with the current default priority. Superuser may use negative values of n
　　to increase the priority of commands.

`nohup [ command ]`
　　Same as in the Korn shell.

`notify [ %job ]`
　　Causes the shell to notify the user asynchronously when the job specified
　　changes state. This is done automatically if the variable `notify` is set.

`onintr [ - ]`
　　　　　`[ label ]`
　　Similar to the Bourne and Korn shell `trap` command. With no argument
　　the command will restore to defaults all of the shells interrupts. If – is

*Command*                                    *Function*

specified it will cause all interrupts to be ignored. If a `label` is specified it will cause the shell to `goto` the label when an interrupt is received, or when a child process terminates because it was interrupted.

If the shell is running in background and interrupts are being ignored, then `onintr` has no effect.

`popd [ +n ]`

Pops the directory stack, returning to the new top directory. With an argument n it discards the nth entry on the stack. The stacked directories are numbered from zero.

`pushd [ name ]`
`     [ +n ]`

With no arguments the command `pushd` exchanges the top two elements of the directory stack. Given a `name` argument, `pushd` changes to this directory and pushes the old working directory on to the top of the stack.

`rehash`

Used when changes to the files present in directories given by the `PATH` environment variable are made, after login. This allows the shell to update its hash table of regularly used commands.

`set [ name ]`
`  [ name=word]`
`  [ name[index]=word]`
`  [ name=(wordlist)]`

Without any arguments displays all shell variables that are set. Variables which have more than a single word value are printed in parenthesized word lists. The variable name on its own sets the value of the variable name to null. The value of `name` is set to a single word with the command `name=word`. The `indexed` word of the variable `name` is set to word by the command `name[index]=word`, but this indexed component must exist. The value of `name` is set to `wordlist` with the command `name=(wordlist)`. The arguments may be repeated to set multiple values with one set command. Note, however, that variable expansion occurs for all arguments before any setting takes place.

`setenv [ name ]`
`       [ value]`

Sets and exports the variable `name` to a value of `value`.

`shift [ +n ]`

Same as in the Bourne and Korn shells.

`source [ -h ]`
`       [ name ]`

Reads shell commands from name. The commands read from name are not normally placed in the history list, but they will be if the -h option is specified.

stop [ %job ]

Stops the job specified by %job or the current job if no argument is given.

suspend

Causes csh to stop as if it had received a suspend signal. Because csh normally ignores the suspend signal, this is the only way to suspend it. The command gives an error message if it is attempted from the login shell.

time [ command ]

Same as in the Korn shell.

umask [ value ]

Same as in the Korn shell.

unalias name

Same as in the Korn shell. name may contain metacharacters, which are expanded.

unhash

The use of the internal hash table used for command lookup is disabled. See hash command.

unset name

Unsets the variables specified by the name argument, as name may contain metacharacters. Unsets variables set by the set command.

unsetenv name

Similar to unset, but unsets variables created or altered by the setenv command.

wait

Similar to the wait command in the Bourne and Korn shells, except that this command waits for all background jobs to complete.

%job

Brings the job %job to the foreground, cf. the Korn shell fg command.

%job &

Sends the job %job to the background, cf. the Korn shell bg command.

# 6
# Comparison of the Bourne, Korn and C shells

The three most widely used shells, the Bourne, Korn and C shells, have several common features and functions. They also have unique features which enable each of them to function more or less effectively in certain development environments. The Bourne shell may be viewed as the UNIX System V standard shell, and the C shell as the BSD 4.x standard shell. The Korn shell is an attempt by AT&T to combine the best features of the C shell and the Bourne shell.

In general, functions found in either the Bourne shell or the C shell will be found in some form in the Korn shell, but similarities between the Bourne shell and the C shell are few.

## 6.1 Generic features of the shells

### 6.1.1 Internal shell commands

The Korn shell has all of the same special commands as the Bourne shell, with some additions. The Korn shell commands differ markedly from those used in the C shell. It is possible to write a generic shell script that will run under both the Bourne shell and the Korn shell, but such a shell script is very unlikely to run under the C shell. Most of the additional internal commands found in the Korn shell are either directly derived from the C shell or are different implementations of the same functionality found in the C shell. Some notable features of the Korn shell are similar but not identical to their C shell counterparts, for example command line history has the same set of generic special commands, but has a different implementation and functionality in the C shell.

### 6.1.2 Environment variables

The Korn shell shares many of the same set of standard environment variables found in both the Bourne shell and the C shell. Its use of the typeset function to

assign a notion of data type to a variable is unique, however, as is the command
`print` which is often used instead of the standard `echo` command.

### 6.1.3   Command reentry

The Korn shell, like the C shell, has the ability to perform command reentry, but
the implementation is quite different. The Korn shell is much more flexible in the
style of command line reentry used, whereas the C shell has its style features fixed.
Although command line reentry is a feature common to the Korn shell and the C
shell, its functionality is quite different in each case.

### 6.1.4   Initialization files

The Korn shell shares the standard initialization files with the Bourne shell. The
Korn shell also has extra security features which enable the administrator to have
closer control over `setuid` programs and the AIX `su` command. The C shell has
very different initialization files.

### 6.1.5   Command line options

The Korn shell shares with the Bourne shell and the C shell some common
command line options which perform the same generic functions in all three
shells.

## 6.2   Usage of the Bourne, Korn and C shells

The question of which of the shells to use for any given purpose is a difficult one to
answer. It depends largely on two main factors; the shell functionality required,
and personal choice.

In terms of functionality the Korn shell is generally superior to both the Bourne
shell and the C shell, having most of the best features of each of the other shells
and some of its own.

Personal choice is greatly influenced by which flavour or flavours of UNIX the
user has been brought up on. The Bourne shell and the Korn shell are both
provided by AT&T and are therefore present on all of the newer versions of
AT&T system V.x. The Bourne shell is of course the *de facto* standard shell, and is
present on nearly all systems, including AT&T's System V.x and BSD 4.x. The C
shell is a more specialist shell, in that it was originally released on the BSD 4.x and
3.x versions of UNIX and has until quite recently remained exclusively in that
domain. However, with the release of AIX and other versions of UNIX which
unify AT&T Systems V.3 and BSD 4.3 (if only in terms of look and feel) the C
shell has been released into what appears to be a System V.x operating environment.

The primary training ground for UNIX software engineers is undoubtedly the universities, and universities tend to use BSD-based systems. University graduates are consequently very likely to be familiar with the C shell and perhaps the Bourne shell. The Korn shell is often a new experience for graduates, but in time nearly all users come to prefer its flexibility and usability when compared with the Bourne shell and C shell. In the author's opinion the Korn shell is the most functionally rich and the most usable of the three shells described in this book.

## 6.3    Shell security

The topic of AIX system security will be discussed at length in the book *AIX 3.x for Administrators* (written by Phil Colledge, to be published by McGraw-Hill, London). However, there are certain shell security procedures that should be observed by the user.

### 6.3.1   *Execution search paths*

All the shells presented above have initialization scripts which are often used to initialize the shell's environment. These scripts typically set the shell execution search path, which the shell will use to look for both AIX utilities and applications programs. This enables the user to initiate a program by name alone, instead of having to specify a full pathname. There are certain instances where it is undesirable, or a potential security breach, to allow the shell to determine the program executed by name alone, using the search path to resolve the full pathname. One such instance is the superuser. As a matter of policy the superuser should have no path set, so that all programs or utilities executed from the command line will need to have a full pathname prefix. The reasons for this are clear. The superuser needs to know that he or she has executed the real rm command for example, and not a shell script called rm in their execution path, before the path of the real rm. This is a common mistake of most UNIX and AIX installations and can potentially lead to a rogue program being executed with superuser permissions. If the superuser needs to have an execution path set, then the directories present in the execution path need to have permissions that forbid other users from modifying any of the executable scripts or code programs present within them.

### 6.3.2   *Inactivity timeouts*

Many users, and unfortunately many professionals as well, tend to leave terminals logged in and unattended for long periods of time. This is a potential security risk, and should be addressed by the administrator. The Korn shell and the C shell provide an environment variable that if set will cause the shell to terminate upon a specified period of inactivity. This feature should be used if it is present. An inactivity set to a reasonable amount of time will seldom upset anyone, but files lost to a malicious hacker will! The Bourne shell does not provide this feature, which presents a slight problem. The implementation of inactivity timeouts does not have to be a shell level, however; a well-written AIX daemon periodically checking device file inactivity can often achieve a similar result. The method used to terminate inactive user shells is irrelevant provided that the aim is achieved.

### 6.3.3   Environment changes

It is often desirable to ensure that certain key environment variables are not changed after the initial values have been assigned to them. With the Korn shell and Bourne shell this is possible by making the variable `readonly`, but using the C shell it is not possible. The environment variables for the execution path and the inactivity timeout features are good examples of variables that the administrator would not wish to have changed.

### 6.3.4   Use of restricted shells

It is most undesirable to give applications users an AIX shell. The usual method is for the initialization script to initiate the application or application menu program, leaving the user only a limited choice of options. However, there may be certain instances where access is required to an AIX shell, and in these cases the restricted versions of the shell should be used if they are supported. The Korn and Bourne shells provide this feature, which limits the functionality of the shell, but the C shell does not.

# Part Two
# The system call interface

# 7
# Programming and development utilities

This part of the book is devoted to the system call interfaces provided by AIX 3.x, and covers a small cross-section of the available system call interfaces within AIX 3.x. It is not a complete reference guide to all the system calls, as most of them are identical to those found in UNIX system V.x and BSD 4.x and only a few are totally specific to AIX. The AIX-specific system calls often provide extended functionality that is not found within other flavours of UNIX, so in the next chapter the AIX-specific system calls are described in some detail.

These system calls are presented in related groups and not in isolation, and the presentation is supported by worked examples to illustrate the use of the calls.

As an introduction we must first look at the development environment of AIX 3.x from the C programmer's viewpoint.

## 7.1    Program development under AIX 3.x

Under AIX 3.x, program development is greatly enhanced by two main features: firstly the wealth of library and system call support available, which aids the speedy development of any application or system utility, and secondly the availability of the XL compiler series. These have common object formats, and cross-language linking between any of the XL series compilers, currently including C, Pascal and FORTRAN, eliminates the complexities of multi-language library and sub-program support. Cross-language procedure calling and formal parameter verification are supported.

All of the XL series of compilers, including IBM's own PL.8 compiler used internally by the IBM Corporation, generate the same intermediate code XIL. This is then transformed by a number of procedures into optimized machine code instructions. Most of these stages, except of course the language parsing, semantic and syntax analysis phases, are common to all of the XL series compilers.

The basic structure of an XL series compiler is to divide the task of compilation into the following four tasks which are processed in this order:

- **Language analysis**   This phase is specific to the specific XL compiler concerned, and is responsible for the formal language analysis and the generation of intermediate code in XIL format.
- **Optimization**   This phase is common to all XL compilers, and will optimize the intermediate code to run on an unlimited register machine.
- **Register allocation**   This phase is common to all XL compilers. It takes the intermediate code generated by the above optimization and produces intermediate code for a limited register machine.
- **Assembly to object format**   This phase is common to all XL compilers. It takes the final intermediate code and transforms it to machine code sequences for the real machine hardware (under AIX 3.x running on the RISC System/ 6000 this would be the POWER RISC chip) and finally links these instructions into a XCOFF object file.

For the majority of software development projects under AIX 3.x the XL C compiler is an obvious choice. However, the compiler technology is only a small part of the development environment provided by AIX 3.x and it would be wrong not to consider the support utilities required for proper software development. Part Four of the book presents a reference to these utilities and some practical guides for usage.

## 7.2    AIX 3.x development environment

One of the design objectives of AIX 3.x is to provide a unifying platform for most of the UNIX industry standards. This objective has led to the creation with AIX 3.x, as far as possible, of a unified system call interface structure for system calls found to be common to one or more standards. This enables the application developer to nominate which standard his or her program will adhere to, and only have to re-link the application with the library support code.

AIX 3.x provides an application development environment which, transparently to the application, provides load-time and run-time dynamic linking of programs and shared libraries. These facilities provide a new dimension of flexibility for the applications programmer which is often not found in other commercial versions of UNIX currently available.

As well as all this, AIX 3.x has features which are not found in any other version of UNIX or perhaps in any other minicomputer-based operating system. These features are often incorporated into interfaces which emulate their UNIX counterparts, but at the system call interface level they are unique to AIX 3.x.

All of these features combine to make AIX 3.x, in the author's opinion, the most powerful and flexible UNIX variant in the marketplace today.

## 7.3    Linking and loading programs

One of the most powerful new features available under AIX 3.x is the ability to have load-time and run-time dynamic linking, in addition to the standard statically linked alternative found in most UNIX implementations.

What are load-time and run-time dynamic linking, and why are they so useful? In order to answer these questions and explain the key philosophical differences between the three types of linking available under AIX 3.x, it is important to understand what linking and object resolution actually are.

Most programs written in a high-level language are translated into machine code instructions using three tools. First, a compiler translates the high-level language into assembly language for the target machine, then the assembler generates the machine code instructions from the assembly language to generate object code, and finally the linker or linkage editor incorporates any library support code that may be required within the object code to generate an executable object. This final executable object contains all of the necessary machine code instructions required to execute its task, including copies of all of the library code required.

### 7.3.1    Statically linked application code

It has been estimated that programs as executable objects are on average composed of 25–50% application code and 75–50% library code required by the application code. In other words, the size of the library code usually exceeds the size of the application code itself. Therefore in the statically linked example in Fig. 7.1 multiple copies of the sample library support code exist in memory at any instant in time, one copy for each user process running the application code. This is inherently wasteful, and also leads to problems for software developers. Today's application programs tend to be object-oriented, or at worst library-orientated programs. This means that each small section of application code may depend on a very much larger section of library code, so each time a library is modified all of the application programs using that library or related libraries have to be re-linked. This process may take many hours or even days. In an attempt to avoid such an unnecessary waste of time, AIX 3.x has incorporated two new linking modes. In *load-time linking* the program loader resolves any library references at load-time, and in *run-time linking* unresolved library references are resolved during the execution of a program .

These features make it possible to implement an additional feature, the shared library, where many copies of application code may share one memory copy of common library code. This often makes enormous savings in the amount of core memory required to execute a number of copies of the application code. With the first generation of RISC technology it was not unusual for the executable object to exceed the size of the source code program, and even with the POWER RISC

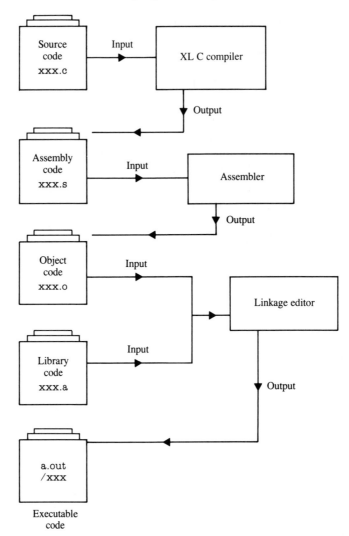

Figure 7.1.  The compilation process for static linking.

technology this can often be the case if statically linked code is used. The ability to use dynamically linked shared libraries enables resource utilization to be optimized and allows libraries to be modified without the long process of re-linking all the application code.

## 7.3.2   Run-time dynamically linked application code

Run-time and load-time dynamic linking are both achieved in the same way with respect to the compilation process. The only difference is that during load-time dynamic linking all external references are resolved before the program begins execution, but with run-time dynamic linking external references are resolved on the fly as the program requires access to the external resources.

In order to enable AIX 3.x to implement both run-time and load-time linking, the UNIX standard object format COFF (common object format file) was replaced with an extended format XCOFF (extended common object format file). These changes allowed the object file to contain the additional information required in order to implement the dynamic linking process. In addition to the changes made to the object file format the linker or linkage editor, the command ld under standard UNIX, was also changed to enable it to function with the new object format. Although there have been some major changes at the implementation level of both the linkage editor and the loader system calls, the semantics have been preserved so that programs compiled under other UNIX variants will have little or no trouble with the transition to AIX 3.x.

The concepts behind dynamic linkage are quite simple. Unlike static linkage, where all of the external references are resolved by the linkage editor at link time, with dynamic linkage the linkage editor just inserts into the object code where the required code may be found. At some later time, either at load-time or run-time, the kernel will resolve these references to objects by loading them into core memory. Thus the application code is totally unaware of the mechanism used to resolve its external references.

In order that the linkage editor at link time can determine where the objects that are externally referenced will reside, so that they may be used later, two files containing information about the objects either exported from the object file (usually a library) or to be imported into the object file (usually an application object code) are used. These files are called *export lists* and *import lists* respectively. It should be noted that an application is not required to import all of the objects exported by a library, and that libraries may contain objects imported from other libraries.

The compilation process for a dynamically linked application will take the path shown in Fig. 7.2. Note that the differences between static linkage and dynamic linkage are found at the linkage editor stage, and at no other stage.

Using dynamic linking has several benefits for the application and systems programmer. The dynamic linking provided under AIX 3.x is used by AIX 3.x itself to allow:

- **Flexible kernel extensions**  Dynamic configuration of sub-systems such as X.25, TCP/IP, etc. are allowed.
- **Dynamic configuration of device drivers**  Device drivers may be configured and new device drivers added dynamically.
- **System call extensions**  New system calls may be added to the kernel after load-time.
- **Ease of program maintenance**  Using dynamically linked library code, application code need not be re-compiled or re-linked each time a change is made

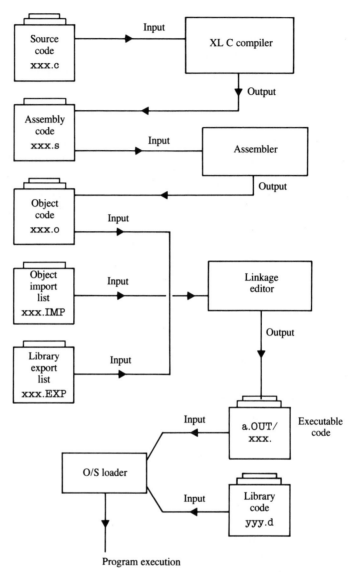

Figure 7.2. The compilation process for dynamic linking.

to the implementation of a library support procedure, provided that the
semantics of the procedure call are not changed.

● **Reduced program size**   RISC-based processors require a larger number of
machine code instructions to achieve a given task than CISC-based processors. The use of dynamically linked shared library code gives the application programmer the ability to have one reusable copy of all library code

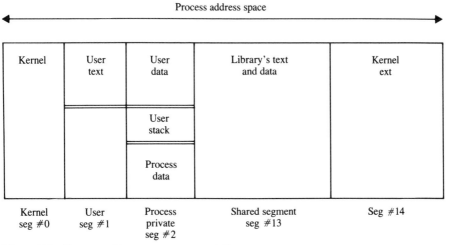

Figure 7.3. Process address space segmentation.

accessible by every application module and all users. This significantly reduces the total amount of core memory required for any given application.

### 7.3.3 How does load-time/run-time linking work?

Under AIX 3.x each process has its own address space, that is its own area of virtual memory. This address space is separated into segments, each of which is accessible to the process by loading and unloading segment registers within the CPU.

A diagrammatic representation of the arrangement of segments within a process is shown in Fig. 7.3.

- The segments labelled kernel and kernel ext are segments which provide the process access to system calls and operating system services. The objects within these segments are exported from the operating system object code.
- The segments labelled user text, user data, user stack and process data are private to the process, and no other process will be allowed to load this segment identifier into a segment register within the CPU.
- The segment labelled shared segment is of the most interest to AIX 3.x application developers and systems programmers. It is often mapped using the virtual memory management functions to a single segment containing one copy of both code and text data for any given library, for example `libc.a`. This mapping is achieved in a similar way to the mapping of shared memory segments as discussed in Part Three of this book.

Libraries that are mapped into this shared memory segment are often not reentrant, in other words their data segments may contain some static data which will be overwritten by each process that may use them. As will be shown later the linkage editor provides the ability to map the data segments of shared libraries into the process's private segment, while still allowing the code segment to be shared.

During load-time or run-time, whichever model is being used, any shared objects not present in the core memory are automatically loaded and mapped by the loader.

The idea with load-time and run-time linking is that applications may be broken down into manageable pieces. Each of these pieces is then page-map-loaded into segments, and pieces that are shared between many processes may be made available to these processes using the memory management functions. Then when all of the pieces are available to a process, externally referenced symbols are resolved.

This mechanism depends on only three main functional units: the linkage editor to enable the use of an extended common object format (XCOFF), a system loader or system call set that will facilitate the resolution of externally referenced symbols at load time, and an advanced memory management system to assist with this task.

The linker, loader and memory management functions are quite separate functional units in AIX 3.x, as shown diagrammatically in Fig. 7.4.

## 7.4    AIX 3.x implementation of dynamic linking

The implementation of dynamically linked code under AIX 3.x is largely transparent to the program code, and requires the programmer to make little or no allowance for this within the code. Under AIX 3.x dynamic linking is achieved using special linker options given at compile-time or link-time to a new linkage

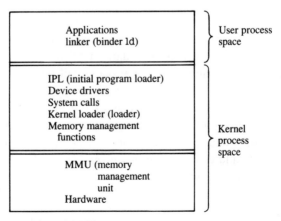

Figure 7.4. The separation of AIX services.

editor (ld), which in turn generates executable object code that may be loaded and executed by the kernel loader.

Let us consider an example of a shared object and dynamic linking under AIX 3.x. The code fragments presented in the text are simple examples, but illustrate the use of shared objects. The first code fragment implements the main procedure of a C program which calls a shared object function defined in the second code fragment.

The following code is contained in a file called main.c:

```
 #include <stdio.h>
/* ************************************** */
/* function prototype for shared object   */
/* function                               */
/* ************************************** */
int shared_func();
int main()
  {
    printf("This was printed by the main procedure\n\n");
    printf("Calling shared function\n");
    shared_func();
    printf("Returned from shared object function\n");
  }
```

In order for the shared object function shared_func() to be known to the linker when the source is compiled and linked, a file must be generated called an *import file* which defines all imported objects and their source. The following definition would be placed in a file called main.imp:

```
  (main.imp)
#! ./sharedobj
shared_func
```

The first line of the import file defines the name of the import file itself. The second line defines the name of the object file in which the shared objects that follow will be found; this name may include a full path to the object file. Finally, one or more lines define the shared objects that may be found in the file specified above. These objects may be of any of the following types, functions, static variables or non-static variables.

The file main.c is then compiled with a special linker option which causes the linkage editor not to attempt to resolve the externally referenced objects at compile time but to do it later, at load-time. The main.c source is compiled with the command line

```
$ cc -b import:main.imp -omain main.c
```

The option -b is a linkage editor option. When passed to the linkage editor it instructs the editor to use the file `main.imp` as the source for its information when trying to locate any externally referenced objects. The compiler generates an executable object file `main` which has an external object `shared_func()` that will reside in a file `sharedobj`.

The generation of the shared object file is achieved as follows. The shared object function is placed in a file called `shared.c`, the text of which is as follows:

```
    #include <stdio.h>
int shared_func()
  {
      static char string[]="SF local variable";
      printf("%s\n", string);
  }
```

This shared object source file is then compiled using the command

```
$ cc -c shared.c -o shared.o
```

As we saw with the main source file which had an import list to define the location of all imported objects, this shared source file has an export list which defines which objects are exported from the object code. This file has a similar form to the import list defined for `main.c—`, but will take the following form and be contained in a file called `shared.exp`:

```
    #! ./sharedobj
shared_func
```

The first line defines the name of the shared object file in which the shared object function will reside, and the subsequent lines define shared objects exported from this object file. Finally the object file `shared.o` is linked using the following command into a shared object file `sharedobj`:

```
$ ld -H512 -T512 -bglink:/lib/glink.o -b export:shared.exp \
     -bM:SRE -osharedobj -lc shared.o
```

The option `-H` defines the boundary number of the output file. This is usually the block size, and ensures that the text, data and loader sections of the output object are aligned.

The `-T` option makes the number which follows it the starting address of the text segment of the object file. If no `-T` value is specified then the text segment starts at zero.

The option `-bglink:/lib/glink.o` causes the linker to use the global linkage interface prototype defined in the object `glink.o` and to generate interface code for all defined external objects.

The -b export:shared.exp defines the file in which the export list is contained for this object. This export list defines all objects exported from this object file.

The -bM:SRE option is used to define the module type. This defines how the data segment of the shared module is to be mapped to individual processes using the module, in that this single shared module code may be used by several processes at the same time and there is no requirement for the shared code to be re-entrant. The options available are listed below.

-bM:S1L
> The library is a single-use library, and a private copy of the data segment will be required for each load. This is the default module type.

-bM:SRE
> The library is reusable and requires a private copy of the data segment for each process that is dependent on the module.

-bM:SRO
> The library is read only, i.e. contains no modifiable data segment objects. This library can, however, be used by multiple processes at once.

The option -lc is used to link the library /lib/libc to the object code to provide the basic C library functions.

Finally, the option -osharedobj is used to output the linked object to a file called sharedobj.

The final executable is the combination of the files main and sharedobj when main is executed using the command line

```
$ ./main
```

The kernel loader determines from the XCOFF file information contained in main that it requires external objects the location of which is defined by main.imp. The loader then determines if this file sharedobj is already page-mapped into memory, if so the loader will resolve the external references by page-mapping the appropriate segments of virtual memory into the current process's address space and resolving the addresses of the shared object. However, if the file sharedobj is not already page-mapped into memory the loader will do this first. The exact sequence of events which the loader follows depends largely on the module type specified when the shared object file sharedobj was linked, but this load-time dynamic linking is often a very useful way of reducing the amount of core memory required to run applications.

These shared objects may also be included in shared libraries, but the format of the import and export files for objects contained within shared libraries is slightly different in that the name of the shared library as well as the shared object file must be specified.

In order to create a shared library the following procedure should be followed:

- Create a shared object file using the method described above.
- Use the ar utility to create a library file:

```
$ ar vq shdlib.a sharedobj.o
```

This creates a shared library file containing one object file, sharedobj.

- Create import and export lists for this shared library. These import and export files are similar to the files created for sharedobj.o, but they also define the shared library file in which the object file containing the shared objects may be found.

The following file is an export file for the shared library and would be placed in the file shdlib.exp:

```
#! shdlib.a(sharedobj.o)
shared_func
```

Notice that the only difference is that the library name is specified and within the brackets the object file in the library where the shared object shared_func is located.

A similar import file for use with applications that use the shared library will also be required, and will be defined as follows in a file called shdlib.imp:

```
(main.imp)
#! shdlib.a(sharedobj.o)
shared_func
```

The use of a shared library by an application is the same as the use of a shared object file, but the library must be present in the standard library search path for the linkage editor ld (usually /usr/lib) unless specified in the import and export files.

An application wishing to use the objects contained in a shared library may be compiled and linked in the following way:

```
$ cc -oapp app.c
$ ld   -b export:shdlib.imp \
            -oapp -lc app.o
```

using the shared library import list to define where the shared objects defined in the application code import list will be found. At run-time the library shdlib.a must be available to the kernel loader.

It should be noted that a shared library may contain object files which do not have shared objects within them and shared objects mixed within one library. As shared objects may be in turn imported from other libraries, this feature is used under AIX 3.x to enable system call functions to be exported from the kernel objects and imported into shared libraries like `libc.a`, so the code for executing a system call does not reside with the `libc.a` object but is imported from the kernel objects already mapped into memory.

# 8
# AIX-specific system calls

It must have been a dilemma for the IBM Corporation when considering the details of their new 'open operating system' AIX 3.x, to have to decide to include software technology that did not, and often still does not, exist in other versions of UNIX in its definition. This, as they must have realized, would lead to the inevitable cry of 'non-standard' from their competitors. However, the design objectives of AIX 3.x required some major re-working of the standard UNIX kernel.

Many of these developments (around 1987–1990) eventually led to the new OSF/1 operating system from the Open Systems Foundation. IBM was a founder member of this organization and in the author's opinion took a bold step in developing new software technology for AIX 3.x which was not a part of the then 'standard', and later many parts of this new technology were included in the definition of the 'new standard' OSF/1.

'Standards' must continually evolve, and provided all contributors to the new standards committees ratify any new features developed then the true spirit of 'open systems' will live on. However, if any single organization within this framework is allowed to impose standards on the other members, then the spirit of 'open systems' will be lost to the lion of commercial advantage.

Let us now consider some of the unique features of AIX 3.x which may be used by the application and systems programmer.

## 8.1    AIX 3.x system calls for load-time/run-time linking

The discussion in the previous chapter outlined the mechanism of load-time/run-time linking, a feature which is almost unique to AIX 3.x. This feature may be used totally transparently to the application or systems program, as described above, or used at the system call level where the application has control of the loading and unloading of objects it requires. Using this feature in this way gives the application or systems program total control over the objects it requires and the system resources they consume. However, the implementation is totally specific to AIX 3.x and portability cannot be assured.

There are four system calls which implement load-time/run-time linking. We now consider each of them in turn, with an example of their use.

### 8.1.1 Loading and unloading objects within the current process

AIX 3.x like all UNIX variants provides the system calls exec() and fork() in some form or another to enable processes to be created and executable code to be loaded and executed by the kernel. These system calls could be considered a fundamental standard for the UNIX operating system.

The exec() system call is provided to load executable objects from secondary storage into virtual memory, but it will completely overwrite the current process's executable code in doing so. This is not always desirable. It may be that objects are only required to be present during certain phases of the execution of a process, and other objects will be required at some later phase. This situation is very common with many application programs which require different modules of library support code at different times in their execution lifespan.

The standard solution to this problem is to load all the required code into one executable program so that all the required objects will be present at all times. This solves one problem, but often poses many others. The executable program size of such programs may be extremely large, particularly on RISC-based processors. This leads to comparatively long load-times.

Alternatively, the program can be split up into separate modules each running as a separate process, each process being significantly smaller than the original executable code. However, each process will require additional code to enable it to communicate with the other processes and to administer its library support needs. This second alternative, although far more sensible than the first, still tends to make the overall size and complexity of the executable code greater.

AIX 3.x provides two system calls that may be called by a process which will load or unload one or more objects found in secondary storage into the process's private segment (#2) (see Fig. 7.3). This object's symbols may then be made available to the current process. When the process has finished with this set of objects it may unload them using another system call. This method avoids the problems of program load size in our first example and also avoids the problems of interprocess communication and coordination found in our second example because all objects are effectively loaded into the same process address space and run as one process.

### 8.1.2 The load() system call

The load system call has the following definition:

```
#include <sys/ldr.h>
```

```
int (*load(ObjectFile,LoadFlags,LibraryPath))()
char *ObjectFile;
unsigned int LoadFlags;
char *LibraryPath;
```

*Parameters*

ObjectFile

> The filename and optionally the path definition of the object file to load. This should be an object file which has been linked but may contain unresolved external references. If this filename contains the character / then the name is used as an absolute filename, but if no / character is found the parameter libraryPath and/or the environment variable LIBPATH will be used be locate the object file.
>
> Here are two examples:

- The filename /usr/phil/part1 is an absolute filename and would be expected to exist in the directory /usr/phil.
- The filename phil is a relative filename and the directories specified in the LibraryPath parameter or the environment variable LIBPATH would be searched for the file phil.

LoadFlags

> Used to modify the behaviour of the load() system call. It can have the following values:

L_NOAUTODEFER

> Causes any unresolved symbols present in the object file to be explicitly resolved using the loadbind() system call, i.e. run-time linking. If the value 0x00000000 is specified then the default action is taken; this is to resolve any unresolved references as soon as possible, i.e. at load-time. This is load-time linking.

L_SHARED_DATA

> Allows the data segments of any object loaded to be shared between all processes that load the module.

L_SHARED_ALL

> Allows both data and code of any object loaded to be shared between all processes that load the module.

LibraryPath

> Used to determine the search path used to locate the ObjectFile if a relative filename is used. If the value of LibraryPath is NULL and the value of the LIBPATH environment variable is defined then the value of LIBPATH is used for the search path.
>
> If the value of LibraryPath is specified it will be used as the default search path for the search for the object.

If neither `LibraryPath` nor the environment variable `LIBPATH` is defined then the path specified in the object file loader section will be used as the default search path which was specified during the linking process.

The `LibraryPath` or `LIBPATH` search directories will not be used if either relative or absolute pathnames are provided within the object file which is being loaded.

*Return value*

The return value of the system call `load()` is a pointer to a function returning an integer value. If the system call fails then the NULL pointer will be returned and the value of `errno` will contain the error code. The system call `loadquery()` may be used to obtain further detail on errors.

If the `load()` system call is successful then a pointer to the function which is the entry point to the object loaded will be returned. This function pointer may be used either by the `loadbind()` system call (see Section 8.1.4) or if this corresponds to the main function in a resolved object then directly within the current process. This will be explained in more detail within the example later in this chapter.

*Errors returned by* `load()`                *Meaning*

EACCES

Either the program specified in the parameter `ObjectFile` is not an ordinary file, or the current process does not have the correct permissions to execute or access this file.

EINVAL

The program specified in the parameter `ObjectFile` does not have the correct 'magic number' and is not identifiable as an object file.

ELOOP

Too many symbolic links were found in translating the pathname to find the object file specified.

ENOEXEC

One of many errors has occurred during the loading process; the `load()` system call cannot load the object specified. Use the `loadquery()` system call to determine the nature of the error.

ENOMEM

The program required more memory than the system-defined limit.

ETXTBSY

The program object is currently open for update by some other process.

ENAMETOOLONG

A proportion of the search path exceeds 255 characters in length or the whole pathname exceeds 1023 characters.

*Errors returned by* load()                    *Meaning*

ENOENT

> Some part of the path prefix given to the ObjectFile does not exist.

ENOTDIR

> Some part of the search path is not a directory.

ESTALE

> Some part of the search path exist on a filesystem that is unavailable or has been unmounted.

### 8.1.3   The unload() *system call*

The system call unload() will unload an object or objects loaded by the system call load. It should be noted that unload will only unload an object if it is not in use. The definition of being in use is quite simple: an object is in use if and only if another object file that is currently in use is importing symbols from it.

It is interesting to note that two modules that import symbols mutually from each other may never be unloaded as they will always be in use; the only time such modules are unloaded will be during process termination.

There is no system call to un-resolve symbols once they are resolved.

The unload system call has the following definition:

```
#include <sys/ldr.h>
int unload(ObjectPointer)
int (*ObjectPointer)();
```

*Parameters*

ObjectPointer

This parameter is the pointer to the entry point to the object to unload returned by the system call load(). It has a definition as a pointer to a function returning an integer value. If a pointer is supplied to this function that was not returned by load() then an error will result.

*Return value*

The return value of the unload() system call is an integer. A value of zero is returned for a successful operation and a non-zero result for an error condition. When an error condition is found the variable errno is set to the error number of the error.

*Error returned by* unload()

EINVAL

> The pointer given in the parameter ObjectPointer was not returned by a call to the load() system call.

## 8.1.4 *The* `loadbind()` *system call*

As specified in the `load()` system call definition, the load system call has a set of flags which modify the load service. One of these flags is `L_NOAUTODEFER`, and if used it has the following effect.

Consider two modules, `main` and `lib`. Module `main` imports several symbols from module `lib`. These modules may be loaded into the current process's address space, using two separate calls to the system call `load()`.

Let us assume that the module `main` is loaded first. Using the `load()` system call without the flag `L_NOAUTODEFER`, this module will have unresolved symbols present within it, i.e. the symbols imported from the module `lib`. The `load()` system call is then called again to load the module `lib`, using the same flags as were used to load the module `main`. At this time the `load()` system call will automatically resolve all symbol references after the load of the module `lib` is complete, but before the system call returns to the calling process. Thus after loading the module `lib` the unresolved references present in the module `main` will have been resolved.

This means that after both modules are loaded the module `main` will be ready to run. However, if the flag `L_NOAUTODEFER` is specified with each `load()` system call then an explicit system call `loadbind()` will be required to resolve any unresolved references present in the loaded modules. This can be useful when application control of symbol resolution is required.

The `loadbind()` system call has the following definition:

```
#include <sys/ldr.h>
int loadbind(BindFlag,ExportPointer,ImportPointer)
int BindFlag;
void *ExportPointer;
void *ImportPointer;
```

*Parameters*

`BindFlag`

>   Not currently used; and a value of zero should be used during the use of `loadbind()`.

`ExportPointer`

>   The pointer returned by the `load()` system call when loading the module `lib` in the example above. It is called an export pointer because the module `lib` exports symbols to other modules.

`ImportPointer`

>   The pointer returned by the `load()` system call when loading the module `main` in our example above. This is called an import pointer because the module `main` imports symbols from the module defined by the export pointer.

It should be quite self-evident that the module `main` may import symbols from several different modules and thus several calls to `loadbind()` would be required to resolve all of its imported symbols, each call having a different value for the `ExportPointer` parameter.

Without the flag `L_NOAUTODEFER` being used during the loading of the module `main`, this would be done automatically by the subsequent `load()` system calls to load the other modules.

### Return value

The `loadbind()` system call will return the value of (-1) on failure, and under these conditions the value of `errno` will be set to one of the values specified below. The system call `loadquery()` may be used to obtain additional information about the error reported by `load()`, `unload()` or `loadbind()` system calls.

*Errors returned by* `loadbind()`         *Meaning*
EINVAL

> An invalid value for one or both of the pointers `ExportPointer` or `ImportPointer` has been specified. These values should only be the values returned by the `load()` system call.

ENOMEM

> The program required more memory than the system will allow.

### 8.1.5   The `loadquery()` system call

The `loadquery()` system call may be used to obtain error information from the use of the system calls `exec()`, `load()`, `unload()` and `loadbind()` and to obtain information about objects loaded within the current process.

The `loadquery` system call has the following definition:

```
#include <sys/ldr.h>
int loadquery(QueryFlags,DataBuffer,BufferLen);
int QueryFlags;
void *DataBuffer;
void *Bufferlen;
```

*Parameters*
QueryFlags

> Specifies the action taken by the `loadquery()` system call. It can have one of two values, and these options will be explored in code examples in Section 8.2.4.
>
> L_GETINFO
>
> > Causes `loadquery()` to return a list of structures providing

information about the objects loaded by the calling process. These structures will be returned in the parameter `DataBuffer` and will be of the type `struct ld_info` as defined in the header file `sys/ldr.h`.

L_GETMESSAGES

Causes `loadquery()` to return error status information in the parameter `DataBuffer`. This information will be relevant to the last call to either `load()`, `unload()`, `loadbind()` or `exec()` system calls.

DataBuffer

A pointer to an area of memory which will be used to store the data returned by `loadquery()`. Its structure is defined by the value of `QueryFlags` and should be obtained via the `malloc()` system call.

BufferLen

Defines the length in bytes of the buffer `DataBuffer`. This should be set to the value used in the `malloc()` system call to obtain this area of memory. The `loadquery()` system call will assume that the area of memory pointed to by `DataBuffer` is the size given by the parameter `BufferLen`.

### Return value

The system call `loadquery()` returns a non-zero result if an error occurs during the system call. When an error occurs the variable `errno` is set to the error code which occurred. It should be noted that additional error information cannot be obtained by using `loadquery()`!

*Errors returned by* `loadquery()`           *Meaning*

EINVAL

Returned if an invalid value of `QueryFlags` is used or `loadquery()` could not access the caller's data buffer `DataBuffer`.

ENOMEM

This error will be returned if the data buffer `Databuffer` is too small to contain the returned data from the `loadquery()` system call. The values returned at this time in the buffer `Databuffer` are not predictable and should not be used.

## 8.2   The use of `load()` and related system calls

The load system call and its related system calls are quite unique to AIX 3.x, and their usefulness may not be immediately apparent to the systems programmer or application programmer.

Many modern application and systems programs are very large and complex, and require a lot of library support code to enable them to function. This library support code may be actually used for only a fraction of the time for which the application code will execute.

With conventional statically linked code, this will consume system resources even when it is not being used. Using the AIX 3.x dynamically linked code and the load() and unload() system calls library support code may be loaded and unloaded at will, thus saving potentially large amounts of system resources.

In the example below a single library module exports a symbol which is imported by a main procedure. In order to achieve this we need the library code, plus its associated export file, and the main procedure, plus its associated import file. With these things in place we can generate a dynamically linked main procedure which will load the required library file at load-time.

Assume that the library file source code exports a function called func_x() and its source code can be found in a file called xlib.c which is as follows:

```
#include <stdio.h>
/* **************************************** */
/* define TRUE and FALSE if not already     */
/* defined                                  */
/* **************************************** */
#ifndef TRUE
#define FALSE 0
#define TRUE ( ! FALSE )
#endif
/* **************************************** */
/* function func_x() has one parameter str  */
/* which it will treat as a string and print */
/* to STDOUT using printf()                  */
/* The function will always return a TRUE    */
/* value                                     */
/* **************************************** */
int func_x(str)
char *str;
{
    /* ************************************ */
    /* print value of str to STDOUT and    */
    /* flush STDOUT                         */
    /* ************************************ */
    printf("%s\n", str);
    fflush(stdout);
    return(TRUE);
}
```

This file xlib.c would be compiled by the XL C compiler using the command line

```
$ cc -c xlib.c -o xlib.o
```

This command would compile the source code into an object file called xlib.o, but this file would not be passed at this stage to the linker ld.

Before we can link this file we must define an export file of symbols which it will export. This will take the form shown below and could be placed in a file called xlib.exp:

```
#! ./xlib
* This defines the final linked file where the following
* symbols can be found, i.e. current directory, in xlib
func_x
* list of exported symbols, only the function func_x
* is listed
```

At this stage we can link the object xlib.o to create the file xlib, and this file can then be used by any executable which wants to import the symbol func_x.

The linking of the object file xlib.o would be done using the following command:

```
$ ld -T512 -H512 -bglink:/lib/glink.o -bE:xlib.exp \
    -bM:SRE -oxlib xlib.o
```

This command will generate the file xlib and place it in the current directory. The options used for the linker ld are explained in Chapter 15.

At this stage we have a file xlib which exports the symbol func_x. Now we can use this exported symbol by importing it into our main procedure, which we will call pgm.c, and which can be defined as follows:

```
#include <stdio.h>
/* *************************************** */
/* define TRUE and FALSE if not already    */
/* defined                                  */
/* *************************************** */
#ifndef TRUE
#define FALSE 0
#define TRUE ( ! FALSE )
#endif
/* *************************************** */
/* prototype function func_x which is defined */
/* externally                                 */
/* *************************************** */
extern int func_x()
int main()
    {
        /* *********************** */
        /* call func_x() with string   */
        /* *********************** */
        func_x("Function func_x called from main");
```

```
    return(TRUE);
}
```

In order to compile this program, and for it to import the symbol exported from
the file xlib, we need to define an import file for the file pgm.c. This file may be
called pgm.imp and have the following structure:

```
(pgm.imp)
#! ./xlib
* define name of import file and source of imported symbol
func_x
* define symbol required to be imported
* it should be noted that not all symbols that
* are exported by a file need be imported by
* any other file
```

Then finally the program pgm.c can be compiled using the following command:

```
$ cc -bI:pgm.imp -opgm pgm.c
```

This defines the import file to be used to locate the imported symbol func_x and
defines that the final executable code is to be placed in a file called pgm in the
current directory.

 At this stage we have two linked files, pgm and xlib. Both files must be loaded
before pgm can execute. However, under AIX 3.x the exec() system call is part of
the system loader and will if necessary automatically load any other supporting
code that may be required when the command pgm is entered as follows:

```
$ ./pgm
Function func_x called from main
$
```

The system loader which is used by the exec() system call uses the load() system
call and its related system calls to achieve this.


## 8.2.1   Loading modules under program control

The above example is a simple use of load-time linking under AIX 3.x, and by now
the reader should be quite familiar with this concept.

 The simple execution of the base module causes the supporting modules to be
loaded, but under program control, we can achieve this result using the load()
system call.

 The following program code, which would be placed in a file called loadm.c,
could be used to load the two above modules and then to execute the main
function in pgm:

```
#include <stdio.h>
 #include <sys/ldr.h>
 /* ************************************************** */
 /* Include the standard header file, and the         */
 /* loader header file ldr.h                           */
 /* ************************************************** */
 /* *********************************** */
 /* define a constant for no load flags */
 /* *********************************** */
 #define NO_LOAD_FLAGS 0x00000000
  /* *************************************** */
  /* define TRUE and FALSE if not already     */
  /* defined                                  */
  /* *************************************** */
  #ifndef TRUE
  #define FALSE 0
  #define TRUE ( ! FALSE )
  #endif
  /* *************************************** */
  /* define parameter to use for default lib */
  /* load path as defined in LIBPATH          */
  /* *************************************** */
  #define DEFAULT_LIBPATH ""
  /* *************************************** */
  /* define NULL pointer return fail value    */
  /* of load() system call                    */
  /* *************************************** */
  #define LOAD_FAIL (int (* )()) NULL
  int main()
     {
         /* *********************************** */
         /* define the variables to contain the */
         /* return result of load() for both    */
         /* the module pgm and xlib             */
         /* *********************************** */
          int (*pgm_start)();
          int (*xlib_start)();
         /* *********************************** */
         /* load module pgm using default lib   */
         /* load path and no load flags         */
         /* symbols will be resolved as soon as */
         /* possible                             */
         /* *********************************** */
         pgm_start=load("./pgm", NO_LOAD_FLAGS,
                        DEFAULT_LIBPATH);
         if ( pgm_start == LOAD_FAIL )
     {
         fprintf(stderr, "can't load pgm\n");
         fflush(stderr);
         exit(FALSE);
     }
```

```
/* ************************************* */
/* load module xlib using default lib    */
/* load path and no load flags           */
/* symbols will be resolved as soon as   */
/* possible                              */
/* ************************************* */
xlib_start=load("./xlib", NO_LOAD_FLAGS,
                DEFAULT_LIBPATH);
if ( xlib_start == LOAD_FAIL )
    {
        fprintf(stderr, "can't load xlib\n");
        fflush(stderr);
        exit(FALSE);
    }
/* ************************************* */
/* At this point the symbol func_x has   */
/* been resolved in the module pgm by    */
/* the use of the NO_LOAD_FLAGS option    */
/* instead of the L_NOAUTODEFER option    */
/* ************************************* */
/* ************************************* */
/* call the function main() in the pgm   */
/* module using the function pointer     */
/* returned from load()                  */
/* ************************************* */
pgm_start();
}
```

This program is then compiled using the following command line:

```
$ cc -oloadm loadm.c
```

The program may then be run to produce the output

```
$ ./loadm
Function func_x called from main
$
```

Some explanation may be required here. The load system call will return to the calling process, a function pointer which will be the main function pointer defined for the module loaded. For an executable module this will always be the function main( ), but for a library module exporting symbols this will be the initialization code used by the loader to obtain the symbols, and not be a pointer to an exported symbol. There may after all be more than one symbol exported! The return value of load( ) when used to load library code is only useful to the system call loadbind( ) and should never be called directly as shown with the pgm_start pointer.

In this case, because the L_NOAUTODEFER flag was not set, the load system call will automatically resolve the symbols exported by xlib and imported by pgm, thus after the load of the xlib module, the main() function within the pgm module can be executed via its returned function pointer.

Another special thing to be aware of in the above example is that the entry point for the module pgm is the main() function by default. Calling a function main() will cause the process to terminate when the function terminates, thus the call made via the pointer pgm_start() in the program loadm will never return to loadm and the whole process will terminate. This will always be the case when calling the function main() in the C programming language; if it terminates, so does the process. However, using the linker/loader directive -estarting_point at compile time it is possible to allow any function to become the entry point for the module, and in this case the function call using this function pointer will return to the calling loadm program.

### 8.2.2 The use of loadbind()

In the above example the load() system call used the constant NO_LOAD_FLAGS which causes all symbols to be resolved as soon as possible. However, if the code were to use the flag L_NOAUTODEFER then an explicit call to the system call loadbind() would be required before the main() function in the pgm module could be called. If we modify the loadm code to use loadbind() then it becomes:

```
#include <stdio.h>
 #include <sys/ldr.h>
 /* ************************************************ */
 /* Include the standard header file, and the       */
 /* loader header file ldr.h                         */
 /* ************************************************ */
 /* ********************************** */
 /* define a constant for no bind flags */
 /* ********************************** */
 #define NO_BIND_FLAGS (int) 0
  /* ************************************** */
  /* define TRUE and FALSE if not alrcady   */
  /* defined                                */
  /* ************************************** */
  #ifndef TRUE
  #define FALSE 0
  #define TRUE (! FALSE)
  #endif
  /* ************************************** */
  /* define parameter to use for default lib */
  /* load path as defined in LIBPATH         */
  /* ************************************** */
  #define DEFAULT_LIBPATH ""
  /* ************************************** */
  /* define NULL pointer return fail value */
```

```
/* of load() system call                    */
/* ********************************** */
#define LOAD_FAIL (int (*)()) NULL
int main()
    {
        /* ********************************** */
        /* define the variables to contain the */
        /* return result of load() for both    */
        /* the module pgm and xlib             */
        /* ********************************** */
         int (*pgm_start)();
         int (*xlib_start)();
         int bind_err;
        /* ********************************** */
        /* load module pgm using default lib   */
        /* load path and no load flags         */
        /* symbols will be resolved using the  */
        /* system call loadbind()              */
        /* ********************************** */
        pgm_start=load("./pgm", L_NOAUTODEFER,
                        DEFAULT_LIBPATH);
        if (pgm_start == LOAD_FAIL)
            {
                fprintf(stderr, "can't load pgm\n");
                fflush(stderr);
                exit(FALSE);
            }
        /* ********************************** */
        /* load module xlib using default lib  */
        /* load path and no load flags         */
        /* symbols will be resolved using the  */
        /* system call loadbind()              */
        /* ********************************** */
        xlib_start=load("./xlib", L_NOAUTODEFER,
                        DEFAULT_LIBPATH);
        if (xlib_start == LOAD_FAIL)
            {
                fprintf(stderr, "can't load xlib\n");
                fflush(stderr);
                exit(FALSE);
            }
        /* ********************************** */
        /* At this point we have xlib_start being */
        /* the exportpointer for loadbind() and   */
        /* pgm_start being the importpointer for  */
        /* loadbind(), then we explicitly bind    */
        /* the modules by calling loadbind()      */
        /* ********************************** */
        bind_err=loadbind(NO_BIND_FLAGS, (void *) xlib_start,
                        (void *) pgm_start);
         if (bind_err)
```

```
            {
                fprintf(stderr, "error binding modules\n");
                fflush(stderr);
                exit(TRUE);
            }
        /* ************************************** */
        /* modules now bound, are free to call   */
        /* ************************************** */
        /* ************************************** */
        /* call the function main() in the pgm   */
        /* module using the function pointer     */
        /* returned from load()                  */
        /* ************************************** */
        pgm_start();
        }
```

## 8.2.3   The use of unload()

The unload() system call may be used to dynamically unload objects loaded by the load() system call. There are, however, certain rules which apply to the unloading of objects.

First, an object may be unloaded if, and only if, none of its exported symbols is currently being imported by an active module. This rule usually means that modules have to be unloaded from the base module through the library modules, as library modules often have symbols imported by the base modules, thus making it impossible to unload a library module with a base module still active.

The unload() system call requires only a pointer to the object to unload in order to free the object's resource utilization. As mentioned before it can become impossible to unload mutually linked library code because both objects may be active at the same time within an executable program.

## 8.2.4   The use of loadquery()

This system call is very useful for obtaining information about the errors returned from any of the following system calls: load(), unload(), loadbind(), and exec().

The system call can be used as in the following example to provide an error handling function for use with the above system calls.

Consider the example given above, but with the error handling function do_error() called to handle errors:

```
#include <stdio.h>
#include <sys/ldr.h>
/* ************************************************ */
/* Include the standard header file, and the        */
/* loader header file ldr.h                          */
/* ************************************************ */
```

```
/* ************************************** */
/* define a constant for no bind flags   */
/* ************************************** */
#define NO_BIND_FLAGS (int) 0
/* ************************************** */
/* define a constant for the MAXIMUM     */
/* number of errors returned from        */
/* loadquery() and the error return      */
/* value from loadquery()                */
/* ************************************** */
#define MAX_ERRORS 500
#define LOAD_QUERY_ERROR ( (int) -1 )
/* *************************************** */
/* Function prototype for do_error function */
/* *************************************** */
 int do_error();
/* *************************************** */
/* define TRUE and FALSE if not already   */
/* defined                                */
/* *************************************** */
#ifndef TRUE
#define FALSE 0
#define TRUE ( ! FALSE )
#endif
/* *************************************** */
/* define parameter to use for default lib */
/* load path as defined in LIBPATH        */
/* *************************************** */
#define DEFAULT_LIBPATH ""
/* ***************************************/
/* define NULL pointer return fail value */
/* of load() system call                 */
/* *************************************** */
#define LOAD_FAIL (int (* )()) NULL
int main()
   {
        /* ********************************** */
        /* define the variables to contain the */
        /* return result of load() for both   */
        /* the module pgm and xlib            */
        /* ********************************** */
         int (*pgm_start)();
         int (*xlib_start)();
         int bind_err;
        /* ********************************** */
        /* load module pgm using default lib  */
        /* load path and no load flags        */
        /* symbols will be resolved using the */
        /* system call loadbind()             */
        /* ********************************** */
```

```
    pgm_start=load("./pgm", L_NOAUTODEFER,
                   DEFAULT_LIBPATH);
    if (pgm_start == LOAD_FAIL)
       {
          do_error("Loading pgm module");
       }
    /* ************************************ */
    /* load module xlib using default lib   */
    /* load path and no load flags          */
    /* symbols will be resolved using the   */
    /* system call loadbind()               */
    /* ************************************ */
    xlib_start=load("./xlib", L_NOAUTODEFER,
                    DEFAULT_LIBPATH);
    if ( xlib_start == LOAD_FAIL )
       {
          do_error("Loading xlib module");
       }
    /* ************************************* */
    /* At this point we have xlib_start being */
    /* the exportpointer for loadbind() and   */
    /* pgm_start being the importpointer for   */
    /* loadbind(), then we explicitly bind     */
    /* the modules by calling loadbind()       */
    /* ************************************* */
    bind_err=loadbind(NO_BIND_FLAGS, (void *) xlib_start,
                      (void *) pgm_start);
    if (bind_err)
       {
          do_error("Binding xlib and pgm modules");
       }
    /* ************************************ */
    /* modules now bound, are free to call   */
    /* ************************************ */
    /* ************************************ */
    /* call the function main() in the pgm   */
    /* module using the function pointer     */
    /* returned from load()                  */
    /* ************************************ */
    pgm_start();
 }
/* ***************************************** */
/* error processing function                  */
/* ***************************************** */
int do_error(err_msg)
char *err_msg;
   {
    /* ******************************** */
    /* define array of errors returned   */
    /* from loadquery()                  */
    /* ******************************** */
```

```
    char *error_list[MAX_ERRORS];
    int query_result;
    int k;
    fprintf(stderr, "***ERROR at %s\n", err_msg);
    /* ************************************** */
    /* call loadquery() to get list of errors   */
    /* into error_list array                     */
    /* ************************************** */
    query_result=loadquery(L_GETMESSAGES,
                   (void *) &error_list[0],
                      MAX_ERRORS-1);
    /* ************************************** */
    /* if loadquery error print message to   */
    /* say no information found              */
    /* ************************************** */
    if (query_result == LOAD_QUERY_ERROR)
        {
            fprintf(stderr, "No additional error information\n");
            fprintf(stderr, "was returned\n");
        }
    else
        {
    /* ************************************** */
    /* if errors returned print all array      */
    /* elements to STDERR until NULL array     */
    /* is found                                */
    /* ************************************** */
      for (k=0; error_list[k]!=(char *) NULL, k++)
          {
            fprintf(stderr, "%s\n", error_list[k]);
          }
        }
  /* ************************************** */
  /* flush STDERR and terminate program    */
  /* ************************************** */
  fflush(stderr);
  exit(FALSE);
}
```

The flag L_GETMESSAGES will cause the array of pointers passed as a parameter to return a list of error messages from the previous system call. These messages will be an ASCII numeric code followed by some error-specific message data. These messages may be output directly to the STDERR as shown above or passed as parameters to the program /etc/execerror which will format the messages and send them to STDERR. The array will be terminated by an array element containing a NULL pointer.

A full list of the error codes contained in these message strings can be found in the header file sys/ldr.h.

Another use for the loadquery() function is to return information about the object files loaded by the calling process. During this call the data stored in the buffer is of the type struct ld_info as defined in the header file sys/ldr.h. To obtain this information the flag L_GETINFO is used. This information is normally used by the program trace functions and will be of little practical use to the applications programmer.

### 8.2.5  The use of load() and unload() by AIX 3.x

AIX 3.x make extensive use of these system calls, which enable AIX 3.x to achieve its stated design goals.

The reader should understand that these system calls provide for a very flexible design for the AIX 3.x kernel. For example, within many UNIX implementations system call interface code is provided with a library called libc.a. This interface code does little more than execute some restricted instructions which enable the CPU to switch from user space to kernel space and supervisor mode. The system call code itself is always present in the kernel code image and not in the code in the library libc.a.

This implementation is quite common but is open to the cunning hacker obtaining the restricted sequence of instructions which implement the system call interface code, and using this sequence to hack the kernel. This is not as easy as it sounds, but given the requisite skill many UNIX implementations can be hacked by obtaining processor supervisor mode in this way.

Under AIX 3.x the implementation of the system call interface is an exported object which is present in the library libc.a and may be imported by any object code which is linked to the library. This has the effect of eliminating this system call interface code from the library libc.a as the objects found in libc.a are exported directly from the kernel object code. In this way the switch from user space to kernel space takes place, at least in concept terms with the kernel itself, and is thus considerably more secure than a library object.

## 8.3    Extensions unique to AIX 3.x

AIX 3.x allows a number of very new extensions which are not found within any other implementation of UNIX.

### 8.3.1  Dynamic configuration of sub-systems

A sub-system in AIX 3.x is any part of the kernel or kernel service which may be configured separately to the kernel itself.

Examples of the sub-systems available are:

- Communications sub-systems including TCP/IP, SNA, X.25.
- Display sub-systems including X11, OSF/Motif and other graphical user interfaces.

These sub-systems and their services may be configured under AIX 3.x, often without the system being taken out of normal service. This is made possible by the ability of AIX 3.x to load and unload the object code within the kernel which supports these functions at run-time.

The AIX 3.x kernel itself makes full use of the `load()` and `unload()` system calls and is itself composed of several separate object libraries which combine to form the kernel object at load-time and if necessary at run-time.

### 8.3.2   Filesystem management

AIX 3.x has a unique filesystem structure which is not found within any other implementation of UNIX. AIX 3.x implements what is known as a journalled filesystem structure (JFS), which provides database-like integrity for files written to them. What this means is that file integrity during a system crash and after a recovery is almost certain. These words have been chosen very carefully: IBM give no assurances about the certainty of intact recovery of any files stored on a JFS, but in the author's experience this system is many thousands of times more secure than a standard System V.x or BSD 4.x filesystem.

Also relevant to filesystem management is the concept of a *logical volume manager*. This is a very complex kernel sub-system, which enables very flexible management of disk units attached to AIX 3.x. The concepts involved within the logical volume manager are to be covered in the book *AIX 3.x for Administrators* (written by Phil Colledge, to be published by McGraw-Hill, London), because this function is primarily administrative. However, the logical volume manager does allow such facilities as dynamic expansion of filesystems, without the requirement to recreate the filesystem in question, and without the requirement to make the system unavailable for use during this time. This type of facility clearly does not exist within the standard system V.x or BSD 4.x environments, where to attempt to do such a thing would be impossible without taking the system out of service.

It is important to state that although these very complex new facilities have been added to AIX 3.x, they are confined to the implementation of the filesystem, and the AIX 3.x filesystem appears to be a standard system V.x filesystem. Thus the user has the flexibility of AIX 3.x and the standard interface of system V.x

### 8.3.3   System management

The first thing that can be said about system management is that non-standard tools are provided within any UNIX environment which enable the administrator to administer the system with a minimum of effort.

Most UNIX administrators are either standard flat file hackers, and all UNIX implementations have flat files, or dedicated vendor-specific administration utility gurus. Most people will tend to use the flat file administration method, and the administrator will edit the system administration files to configure the system. This method is fine if you know exactly what you are doing, and can master the wonders of the vi editor. The author finds that most people have more problems with the latter than with the former!

AIX 3.x provides two extensions to this basic concept. First it provides its own administration tool, the system management interface tool (SMIT) which enables the administrator to administer the system easily, or at least more easily than by editing flat files. This tool is of course totally specific to AIX 3.x, and is found only under AIX 3.x.

The second extension includes the object data manager (ODM) and the object data library (ODL). These facilities provide a database-like structure which holds all of the management information contained within the system, with the ability to manipulate this information. This facility is largely transparent to the administrator of the system, and is maintained automatically by the use of the administration tools and utilities.

Its function is quite clear: it provides a structured way of defining the relationships between different administrative objects present within the operating system, while also providing the ability to extend and redefine these relationships in a controlled way.

In order to implement this a large number of utilities are provided, and these together with the SMIT tools will be presented in the book *AIX 3.x for Administrators* (written by Phil Colledge, to be published by McGraw-Hill, London).

### 8.3.4 System security

AIX 3.x also provides extensions to system security, such as trusted computing base (TCB), which enable the security of the system to be greatly improved.

The most significant extension is the terminal state monitor (TSM) which enables a secure data path to be established between the terminal user and the system, thus eliminating the security problem posed by 'fake login' programs.

The extensions to the security are quite complex and are again largely administrative. These, like other administrative functions, will be covered in the book *AIX 3.x for Administrators* (written by Phil Colledge, to be published by McGraw-Hill, London).

# 9
# Memory management system calls

Memory management under AIX 3.x is by no means specific to AIX. The system calls that implement the memory management functions are quite standard throughout all UNIX implementations, but it is interesting to look at the implementation of these system calls from the viewpoint of the unification of the system call interfaces from System V.x and BSD 4.x.

Most applications and systems programs will from time to time make use of the dynamic memory allocation system calls provided by the underlying operating system. It is often quite practical for the application program not to have to impose artificial limits and restrictions based solely on an estimate of the amount of memory a process may require during its execution.

## 9.1    Types of virtual memory

All processes have the three basic types of memory (or more correctly, virtual memory) allocated to them. These are static memory, stack memory and dynamic memory.

### 9.1.1    Static memory

Allocated in the process data segment (seg #2), this contains variables and data declared with fixed static size characteristics within an application program. As an example, consider the C declaration

```
static char array[100];
```

This variable is not only static in nature in the sense of the C programming language but is placed with the process's data segment.

136

### 9.1.2 Stack memory

Allocated on the process stack and placed in the process stack segment (seg #2), this contains data declared as automatic variables within C function and function parameters. An example is the C declaration

```
int func(p1,p2)
char *p1;
char *p3;
{
    int k;
}
```

In this case the parameters p1 and p2 and the automatic variable k are allocated on the process stack within the process stack segment. It should be noted that automatic variables with the type class static would be allocated within the process data segment and not the stack segment.

In the C programming language the stack frame is 'pushed' and 'popped' during the calling and returning from any function, so these stack allocated variables are allocated only for the duration of the function's life, and are re-allocated for each call to the function.

### 9.1.3 Dynamic memory

This memory is allocated by the process at run-time, and is returned by the memory management system calls. This memory is allocated to the process from the kernel memory pool and is used to extend the current process's memory segments (often seg #2) using system calls brk() and sbrk() which will be described in Section 9.4. This memory is then allocated to the process using additional memory management functions, which will also be described below.

This memory is often accessed by the use of memory addresses or pointers in the C programming language. The rules of scope and the data types which may be stored in this memory are implied by the type of the pointers used to access the data area. These pointers are allocated in either stack memory or static memory.

The major difference with this type of memory is that it will remain allocated to the requesting process until that process either terminates or explicitly returns this memory using any other system call.

## 9.2 Allocation of dynamic memory to a process

The simple statement made above that dynamic memory is allocated to a process at run-time is often more complex than it might at first appear. Many chapters of many books have been totally dedicated to memory management algorithms which endeavour to allocate and de-allocate memory within a process. The implementation details of the memory allocation functions are known only to the vendors of the operating system. This information is often regarded as commercially confidential, such is the importance of this system call not only to the applications but to the operating system itself. AIX 3.x is no exception to this rule; the underlying algorithms used for memory allocation are not published outside IBM. However, the system call interfaces which provide the service to the applications, etc., are well known and documented.

As a simple overview of the memory allocation process, we now consider some of the issues that would be faced by our memory management system calls.

### 9.2.1  Memory block sizes

Any memory management system call will be either limited or enhanced by the underlining hardware. Some systems have fixed memory segment sizes which limit the amount of memory that can be allocated in one call.

### 9.2.2  Memory alignment

Many modern CPUs require memory to be aligned on even or odd addresses, or any particular type of memory boundary address. This often limits the size and location of memory blocks allocated.

### 9.2.3  Memory continuity

This is largely linked to the memory block sizes, but any memory returned by our allocation system calls must be in a contiguous block in order for it to be any use to most applications or systems programs.

### 9.2.4  Memory allocation/de-allocation

This is far more complex than it might seem. A procedure which is required to keep track of all of the memory that has been allocated in random size chunks from the kernel memory pool, and then return them to this pool so that they form a contiguous block of memory, has a considerable problem on its hands. Several algorithms exist to carry out this process, but it is beyond the scope of this book to discuss them.

The above list does not include all of the potential problems a memory allocation/de-allocation function may face, but it does outline some quite complex

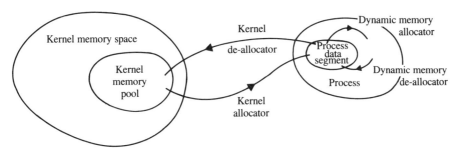

Figure 9.1. Dynamic memory allocation.

issues. Many UNIX implementations, and AIX 3.x is no exception, use a mechanism similar to the mechanism outlined in Fig. 9.1.

Dynamic memory allocation is often a two-stage process. Under the direct control of the dynamic memory allocator/de-allocator, these functions provide addresses or pointers to memory blocks within the calling process's data segment for use by the process during its execution. These functions also control the de-allocation of the memory blocks by the process and control the overall memory allocated from the kernel pool to the process data segment. They are often quite complex functions which optimize the allocation, de-allocation and re-allocation of memory within the process data segment. These functions may if required call the kernel allocator/ de-allocator functions to extend or reduce the size of the process data segment. This additional memory will, if possible, be allocated from the kernel memory pool to the process data segment.

This two-stage memory allocation process ensures that memory within the kernel memory pool is allocated and de-allocated in fixed known block sizes which may be re-used quickly and easily if required.

This is not necessarily true or even desirable at the memory allocation/de-allocation function level, where memory can be allocated and de-allocated in blocks of varying size and at random intervals. The purpose of these functions is to manage this requirement without continuously requesting additional memory resources from the kernel memory pool.

The kernel memory pool is under the direct control of the operating system kernel itself, and is thus available to any process. It should be recognized that until memory is returned to the kernel memory pool by the kernel de-allocator it is only available for use by the process in whose memory segment it currently resides. Thus freeing memory by use of the dynamic memory de-allocator may not free this memory for use by other processes, but hold it in reserve for use by further allocation requests made within the current process.

This difference between the two allocators can cause problems when applications use the dynamic memory allocators. However, the implementation of these allocators and de-allocators is totally vendor specific so problems encountered on one system may not occur on others and vice versa.

All implementations of UNIX, and of course AIX 3.x is no exception, will de-allocate any memory allocated to a process from whatever source when the process terminates. Thus the programmer may be sure that memory will be returned to the kernel memory pool after termination of the process.

The kernel memory allocation and de-allocation functions may be called from within any process, to allocate and de-allocate memory from the kernel memory pool to the process data segments. It is not advisable for any process to call these functions when calls to the dynamic memory functions are being used. This can lead to the kernel memory pool experiencing some of the problems which the dynamic memory allocator/de-allocator was designed to protect it from, thus making it difficult or impossible to re-use memory resources efficiently.

## 9.3      Implementation of dynamic memory functions under AIX 3.x

Dynamic memory functions can be grouped into five main groups:

- allocation functions
- de-allocation functions
- re-allocation functions
- allocation optimization functions
- allocation information functions

Under AIX 3.x these functions are implemented as follows.

### 9.3.1   Allocation functions

```
#include <sys/types.h>
#include <malloc.h>
void *malloc( MemSize )
size_t Memsize;
char *alloca( MemSize )
int MemSize;
char *valloc( MemSize )
unsigned int MemSize;
void *calloc( NoOfElements, ElementSize)
size_t NoOfElements
size_t ElementSize
```

Most of the above functions all have a common parameter MemSize which is the number of bytes of memory that the process is requesting the allocator to return to it.

All of the above functions will return a pointer to the first byte of the memory block allocated if successful, or a pointer to NULL if the request cannot be satisfied.

The general function malloc() will return a pointer to a memory block that has all of the correct alignments to be used for the storage of any type of data. This function returns a void pointer, which should be type-cast within the C programming language to the data type required.

The function `valloc()` is provided for BSD compatibility and requires the library `libsd.a` to be linked to any executable using this function. This function, although in many ways identical to `malloc()`, does not return a pointer that is correctly aligned for any data type, but a pointer to the data type character. This can cause some problems if alignments are important for the processor, which in many cases they are! This function should only be used for compatibility purposes, and a call to `malloc()` should be substituted wherever possible.

The function `calloc()` allocates the space for a number of array elements specified by the parameter `NoOfElements`, the size of each element in bytes being specified by the parameter `ElementSize`. A pointer to the first element of this array is returned by `calloc()` and all elements are initialized to have zero values. This system call is very similar to `malloc()` except that it returns a pointer to an array object and not a standard object as does `malloc()`. It would not be valid to use `malloc()` to allocate the memory required for the array elements and then to type cast the returned value, because there are some hidden administration overheads with array processing. The `calloc()` system call also returns a NULL pointer on failure.

`malloc()`, `valloc()` and `calloc()` all potentially extend the data segment of the calling process, and the memory which they return must be explicitly returned to the system after use (see `free()` in Section 9.3.5). However, the system call `alloca()` causes the process stack segment to be extended and this memory is freed automatically as soon as the calling function terminates.

## 9.3.2 De-allocation functions

```
#include <sys/types.h>
#include <malloc.h>
void free( MemoryPointer )
void *MemoryPointer
```

This function takes a pointer returned by `malloc()`, `calloc()`, `valloc()` or `realloc()` and returns this memory to the process data segment, under the control of the dynamic memory allocation functions. Undefined results will occur if a pointer is supplied which was not returned by `malloc()`, `calloc()`, `valloc()` or `realloc()`. As mentioned before this may not automatically return this memory to the kernel memory pool and thus it may not be re-usable by other processes.

## 9.3.3 Re-allocation functions

```
#include <sys/types.h>
#include <malloc.h>
```

```
void *realloc(MemPointer, NewSize )
void *MemPointer;
size_t NewSize;
```

This function has two parameters. The first is a pointer to an area of memory returned by `malloc()`, `valloc()` or `realloc()`, and the second is the new size in bytes which this area of memory is desired to be.

This re-allocates the memory, pointed to by `MemPointer` to be larger or smaller than it currently is, depending on the value of `NewSize`. Any data contained within the memory will be preserved up to the last location of the new memory block; that is, if the memory block is expanded then all data will be preserved, but if the memory block is reduced the data up to the last reduced location will be preserved.

The `realloc()` system call returns a pointer to the location of the first type of the new memory block. It should not be assumed that the memory block will be expanded leaving its starting location constant. This value may change as `realloc()` may move memory blocks to achieve the required result. In short, after a call to `realloc()` only the pointer returned by `realloc()` should ever be used to access the memory block, and not the original pointer given as a parameter to `realloc()`.

The system call `realloc()` also returns a NULL pointer if the re-allocation of the memory block fails. This should of course be checked before any use is made of the pointer returned. When this situation occurs the data in the block given in `MemPointer` may be lost.

Unpredictable results will occur if a pointer other than one returned by `malloc()` or `realloc()` is used for the parameter `MemPointer`.

### 9.3.4   Allocation information functions

The dynamic memory allocation functions also maintain an information structure which contains useful information that may be used to optimize the use of the memory allocation functions. The meaning of this information becomes apparent when considering the function `mallopt()`:

```
#include <sys/types.h>
#include <malloc.h>
struct mallinfo mallinfo();
```

This function should only be called after the first call to a dynamic memory allocation function within a process. The function returns a structure `mallinfo` which is defined in `malloc.h`. The structure is defined as follows:

```
struct mallinfo {
        int arena;   /* total space in arena */
        int ordblks;  /* number of ordinary blocks */
```

```
int smblks;   /* number of small blocks */
int hblks;    /* number of holding blocks */
int hblkhd;   /* space in holding block headers */
int usmblks;  /* space in small blocks in use */
int fsmblks;  /* space in free small blocks */
int uordblks; /* space in ordinary blocks in use */
int fordblks; /* space in free ordinary blocks */
int keepcost; /* cost of enabling keep option */
};
```

The meaning of the definitions within this structure will become clear after considering the function `mallopt()`.

## 9.3.5   Allocating optimization functions

Under AIX 3.x the memory allocator function performs internal optimization of memory allocation, so the system call `mallopt()` is only included as a System V.x interface. Any values set by this system call will not affect the values used by `malloc()`, `calloc()`, `valloc()` and `alloca()`, and thus will not affect the values returned by `mallinfo()`.

Before considering this function and its parameters it would be useful to consider certain concepts used in memory allocation functions. The memory allocation functions do not simply allocate memory and return it to the calling process; they are much more sophisticated than that. For each pointer returned an information block is held internally which contains information about the size of the data area and other performance-related information. The reader may have wondered how the `free()` system call determines the size of the data area pointed to by the pointer given to it. The answer of course is that the pointer actually points to the control information which contains a pointer to the data block. That is the reason why it is not advisable to call `free()` with any other pointer type!

As previously mentioned, the dynamic memory allocator functions must administer the memory allocated to the process data segment. This task is far from simple. I would suggest any interested reader consults *Operating Systems Design and Implementation*, by A. S. Tanenbaum, Prentice-Hall, USA, 1987, for further information on memory algorithms. What follows here is a very simple explanation of how memory is allocated by the memory allocation functions. This may not in fact be how AIX 3.x actually allocates memory; for the reasons mentioned above, the author does not have access to this information.

It can be shown (although no attempt is made to prove it here) that if a given area of memory such as the process's data segment is used for dynamic memory allocation, it is more efficient to allocate memory of similar sizes from the same contiguous memory block. Thus if a process can allocate memory in blocks of multiples of 16 bytes then it is efficient to split the allocation of these memory blocks into separate large memory areas, which can be sub-divided into blocks of

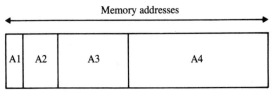

Figure 9.2. Memory map for dynamic memory allocation.

similar size. These large areas should also be related to each other by allocating blocks with sizes of successive multiples of 2 within each area.

For example, consider an area of memory of 2400 bytes in length which we wish to use to allocate memory. We assume that the minimum allocation unit is 16 bytes, then we may decide to sub-divide this large area into four contiguous areas each large enough to hold 10 allocations of 16, 32, 64, 128 bytes respectively.

Diagrammatically this would look like Fig. 9.2. The figure represents four large memory areas, A1, A2, A3, A4, which are allocated in contiguous memory with our data area of 2400 bytes. The first area, A1, will be large enough to hold 10 blocks of 16 bytes each, the second area, A2, will hold 10 blocks of 32 bytes each, and so on; the last area, A4, will hold 10 blocks of 128 bytes each. The total area will thus be given by

$$area = A1 + A2 + A3 + A4$$

$$area = (16 * 10) + (32 * 10) + (64 * 10) + (128 + 10)$$

$$area = (16 + 32 + 64 + 128) * 10$$

$$area = 2400 \text{ bytes}$$

Then when the dynamic memory allocator gets a request to allocate 23 bytes of memory it will allocate it in area A2 as a 32 byte area, a request for 48 bytes of memory would be allocated in area A3 as 64 bytes and so on. Allocating a 1200 byte area would mean extending our total area and the number of sub-areas within it so that an area with 2048 blocks allocated within it could be used.

This system ensures that when memory is freed using the memory de-allocator it is returned to an area where it will form a contiguous area of memory, thus making re-allocation of this memory very much easier.

This explanation is very simplistic, and there are really many more considerations involved, but it gives an indication of the complexities of memory management.

The areas A1–A4, as I have called them, are often referred to as *holding blocks*, and the minimum allocation unit size in my example of 16 bytes is often referred to as the *grain size* for small blocks.

The example did not take account of the administrative information that each memory block also requires to be stored with it. These are often called *block headers*, and are stored with each memory block allocated.

Finally, for efficiency the areas described above are often allocated into two main groups, a group of areas for small blocks, perhaps from 16 bytes to 2048 bytes, and a group of areas for large blocks, perhaps from 4096 bytes to 32768 bytes, omitting all the areas between these values. These are often simply called *small blocks* and *ordinary blocks*.

A list is maintained for each area or block of memory, which contains used and free blocks within that area (a useful list!) and this is used to re-allocate freed memory blocks.

It should now be quite apparent what the following structure defined in `mallinfo()` means:

```
struct mallinfo {
  int arena;      /* total space in arena (total memory space) */
  int ordblks;    /* number of ordinary blocks */
  int smblks;     /* number of small blocks */
  int hblks;      /* number of holding blocks (number of areas)*/
  int hblkhd;     /* space in holding block headers */
  int usmblks;    /* space in small blocks in use */
  int fsmblks;    /* space in free small blocks */
  int uordblks;   /* space in ordinary blocks in use */
  int fordblks;   /* space in free ordinary blocks */
  int keepcost;   /* cost of enabling keep option */
};
```

### 9.3.6 The `mallopt()` system call

Under AIX 3.x the system call `mallopt()` is used only as an interface, but does have the following definition. It should be noted that it does not affect the memory allocation method used by the dynamic memory allocators.

```
#include <sys/types.h>
#include <malloc.h>
int mallopt(OptCmd, Parameter)
int OptCmd;
int Parameter
```

The parameters are listed below.

OptCmd

This is the optimization command to be used with this call to `mallopt()`, and can take the following values.

*Command value*                                *Action*

M_GRAIN

> Sets the small block size gain. The value used is that specified in the parameter Parameter, and must be larger than zero and smaller than the pre-defined value of MAXFAST as set by this command. This parameter is roughly equivalent to the minimum allocation unit in our example above, i.e. 16 bytes.

M_KEEP

> If this option is set it will preserve that data in the last freed block of memory until the next call to one of the memory allocators. When this option is used the value of Parameter has no meaning. This option is included only for compatibility with older versions on malloc( ) and should not be used by new software.

M_MXFAST

> Sets the maximum size of memory blocks MAXFAST that will be allocated in small memory blocks; in our example this value is 128 bytes. Memory blocks of this size or less are allocated in large holding blocks and then allocated one at a time. If MAXFAST is set to zero then no small block allocation is done. The value to set for MAXFAST will be taken from the parameter Parameter.

M_NLBLKS

> Sets the value of NUMBLKS which will be the number of small blocks allowed in each holding group, in our example the value is 10. This value may take any value larger than 1, the default being 100. The value taken to set NUMBLKS is that found in the parameter Parameter.

## 9.4    Kernel allocators/de-allocators under AIX 3.x

Like most UNIX implementations, the dynamic memory allocators call the system calls sbrk( ) and brk( ) to obtain additional memory from the kernel memory pool. The implementation of these system calls is standard throughout the UNIX world, but under AIX 3.x they are defined as follows:

```
int brk(EndSegmentAddress);
char *EndSegmentAddress;
char *sbrk( SizeChange )
int SizeChange;
```

The system call brk( ) sets the value of the 'break value' for the calling process. This value is the address of the first location after the end of the current data area in the process private segment (seg #2). As the value of this address increases the amount of available space also increases. However, it should be noted that the memory addresses which are used to increase this segment, although shown as contiguous in the diagram, may not always be so. This makes the direct use of this system call quite difficult, and the dynamic memory allocators should be used in preference.

The parameter EndSegmentAddress is used to set the value of the symbol _edata for the calling process. This symbol defines the end of the process data segment. If the value of the symbol _edata can be set to the value specified the system call brk() returns a zero result, otherwise a value of (−1) is returned and the variable errno is set as shown below.

The system call sbrk() is used to increment or decrement the value held within the symbol _edata by the value specified in parameter SizeChange in bytes. This value if positive will extend the segment, and if negative will contract the segment. The returned value of the system call sbrk() is the new address allocated for the memory requested, or the value (char *) (−1) if any error occurred. If an error occurred then the error value can also be found in the variable errno.

This system call may also use non-contiguous memory addresses, so its use by the programmer directly is not very easy. Again the use of the dynamic memory allocator/de-allocators is recommended.

Very unpredictable results will occur if an address not returned by the system call sbrk() is used in a call to the brk() system call. The only exception to this is the value of the symbol _edata itself.

The actual values by which the segment is incremented or decremented will be rounded up to a multiple of the system page size which can be obtained by calling the system call getpagesize(); this is the minimum allocation unit of the kernel memory allocators.

## 9.4.1 Error returned

If either of the above system calls fail then the value of errno will take one of the following values, which are defined in the file sys/errno.h.

*Value of* errno                                        *Functionality*
ENOMEM

The request requires more memory than is allowed by the current system limit. This limit is imposed using the system call ulimit() using the command SET_DATALIM. The maximum allowable break address may be found by calling the system call ulimit() as follows:

```
   #include <ulimit.h>
#include <sys/types.h>
off_t maxlimit;
ulimit(GET_DATALIM, maxlimit);
```

Each process has a pre-defined limit to the maximum size of the data segment area.

This error is also returned by attempting to change the break value to an address which is already attached as a shared memory segment. See Chapter 10 for more information on shared memory segments.

## 9.5    Use of memory allocation functions: potential problems

Memory allocation functions provide great flexibility in programming style and techniques that may be employed to solve many complex programming problems.

Examples of the use of memory allocation functions could fill another book, because their use is so wide, but space restrictions mean that we must concentrate on a few specific examples.

The most common use of the memory allocation function is to allocate storage space for variables. This is perhaps the most natural use of these functions, and is illustrated very well using the C programming language.

Consider the following program fragment which reads a string of characters from the STDIN, the length of which is unknown and may vary at each execution. An elegant solution would be to define a function get_string() which accepts a pointer to a string of characters as a parameter. This function then allocates memory as required as each character is typed at the keyboard, finally returning a pointer to the string containing the function.

The code might look something like this:

```
    #include <stdio.h>
#include <malloc.h>
/* ************************************* */
/* define initial maximum size of a string */
/* ************************************* */
#define MAX_STRING_DEF 10
/* ************************************* */
/* define the returned value of get_string */
/* if not enough memory could be found     */
/* to contain the string                   */
/* ************************************* */
#define NO_STRING (( char *) NULL )
/* ************************************* */
/* define character used to terminate string */
/* input                                   */
/* ************************************* */
#define END_OF_STRING '\n'
/* ************************************* */
/* function prototype for function get_string() */
/* ************************************* */
char *get_string(void);
/* ************************************* */
/* main function calling get_string       */
/* and printing results                   */
/* ************************************* */
```

```
main()
  {
      char *string;      /* pointer to contain pointer to  */
                         /* the memory allocated to string */
      string=NO_STRING;  /* initialize this pointer to
                                                    point to */
                         /* no value before using          */
      /* ***************************************** */
      /* prompt for a string and call set_string() */
      /* assign the value returned to string       */
      /* ***************************************** */
      printf("Enter string : ");
      string=get_string();
      /* ***************************************** */
      /* if a string was returned the print it value */
      /* then deallocate its memory                   */
      /* ***************************************** */
      if ( string != NO_STRING )
         {
         printf("String value = [%s]\n", string);
         free(string);
         }
  }
/* ***************************************** */
/* function get_string returns pointer to  */
/* memory in which string is contained      */
/* ***************************************** */
char *get_string()
{
    char *ptr;          /* pointer to current string
                                                    location   */
    int len ;           /* current character position in
                                                    string */
    int current_len;    /* current max length of
                                                    string     */
    int ch;             /* current character input from
                                                    STDIN    */
    /* ***************************************** */
    /* init pointer to MAX_STRING_DEF length    */
    /* as our first estimate                    */
    /* ***************************************** */
    ptr=(char *) malloc ( MAX_STRING_DEF * sizeof(char));
    /* ***************************************** */
    /* if no memory return NO_STRING            */
    /* ***************************************** */
    if ( ptr == NO_STRING )
       {
          return( NO_STRING );
       }
```

```
/* **************************************** */
/* set current Max length of string to      */
/* MAX_STRING_DEF -2, allow for '\0' char    */
/* terminator                                */
/* set current position in string to zero    */
/* **************************************** */
current_len=MAX_STRING_DEF-2;
len=0;
/* ******************************************* */
/* while not input END_OF_STRING character read */
/* characters from the STDIN stream             */
/* ******************************************* */
while ( ( ch=getchar() ) != END_OF_STRING )
    {
        /* ************************* */
        /* put current character in    */
        /* current position in string  */
        /* and increment position by 1 */
        /* ************************* */
        ptr[len]=ch;
        len++;
        /* ************************* */
        /* if the current position is */
        /* larger or equal to the     */
        /* maximum string length then */
        /* we need to allocate more   */
        /* space                      */
        /* ************************* */
        if ( len >= current_len )
    {
        /* ***************************** */
        /* reallocate space for string    */
        /* to be current maximum space    */
        /* plus MAX_STRING_DEF characters */
        /* if no space return NO_STRING   */
        /* ***************************** */
        ptr=realloc(ptr,
              (current_len+MAX_STRING_DEF) * sizeof(char));
        if ( ptr == NO_STRING )
          {
          return( NO_STRING );
          {
        /* ************************* */
        /* set the current max string */
        /* value to new length        */
        /* ************************* */
        current_len=(current_len+MAX_STRING_DEF);
    }
}
```

```
/* *************************** */
/* terminate string with '\0'   */
/* and return pointer to string */
/* *************************** */
ptr[len]='\0';
return(ptr);
}
```

The function get_string() is therefore able to accept the entry of an undefined and variable-length string from STDIN. This function could of course be extended to accept a parameter of a character pointer and to use this as its initial storage space, and to extend this where necessary. This function could also be extended to take its input from any file pointer, not just STDIN. It is left as an exercise to the reader to extend the function to do this.

This function in itself is a great improvement over the standard library function gets() which merely accepts characters into a character pointer supplied, and assumes that the memory space is allocated correctly. Unfortunately in most cases this is a fatal assumption.

The simple example above should be familiar to most C programmers. The problems that functions like this solve are commonplace, but from such simple beginnings complex structures can be built. The use of the allocation functions to make it possible to use a multidimensional array of any data type, defining the dimensions of the array at run-time, can also be coded.

The example which follows shows how a two-dimensional array of integers may be coded and used within a program. This program allows the user to define the dimension sizes of the two-dimensional array at run-time and then to enter values into elements selected by the user. Finally the program will print out these values, before de-allocating the memory allocated to them.

```
#include <stdio.h>
#include <malloc.h>
/* *************************************************** */
/* use of malloc.c to implement a two dimensional     */
/* dynamic array of integers                           */
/* *************************************************** */
/* *************************** */
/* define TRUE and FALSE if not   */
/* already defined                */
/* *************************** */
#ifndef TRUE
#define FALSE 0
#define TRUE ( ! FALSE )
#endif
/* *************************** */
/* defined failure return value   */
/* from malloc()                  */
/* *************************** */
```

```
#define MALLOC_FAIL ( (char *) NULL)
/* ********************************* */
/* define initialization value for     */
/* array elements                       */
/* *************************************/
#define INIT_VALUE (int ) 0
/* *********************************** */
/* define value for termination of input */
/* loop                                 */
/* *********************************** */
#define END_VALUE (int) —1
/* ******************************** */
/* function Prototype for error()    */
/* ******************************** */
int error(char * );
main()
  {
      int **array;   /* pointer to the first element of the
                                                    array */
      int max_cols; /* maximum number of columns in 2D
                                                   array      */
      int max_rows; /* maximum number of rows in 2D
                                                   array      */
      int row;       /* current row number */
      int col;       /* current column number */
      int value;     /* element value */
      /* *********************************** */
      /* get from the user the maximum number */
      /* of rows and columns in the 2D array  */
      /* *********************************** */
      printf("Enter Number of columns required : ");
      fflush(stdout);
      scanf("%d", &max_cols);
      printf("Enter Number of rows required : ");
      fflush(stdout);
      scanf("%d", &max_rows);
      /* ********************************** */
      /* allocate an array of (max_rows in size)*/
      /* of pointers to pointers to integers and*/
      /* make array point to the first element  */
      /* ********************************** */
       array=( int ** ) malloc ( (max_rows )   *
                                            sizeof( int *) );
       if ( (char *) array == MALLOC_FAIL )
          {
             error("failed to allocate rows");
          }
```

```
/* **************************************** */
/* for each pointer allocate max_cols      */
/* integers                                */
/* initialize all integers to INIT_VALUE   */
/* **************************************** */
for ( row=0; row < max_rows ; row ++ )
    {
        *(array+row)=(int *) malloc((max_cols ) *
                                          sizeof(int));
        if (((char *) *(array+row)) == MALLOC_FAIL)
           {
             error("failed to allocate columns");
           }
         /* **************************************** */
         /* set all values to INIT_VALUE             */
         /* **************************************** */
         for ( col=0; col < max_cols ; col ++ )
            {
              *(*(array+row)+col)=INIT_VALUE;
            }
    }
/* ****************************************** */
/* allow user to enter any column or row value  */
/* and insert into array                     */
/* Enter END_VALUE in both col and row to end  */
/* ****************************************** */
while ( TRUE )
  {
    printf("Enter row value from [0-%d], −1 to end : ",
                                        max_rows−1);
    fflush(stdout);
    scanf("%d", &row);
    printf("Enter column value from [0-%d], −1 to end :",
                                        max_cols-1);
    fflush(stdout);
    scanf("%d", &col);
    if ( ( row == END_VALUE ) && ( col == END_VALUE ) )
       {
         break;
       }
    if ( ( row < 0 ) || ( row > max_rows -1 ) )
      {
        fprintf(stderr, "ERROR row value %d out of range
                                           \n", row);
        fflush(stderr);
        continue;
      }
    if ( ( col < 0 ) || ( col > max_cols −1 ) )
```

```
          {
            fprintf(stderr, "ERROR column value %d out of
                                             range \n", col);
            fflush(stderr);
            continue;
          }
       printf("Enter value for array[%d][%d] : ", row, col);
       fflush(stdout);
       scanf("%d", &value);
       /* ********************************************* */
       /* assign value to element                       */
       /* ********************************************* */
       *(*(array+row)+col)=value;
   }
/* ********************************************* */
/* print out all values                         */
/* ********************************************* */
for ( row=0 ; row < max_rows  ; row ++ )
   {
     printf("Row[%d] :", row);
     fflush(stdout);
      for ( col=0 ; col < max_cols ; col++ )
         {
             printf("%4d ", *(*(array+row)+col));
         }
     printf("\n");
     fflush(stdout);
   }
/* ********************************************* */
/* free up all elements                         */
/* and array of pointers                        */
/* ********************************************* */
 for ( row=0 ; row < max_rows ; row ++ )
    {
       free(*(array+row));
    }
    free(array);
}
/* ********************************************* */
/* print error to stderr and terminate program  */
/* ********************************************* */
int error(str)
char *str;
{
   fprintf(stderr, "ERROR : %s\n", str);
   fflush(stderr);
   exit(1);
}
```

As the above example shows, what might at first be a simple concept can soon become a complex program, thanks mostly to the syntax of the C programming language. However, this point should be taken to heart by the reader, who should learn the lesson that a complex solution is not always the one that will work.

As mentioned before, the memory allocators are useful in providing a flexible programming environment. However, there is a cost to this flexibility, that is complexity and verifiability. It would be true to say that most bugs in C programs can often be traced to the inappropriate use of pointers within the program. This problem is more often than not directly associated with the memory allocation functions.

The problems can be divided into two main categories: misuse of pointers and poor memory management. The first category is a very large one, and all good programmers learn very quickly to treat pointers with respect, but there are a few classic examples.

The use of the pointer whose status is not known by the programmer is very common, and in AIX 3.x and UNIX will almost certainly cause the programmer's nightmare, the 'core dumb', to occur. This very often happens because the value of the pointer used is so undefined that it attempts to access address space outside that allocated to the process. AIX 3.x takes a very dim view of this and terminates the offending process.

If the programmer is lucky when this situation occurs, it is possible to overrun the memory allocated to a pointer and not cause the process to 'core dumb'. This is because memory is allocated from the kernel in fixed size blocks, so AIX 3.x usually does not notice that a memory area has overrun until it overruns past the end of this block. In this situation other pointers which have been allocated memory locations within the same block of memory may have the contents of their memory changed by this action. This error can take many happy hours with a debug tool to locate and fix, and may even go undetected for many years.

This type of mistake is totally avoidable and should never happen if good programming practice is followed. However, a simple standard rule applies: whenever a program is to access memory pointed to by a pointer, or change the value of a pointer, it is vital that the programmer is certain that *he or she knows the current value of the pointer is a valid one, and he or she makes no assumptions as to its value if the value is not known*. The second kind of mistake is more concerned with the memory allocation functions than with programming practice, and is therefore of direct concern to the user of these functions. Memory allocated by these functions is often not returned to the kernel memory pool until the process that requested this memory terminates; it is simply held for re-use within the process address space. It is therefore very important that memory allocated by the memory allocation functions is freed using the de-allocation functions, thus allowing its re-use by the allocation functions. If memory is not de-allocated then the allocation functions will make successive requests for more kernel memory, thus using large amounts of system resources which are not strictly required. The process's own address space contained enough memory to satisfy the request, but this was erroneously unavailable.

The problem can be serious, both to the programmer and to the AIX 3.x administrator. Rogue programs which eat memory like this can soon cause any system to come to a very slow stop.

Quite simple mistakes can cause this problem; consider the following function which removes spaces from a string and returns the string back to the calling process.

```c
    #include <stdio.h>
#include <malloc.h>
/* ********************************* */
/* failure return for malloc()       */
/* ********************************* */
#define NO_STRING ((char *) NULL)
/* ********************************* */
/* success and failure for strip_space */
/* function                           */
/* ********************************* */
#define FAIL 0
#define OK   1
/* *********************************** */
/* strip spaces from str and return string */
/* in str                              */
/* *********************************** */
int strip_space(str)
char *str;
{
    int len;          /* length of string in characters      */
    char *temp,*old; /* temporary and old pointers to string */
    int pos;          /* current position on temporary string */
    /* ********************************* */
    /* allocate temporary string to be the */
    /* same size as that of str           */
    /* ********************************* */
    len=strlen(str)+1;
    temp=(char *) malloc(len * sizeof(char));
    if ( temp == NO_STRING )
        {
          return(FAIL);
        }
    /* *********************************** */
    /* set old to pointer to the beginning of */
    /* the old string and reset pos to zero   */
    /* *********************************** */
    old=str;
```

```
pos=0;
/* ************************************** */
/* skip through str deleting all spaces */
/* and copying other characters to temp */
/* ************************************** */
while ( *str != '\0' )
  {
     if ( *str == ' ')
       {
          str++;
          continue;
       }
     temp[pos]=(*str);
     str++;
     pos++;
  }
/* *************************** */
/* add terminator to temp and  */
/* copy temp back to the old   */
/* string pointer memory       */
/* *************************** */
temp[pos]='\0';
strcpy(old, temp);
return(OK);
}
```

At first sight this function's mistake may go unnoticed. The alert reader has probably already observed that the variable temp is an automatic variable within the function strip_space(), and its value is lost after the function returns. This function only uses the space allocated to this pointer as a temporary storage space. It then copies the contents of this back to its original memory storage space, without changing the pointer which locates this area, so after the function strip_space has returned there is no possible way to locate the pointer value used by the variable temp and thus this memory can never be freed by the de-allocator function. After many successive calls to strip_space() many of these un-freeable memory blocks will exist, and this will of course tend to cause the problem described above.

The solution is equally simple. The function should explicitly free the memory pointed to by the variable temp before returning to the calling process, thus allowing the next call to the allocator function to re-use this space if appropriate.

The above problem could of course be solved by using the allocator alloca() to allocate the memory for the variable temp. In this case this memory will automatically be freed when the function strip_space() returns, because it will be allocated in the process stack segment which is of course 'popped' on return from functions.

This again is one of the more obvious mistakes that can be made while using the memory allocators. Many other possible mistakes are more difficult to spot.

Not only do coding mistakes cause problems when using the memory allocators, but their use can prove very difficult when a set of interrelated functions need to abort their operations. Each function may be unaware of the memory allocated by the other functions, and may not even have access to their pointers. This usually presents itself as a problem to be addressed in 'error-processing routines', and as not all error-processing routines will terminate the process, it is often not safe to assume that all memory allocated by the process so far has been de-allocated.

This problem is compounded by the need, which is of course good practice, to check the return result of the memory allocator functions for a failure after each call to these functions. It can often prove quite difficult to decide how to notify all of the calling functions of a failure of this type within a lower-level function. This can at best complicate the code of all of the functions, to allow a cascade of abort conditions supporting this type of event.

Some applications solve this problem quite simply; they do not check the return result of the allocator and assume it will always be successful in returning the memory required. This is rather like carrying a bomb in your pocket—one day it will go off! Thankfully most applications programs do not take this approach. Many surround the memory allocators and de-allocator functions with program-defined functions which enhance the error-handling capabilities of the program. The goal of such functions is to be as far as possible functionally identical to the functions they encapsulate. This enables easy substitution of these functions for their standard counterparts within applications that already exist, but also provides additional functions which enable error processing and extra error trapping to be performed.

Let us consider a set of such functions that could be used instead of `malloc()` and `free()` but would allow all allocated pointers to be freed with one call to its `free()` function and, if required, an error-handling function to be nominated and called upon an error condition. This will eliminate the extra code required to check for failure after each call to the allocator, as one error-processing function can be nominated to do this for all calls to the allocator. This would also ensure that within this error function all allocated memory could be freed without requiring direct access to the pointers which point to the memory areas.

The simple code which follows has the six functions listed below.

| *Function* | *Action* |
|---|---|

`get_mem_error()`

        Accesses the private copy of the structure `mem_info` to return the value of `last_error` to the calling process. This allows the caller to determine the status of the last call to any of the memory allocator or de-allocator functions.

`set_mem_err_action()`

        Allows for a function pointer to be nominated which will be called if an error occurs within the memory allocators or de-allocator. This function may be user defined, and may call any of the memory functions. If it is defined as a NULL function then the functions return the error status in a similar way to malloc() and free(). If this error function returns then the functions will return also, returning the normal error values which malloc() and free() would return.

set_free_action()

> Sets the action taken by the de-allocator when called. This allows the de-allocator to free all memory allocated by setting this value to FREE_ALL or only the memory pointed to by the current pointer if this is set to FREE_THIS.

init_mem()

> Initializes some of the internal values held within the structure mem_info to their default values, and should be called before any other memory function is called. This is also called by the de-allocator function if the FREE_ALL flag is set by set_free_action().

get_mem()

> Behaves in the same way as malloc() in that it returns a pointer to the memory allocated or NULL if an error occurred.

free_mem()

> Behaves like free() but has the added security of only attempting to free pointers that were allocated using get_mem(). This can be very useful in tracking down those 'core dumb' bugs. This function also uses the flag free_action within the structure mem_info to control the action it takes with the pointer it is given. When the flag FREE_ALL is set the pointer given to this function is not used.

This set of functions would be divided up into a separately compiled library of objects. Let's call the code for this library xmem.c and the header file required by all processes using it to be xmem.h. Then xmem.h would be as follows:

```
/* *********************************************************** */
/* extended memory handling functions to show the use of    */
/* malloc() and free()                                       */
/* *********************************************************** */
/* ***********************************************************/
/* Structure used to keep track of all memory allocations    */
/* made by get_mem(), using a linked list structure          */
/* *********************************************************** */
static struct mem_used   {
                          struct mem_used *next;
                          char *memory;
                          };
/* *************************************** */
/* NULL pointer for mem_used pointer       */
/* *************************************** */
```

```
#define INIT_VALUE ( (struct mem_used *) NULL )
/* ***************************************************** */
/* Structure used for memory function extensions         */
/*                                                        */
/* Such as   :  get_mem_error()                           */
/*              set_mem_err_action()                      */
/*              set_free_action()                         */
/*              init_mem()                                */
/* ***************************************************** */
static struct mem_info {
                        int free_action;
                        int (*error_func) ();
                        int last_error;
                        };
/* ***************************************** */
/* constants used in mem_info by functions   */
/* ***************************************** */
/* **************************** */
/* define free_action           */
/* **************************** */
#define FREE_ALL  1  /* free all known pointers on call to
                                               mem_free */
#define FREE_THIS 0  /* free only this pointer on call to
                                               mem_free */
/* *********************************************/
/* define defaults for error function pointer */
/* ******************************************* */
#define NO_ERROR_FUNC ((int (*)()) NULL)
/* *******************************************/
/* define ERRORs for get_mem_error()          */
/* ******************************************* */
#define ERR_NONE   0  /* no error found */
#define ERR_INTER  1  /* internal error in memory functions */
#define ERR_ALLOC  2  /* allocation failure                 */
#define ERR_FREE   3  /* free given bad pointer              */
/* ****************************************** */
/* function prototypes                        */
/* ****************************************** */
int free_mem( char *);
char *get_mem( int );
void set_mem_err_action( int (*)()  );
int set_free_action( int );
int get_mem_error( void );
void init_mem( void );
```

The contents of the file xmem.c would be as follows:

```
  #include <malloc.h>
#include "xmem.h/
#include <stdio.h>
```

```
/* ************************************************************ */
/* extended memory handling functions to show the use of    */
/* malloc() and free()                                        */
/* ************************************************************ */
/* ********************************************** */
/* define TRUE and FALSE if not defined            */
/* ********************************************** */
#ifndef TRUE
#define FALSE 0
#define TRUE ( ! FALSE )
#endif
/* ****************************************** */
/* Root pointer to linked list of memory    */
/* blocks                                    */
/* local memory information structure        */
/* ****************************************** */
static struct mem_used *mem_root=INIT_VALUE;
static struct mem_info info;
/* ********************************************** */
/* internal functions to handle linked list      */
/* ********************************************** */
/* ********************************************** */
/* add pointer defined in structure item         */
/* to linked list of pointers held internally    */
/* return a pointer to the new root to the        */
/* calling process                                */
/* ********************************************** */
static struct mem_used *add(root, item)
struct mem_used *root;
struct mem_used item;
{
    struct mem_used *new;
    if ( root == ( struct mem_used *) NULL )
        {
            new=(struct mem_used *) malloc( sizeof(struct
                                                 mem_used ));
            if ( (char *) new == (char *) NULL )
              {
                  info.last_error=ERR_INTER;
                  return( (struct mem_used *) NULL);
              }
            new->next=(struct mem_used *) NULL;
            new->memory=item.memory;
            return(new);
        }
        new=(struct mem_used *) malloc( sizeof(struct
                                             mem_used ));
        if ( (char *) new == (char *) NULL )
          {
              info.last_error=ERR_INTER;
```

```
                    return( (struct mem_used *) NULL );
              }
          new->next=root;
          new->memory=item.memory;
          return(new);
   }
   /* ****************************************** */
   /* remove specified memory pointer from memory */
   /* also clean up internal structures          */
   /* ****************************************** */
   static struct mem_used *del(root, item)
   struct mem_used *root;
   struct mem_used item;
   {
     struct mem_used *last, *this;
     this=root;
     last=this;
     while ( this != (struct mem_used *) NULL )
         {
           if ( this->memory == item.memory )
             {
                 free(this->memory);
                 if ( this == root )
                   {
                       free(this);
                       return((struct mem_used *) NULL );
                   }
                 last->next=this->next;
                 free(this);
                 return(root);
             }
           last=this;
           this=this->next;
         }
       return((struct mem_used *) -1 );
   }
   /* ****************************************** */
   /* remove all memory plus memory management */
   /* data structure                            */
   /* ****************************************** */
   static struct mem_used *del_all(root)
   struct mem_used *root;
   {
     struct mem_used *this,*last;
     this=root;
     while ( this != ( struct mem_used *) NULL )
         {
           if ( this->memory != ( char *) NULL )
             {
```

```
                free(this->memory);
            }
          this=this->next;
        }
    this=root;
    last=this;
    while ( this != ( struct mem_used *) NULL )
        {
          last=this->next;
          free(this);
          this=last;
        }
    init_mem();
}
/* ********************************************** */
/* init memory function called before any other */
/* function                                      */
/* ********************************************** */
void init_mem()
  {
    /* *********************************** */
    /* init the root of the linked list    */
    /* error function to NULL              */
    /* free action to only one pointer     */
    /* reset error value                   */
    /* *********************************** */
    mem_root=INIT_VALUE;
    info.error_func=NO_ERROR_FUNC;
    info.free_action=FREE_THIS;
    info.last_error=ERR_NONE;
  }
/* *********************************** */
/* set memory error function to function */
/* pointer supplied                      */
/* *********************************** */
void set_mem_err_action(func)
int (*func)();
{
    info.error_func=func;
}
/* *********************************** */
/* set free_action flag to free action   */
/* specified                             */
/* *********************************** */
int set_free_action(value)
int value;
{
    if ( (value != FREE_ALL ) && ( value != FREE_THIS ) )
```

```
      {
         return(FALSE);
      }
   info.free_action=value;
   return(TRUE);
}
/* ************************************** */
/* Return the value of the last error    */
/* found by the memory allocation        */
/* functions to the calling process      */
/* The value of ERR_NONE is returned if */
/* the last operation was successful     */
/* ************************************** */
int get_mem_error()
{
   return(info.last_error);
}
/* ******************************************* */
/* memory allocator function, Update linked    */
/* list of structures while allocating memory  */
/* ******************************************* */
char *get_mem( size )
int size;
{
   struct mem_used new, *new_root;
   char *ptr;
   ptr=(char*) malloc( size);
   if ( ptr == (char *) NULL )
     {
         info.last_error=ERR_ALLOC;
         if (info.error_func != (NULL))
           {
              info.error_func();
           }
         return((char *) NULL );
      }
   new.memory=ptr;
   new_root=add(mem_root, new);
   if ( new_root == ( struct mem_used *) NULL )
      {
         free(ptr);
         info.last_error=ERR_INTER;
         if ( info.error_func != ( NULL ) )
           {
              info.error_func();
           }
         return((char *) NULL);
      }
```

```
      mem_root=new_root;
      info.last_error=ERR_NONE;
      return(ptr);
 }
/* ********************************************** */
/* free up memory and remove internal structures */
/* If the FREE_ALL flag is set all known pointers*/
/* are free irrespective of the value of the     */
/* pointer supplied, if a pointer is supplied     */
/* which was not allocated by get_mem() then an   */
/* error is returned                              */
/* ********************************************** */
int free_mem( ptr )
char *ptr;
{
     struct mem_used this, *new_root;
     if ( info.free_action == FREE_ALL )
       {
          del_all(mem_root);
          return(TRUE);
       }
     this.memory=ptr;
      new_root=del(mem_root, this);
      if ( new_root == ( struct mem_used *) -1 )
        {
           info.last_error=ERR_FREE;
           if ( info.error_func != ( NULL ))
             {
                 info.error_func();
             }
           return(FALSE);
        }
     else
        {
           mem_root=new_root;
        }
     return(TRUE);
}
```

This library may be compiled under AIX 3.x using the following command:

```
$ cc -c -oxmem xmem.c
```

This will produce a file called xmem.o which will contain the compiled library functions as described in the header file xmem.h. This file can then be incorporated into a library archive using the ar command or used on the compiler command line as an object.

The use of these functions can be illustrated by the following code, which shows the structure of a very simple program using memory allocators

Let us assume the following code would be contained in a file called `pgm.c`.

```c
#include <stdio.h>
/* ****************************************** */
/* include header information for xmem.o     */
/* ****************************************** */
#include "xmem.h"
/* ****************************************** */
/* function prototype for error() function   */
/* ****************************************** */
int error(void);
/* ****************************************** */
/* define the number of characters allocated */
/* to pointers                               */
/* ****************************************** */
#define MAX_CHARS 30
main()
{
   /* four pointers to be used by allocator */
   char *str1, *str2, *str3, *str4;
   /* ******************* */
   /* call init_mem() before */
   /* we start               */
   /* ********************* */
   init_mem();
   /* *************************** */
   /* set error action to call the */
   /* function error when an error */
   /* occurs                       */
   /* *************************** */
   set_mem_err_action(error);
   /* ****************************** */
   /* allocate str1, str2, str3 memory */
   /* to pointer to MAX_CHARS         */
   /* characters memory location      */
   /* ****************************** */
   str1=get_mem( MAX_CHARS * sizeof(char) );
   str2=get_mem( MAX_CHARS * sizeof(char) );
   str3=get_mem( MAX_CHARS * sizeof(char) );
   /* ******************************************* */
   /* copy values in str1, str2, str3 and print */
   /* to STDOUT                                  */
   /* ******************************************* */
   strcpy(str1, "string number 1");
   strcpy(str2, "string number 2");
   strcpy(str3, "string number 3");
   printf("values are: \n [%s] \n [%s] \n [%s]\n",
                                    str1, str2, str3);
   /* ********************************** */
   /* set free action to FREE_THIS and  */
```

```
    /* free all pointers str1, str2, str3 */
    /*                                     */
    /* also free str4 which was not        */
    /* allocated, this will cause an        */
    /* error and error() will be called    */
    /* ******************************** */
    set_free_action(FREE_THIS);
    free_mem(str1);
    free_mem(str2);
    free_mem(str3);
    free_mem(str4);
}
/* ******************************** */
/* error handling function           */
/* ******************************** */
int error()
{
 /* ********************************/
 /* print error to screen that caused */
 /* jump to error handler            */
 /* ******************************** */
 printf("ERROR number was [%d]\n", get_mem_error());
 fflush(stdout);
 /* ******************************** */
 /* let's get rid of any memory that  */
 /* is still allocated               */
 /* ******************************** */
 set_free_action(FREE_ALL);
 free_mem( (char *) NULL);
 /* ******************************** */
 /* terminate program with error status */
 /* ******************************** */
 exit(1);
}
```

This simple example shows the advantage of having the error function and the ability to detect the use of invalid pointers used by the memory de-allocators. It could be improved to allow memory to be freed by function groups or even function names, using a simple extension to the get_mem() and free_mem() calls. The potential of this type of library is left to the reader to exploit.

The above program could be compiled using the following command

```
$ cc -opgm pgm.c xmem.o
```

and executed using the command

```
    $ ./pgm
```

```
    values are:
 [string number 1]
 [string number 2]
 [string number 3]
ERROR number was [3]
```

The output produced shows the error generated by the use of free_mem( ) with an invalid pointer.

# Part Three
# Interprocess communication

# 10
# Processes and communications

AIX and UNIX are both examples of multitasking operating systems. But what does this term mean? A multitasking operating system could be defined as

*an operating system that simulates the exclusive use of one or more machine resources by one or more processes, apparently simultaneously.*

This is all very well, but what do we mean by a 'process' and a 'resource'. The definition of a process is not as simple as one might imagine. Often people give the simple but technically incorrect definition 'a process is equivalent to a program', whether the program is a user program or a system program. This is far too simplistic, and leads to lots of misunderstandings between systems programmers and application programmers. A process is most certainly not equivalent to a program. The difference between them is very subtle, but quite crucial to the programmer's understanding of the operating environment. The best way to understand the difference is by an analogy.

Consider a DIY enthusiast who is constructing a kitchen cupboard from a self-assembly kit. The kit's assembly instructions can be considered as 'the program' which is expressed in some language which the CPU (the hobbyist's brain) can understand. The components of the cupboard constitute the input to the program. The DIY enthusiast follows the instructions or program, using up input, i.e. the components, to produce the output, the finished cupboard. The process is the activity of reading the instructions, fetching the input and constructing the cupboard to produce the output, the finished unit. Now, consider what happens if the telephone rings during the construction process. Our DIY enthusiast stops what he is doing, notes his position in the instruction list (i.e. the process state is saved), and then walks over to the telephone and answers it. To do this he uses another set of instructions, 'how to answer a telephone', which by our analogy is a new 'program'. The input now is the voice on the telephone, and the output is the verbal responses. When the telephone call is finished the hobbyist replaces the telephone and walks back to his cupboard construction, where he restarts the process at the instruction where he left it (i.e. the process state is restored).

The key idea is that a process is an 'activity' and not a program. By this we mean that

*a process is defined as being a program together with all of the resources it requires to complete its instructions and its current state with respect to its instructions.*

The definition of a 'machine resource' is a lot simpler:

*a machine resource is any object used by the program to constitute a process,*

in simple terms it consists of the central processor unit (CPU) and disks, the RAM, etc.; all of these objects can be considered as a machine resource. A multitasking operating system is primarily concerned with sharing these machine resources between one or more processes in such a way that each process is given the illusion of exclusive access to the resource.

## 10.1    Why do processes need interprocess communications?

In order to achieve the stated goal of multitasking operating systems, processes are often created or appear to be created with their own private set of machine resources. These may be virtual machine resources, simulated by the operating system, or real machine resources. The process is forbidden by the operating system to access in any way the machine resources allocated to another process. Thus if one or more processes wish to communicate with each other, under these rules they will have a problem; they have no common resource area, which they may all access, to exchange information.

Before we may consider how the interprocess communication mechanisms are defined, we must fully understand their importance. Under AIX and UNIX the operating system itself consists of several processes running apparently simultaneously, together with many user processes in the form of applications programs and their resources. If we accept the primary axiom that the operating system is the controller and provider of all resources to all processes then it is self-evident that there must exist a mechanism for separate processes to communicate, at least within the operating system processes.

One such mechanism might be to statically link all of the necessary operating system code to each user process, so that the interprocess communication problem between user process and operating system simply does not exist, but this has certain disadvantages. Firstly, the multitasking is then dependent on a lower layer of code which is not statically linked, which provides a 'virtual machine' environment to the user processes, thus allowing each user process to believe it has exclusive access to a 'real machine'. Secondly, the size of code required to be linked to the user processes tends to be very large.These processes are shown diagrammatically in Fig. 10.1.

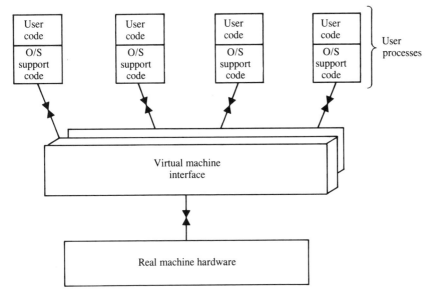

Figure 10.1. The virtual machine environment.

In the example shown in the figure each user process, and by implication each program, will have all of the operating system code necessary to communicate with the virtual machine interface, which will present each user process with a simulated copy of the real machine hardware. Thus in this situation all the user processes can coexist on the same real hardware, but are often unaware of other user processes. The only communication a process does is via its own statically linked copy of the operating system code. Thus although interprocess communications between the user process and the operating system have been removed, there still exist a requirement for the virtual machine interface to communicate with each user process. This, although far simpler to achieve, still requires interprocess communication. A mechanism similar to the above is used by mainframe computer operating systems such as VM to allow one or more operating systems to coexist on the same real machine hardware. In this case the user process becomes an operating system in its own right and will be internally responsible for its own resource management. This mechanism, although quite refined today, is not found in AIX or UNIX; however, a similar mechanism is used. In AIX a process may be conceptually considered to consist of two main parts, user code and operating system interface code, often termed the *system call interface*. This system call interface code is relatively small in comparison with the operating system code of our virtual machine example. Its only function is to allow the user process to execute operating system code, which resides in the operating system layer below. The operating system layer is then responsible for the implementation of resource management and the multitasking environment on the real machine hardware.

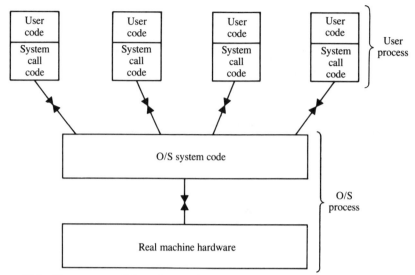

Figure 10.2. The system call interface environment.

Diagrammatically our processes may look like Fig. 10.2. In this environment, whenever a user process wishes to communicate with the operating system it executes one or more of the 'system call interfaces'. This code causes the user process to transfer from the conceptual 'user space' to the conceptual 'operating system space', passing with it any information it requires. While executing in the operating system space the user program has controlled access to the real machine hardware. After the system call is complete, the operating system returns the process back to the user space code where it will continue to execute the instructions that follow the system call. The operating system itself, although shown in this simplistic diagram as one process, is always more than one and therefore it too requires interprocess communication. All good operating systems are layered into discrete functional units, with defined interfaces between them. This is of course the case with AIX and is the major factor in the operating system's portability and compatibility with other UNIX offerings from other manufacturers.

It should now be clear that there is a requirement for user processes to communicate, and it is a fundamental requirement for the implementation of a multitasking operating system.

## 10.2  Fundamental axioms for interprocess communication under AIX

In order for any process to communicate with another one, each process must be able to have access to an area of common resource. As stated earlier, in order to implement a multitasking environment each process is created with its own private resource area to which only it has direct access. Thus under AIX and UNIX the general principle by which information is passed from one process to another is via the operating system and the system call interface. Using this method the operating system is responsible for the safe transfer of data from one process's private resource area to that of another process.

A problem arises, however, when one or more processes have access to a common resource—the problem of mutual exclusion. This requires that only one process may modify the resource at any one time, and it is vital for interprocess communication.

# 11
# Mutual exclusion and semaphores

All interprocess communications mechanisms require a method of providing mutual exclusion between processes, if only when the internal structures of the interprocess communication abstraction are being updated.

In 1965 E. W. Dijkstra (see *Co-operating Sequential Processes in Programming Languages*, ed. F. Genuys, Academic Press, London, UK, 1965) suggested a mechanism by which mutual exclusion could be achieved by many processes. He called this mechanism a *semaphore*. The word has Greek roots: *sema*, means to flag or signal, and *phore* denotes a bearer or producer. The essence of a semaphore is quite simple; it is an integer variable which may have a value of 0 or any positive value. Two conceptual operations can be defined on a semaphore, which Dijkstra called DOWN and UP. The key property of these functions is that their operation is guaranteed to be one single uninterrupted action, i.e. a DOWN or an UP operation proceeds to its conclusion without being interrupted by any multitasking context switches from process to process. That is an *atomic action*. With this single property, the DOWN and UP operations are defined as follows:

- The DOWN operation on a semaphore will first check the value of the semaphore to be determined. If it is zero, the DOWN operation will cause the calling process to 'go to sleep' or 'block', waiting for the semaphore to become non-zero, after which it will be decremented by 1, and the DOWN operation will then return to the calling process. If the value is greater than 0 the DOWN operation will decrement the semaphore by 1 and return to the calling process immediately.
- The UP operation will simply increment the semaphore by 1 and return to the calling process.

Using semaphores we may thus allow two processes to have exclusive access to a shared data area. The classic producer/consumer problem where one process produces data items to be used by the other process, using a shared data area as a buffer, can be implemented in the C programming language as follows:

```
    #define NumberOfItems 100
typedef int semaphore
semaphore mutual = 1;
semaphore empty = NumberOfItems;
semaphore full = 0;
producer()
 {
     int item;
     while (TRUE)
       {
         produce_item(&item);
         DOWN(&empty);
         DOWN(&mutual);
         add_item(item);
         UP(&mutual);
         UP(&full);
       }
}
consumer()
{
    int item;
  while (TRUE)
     {
       DOWN(&full);
       DOWN(&mutual);
       get_item(&item);
       UP(&mutual);
       UP(&empty);
       process_item(item);
     }
}
```

There are two main functional processes, which can be considered as separately executing processes although they are defined as C functions. One called producer() obtains items and places them into a shared items buffer, and the other called consumer() extracts items from the shared buffer and processes them.

There are four library support functions used by the two main processes:

- produce_item() Obtains a new item from the input stream of the process which calls it, and returns that item in the parameter given.
- add_item() Adds the item given as a parameter to the shared item buffer.
- get_item() Removes an item from the shared buffer and returns it to the calling process in the parameter given.
- process_item() Performs some processing on the item given as a parameter.

There are two major problems with the producer/consumer syndrome. Firstly the shared data area accessed by functions add_item() and get_item() needs to be accessed exclusively by these functions at any instant in time. Secondly, because the `producer()` and `consumer()` processes are totally independent of each other and may execute at different rates, a semaphore `mutual` is required to achieve this mutual exclusion.

The semaphore `mutual` is initialized to a value of 1, and a simple rule exists for any process wishing to use either of the functions `get_item()` or `add_item()`: simply issue a DOWN operation on the semaphore `mutual` before calling either function, and an UP operation after the function has returned.

Consider what happens if the producer process calls the DOWN operation on semaphore `mutual`. It initially has a value of 1, so the down operation will decrement its value to 0 and return to the calling process, i.e. the producer process. At that moment a process context switch takes place and the operating system switches to the consumer process. The consumer process again calls the DOWN operation on the semaphore `mutual` and is 'blocked' because the semaphore has a value of 0. Thus the operating system may restart the producer process which eventually calls the UP operation on the semaphore `mutual`, thus unblocking the consumer process which then continues after its DOWN operation has decremented the value of the semaphore `mutual` to 0. Mutual exclusion is guaranteed if the semaphore operations are used in this way.

The second problem is that the shared item buffer used by the functions `add_item()` and `get_item()` is finite in size. What should the `add_item()` function do if the buffer is full, and what should the `get_item()` do if the buffer is empty? A neat solution would be for the calling process to 'go to sleep' or 'block' in these cases. In order to achieve this we need two further semaphores, one called `full` and the other called `empty`. The `full` semaphore is initialized to 0 and `empty` is initialized to the maximum number of items allowed in the shared item buffer (`NumberOfItems`). The semaphore `empty` is used to count the number of empty places left in the buffer and `full` is used to count the number of full spaces currently in the buffer. Then using these two semaphores the producer process will do a DOWN operation on the semaphore `empty` before it attempts to call `add_item()`, causing it to block if there are no empty spaces in the buffer. If all is well the producer will call `add_item()` and add an item to the buffer, then it will do an UP operation on the semaphore `full` to signify that there is now one more full space in the buffer. Thus the producer will continue to decrement the number of empty spaces and increment the number of full spaces as it adds items to the buffer.

The consumer process on the other hand reverses the semaphore calls. It does a DOWN on the semaphore `full` before it calls `get_item()`, which will cause it to block if there are no full spaces in the buffer, and does an UP operation on the semaphore `empty` on return from `get_item()` to signify that a new space is now vacant in the buffer.

The above example, although quite simple to understand, illustrates the power of semaphores and the need for them in everyday systems programming.

## 11.1    Semaphores under AIX 3.x

Under AIX 3.x, as with UNIX system V.x, semaphores are implemented in what seems at first sight to be an unnecessarily complex way. In the light of the previous discussion, however, the semaphore system call interface provides a much more powerful tool than could be achieved with the simple implementation presented above. Although the system call interface may be quite different, the underlying principles of the semaphores still hold true.

There are primarily four operations:

- Creating a semaphore
- Using and testing a semaphore
- Deleting a semaphore
- Changing or examining the characteristics of a semaphore

These operations are provided under AIX 3.x by three system call interfaces, `semget()`, `semop()` and `semctl()`.

Each semaphore has two identifiers. One of them is created by and known to the semaphore's creator process. This is analogous to the filename in the system call `fopen()`. The second identifier is assigned by the AIX kernel and is analogous to the file pointer returned by `fopen()`. This is used in all subsequent accesses to the semaphore by all cooperating processes. The initial identifier (the filename) must be chosen very carefully. In any system using any interprocess communications mechanism a standard for choosing this identifier must be followed, as the generation of unique identifiers is vital for the proper operation of the interprocess communications. Any method may be used to choose such an identifier, but a library function called `ftok()` is provided to generate unique keys.

## 11.2    Creating a semaphore

The system call used to create a new semaphore is

```
#include <sys/types.h>
#include <sys/ipc.h>
#include <sys/sem.h>
#include <sys/mode.h>
int semget(semkey, nosem, semflag)
key_t semkey;
int nosem;
int semflag;
```

The parameter `semkey` is of the predefined system type `key_t`; this type is the return type of the library function `ftok()`, but any scalar type may be type cast and used. The value of `semkey` must be unique within the system as its value determines the returned system identifier for the semaphore. A predefined key `IPC_PRIVATE`, is defined to create a semaphore which will initially only be known to the creating process and is not accessible by other processes using the same value of semkey.

The parameter nosem specifies the number of semaphores to be created as a set with this call. If more than one semaphore is created in this way, all subsequent actions on the system semaphore identifier returned by the function will act upon all semaphores in the set, and each operation must succeed before the overall operation is considered a success. Any operation on the set of semaphores is guaranteed to be an atomic process.

The parameter semflag is a semaphore flag created by logically ORing any of the following values. This flag may also have no value, which is specified using the value of ZERO.

| Parameter value | Functionality |
|---|---|

IPC_CREAT
Creates a semaphore data structure for the semkey specified, if one does not exist.

IPC_EXCL
Causes the semget() call to create the semaphore with the key semkey exclusively in the system, i.e. to cause semget to fail if the semaphore already exists.

S_IRUSR
Allows read access for the owner of the semaphore.

S_IWUSR
Allows write access for the owner of the semaphore.

S_IRGRP
Allows read access to owner's group to the semaphore.

S_IWGRP
Allows write access to owner's group to the semaphore.

S_IROTH
Allows read access to other process outside the owner and the owner's group.

S_IWOTH
Allows write access to other process outside the owner and the owner's group.

The parameters that begin with S_I may be considered as a subset of the permissions used by the system call chmod() on files.

The system call semget() can be used to return the system identifier to other processes using the following rules.

In order for a co-process to obtain the system identifier of a semaphore all of the following conditions must be met:

• Each process must use the same semkey. Each process must use the same value of semkey as was used by the creator of the semaphore; however, this value cannot be IPC_PRIVATE as in this case the semaphore will be created privately to the creator and will not be accessible by other processes.

- The semflag parameter must not contain IPC_EXCL. The IPC_EXCL flag will cause the semget() system call to fail if the semaphore with the key semkey already exists, thus for co-processes wishing to obtain the system identifier of the semaphore this flag must be absent.
- The co-process must have read permissions on the semaphore. The co-process making the request must have at least read permissions on the semaphore.
- The value of nosem must be set correctly, either to 0 in which case it will always match the created semaphore, or to the same number of semaphores as was used in the creation operation.

If any of these conditions is not met then the co-process's call to semget() will fail.

The returned value of the semget() function is (−1) for failure, in which case the global variable errno will be set to an error code that describes the condition. These are defined in the file sys/errno.h. If the operation was successful the returned value of semget() is the system identifier for the semaphore.

For example, here is a simple program to create a semaphore using the semget() system call:

```
 #include <stdio.h>
#include <sys/types.h>
#include <sys/ipc.h>
#include <sys/sem.h>
#include <sys/mode.h>
/* ********************************** */
/* random semaphore key ?             */
/* ********************************** */
#define SEMA_KEY ( key_t ) 0x405
/* ********************************** */
/* semget() returns this on           */
/* failure                            */
/* ********************************** */
#define SEM_FAIL (int ) -1
/* ********************************** */
/* number of semaphores to            */
/* try to allocate                    */
/* ********************************** */
#define SEMNO 1
main()
 {
     int SemaphoreId;
     /* ********************************************* */
     /* create SEMNO semaphores with key SEMA_KEY     */
     /* and allow the owner read/write permissions    */
```

```
    /* and others read/write permissions              */
    /*                                                 */
    /* place the system semaphore id in the variable  */
    /* SemaphoreId                                     */
    /* *********************************************** */
SemaphoreId=semget(SEMA_KEY,SEMNO,IPC_CREAT | IPC_EXCL |
                            S_IRUSR | S_IWUSR |
                            S_IROTH | S_IWOTH );
    if ( SemaphoreId == SEM_FAIL )
       {
        fprintf(stderr, "ERROR creating Semaphore\n");
        fflush(stderr);
        exit(1);
       }
    printf("semaphore was created ok\n");
    fflush(stdout);
    exit(0);
}
```

The above program creates a semaphore set, i.e. one or more semaphores, and the semaphore key SEMA_KEY, the number of semaphores in the set, is given by the parameter SEMNO. The semaphore is created exclusively because of the combination of the parameter flags IPC_CREAT and IPC_EXCL which together ensure that the semget() system call will fail if the semaphore with the key of SEMA_KEY already exists. The other parameter flags supplied in the call set the access permissions for the semaphore to read/write for the owner and read/write for other users.

The program above may be one of many programs wishing to access this semaphore, and as all of the semaphore functions require the system identifier assigned to the variable SemaphoreId there must be a way for other processes to access this value.

The semget() system call detailed above creates a set of semaphores; these will later be represented by an array of semaphore structures. But what is a semaphore in the context of the semget() system call? The semaphore as defined in the file sem.h is quite different from the conceptual example shown at the beginning of the chapter. The structure sembuf in the file sem.h defines a C structure for a semaphore, as follows:

```
struct sembuf {
            unsigned short sem_num;
            short          sem_op;
            short          sem_flg;
          };
```

The first field within the structure sembuf is sem_num which is the semaphore number within the set of semaphores; this number by convention starts with 0 up to the value of semno–1, where semno was specified in the creation of the semaphore set. Thus valid values for sem_num are 0..semno-1.

The second field is the operation that will be carried out on the semaphore. The conditions under which this action will take place are covered later when we look at the system call semop(). This is usually a positive, negative or zero value which will be added to the semaphore value under certain conditions.

The third field is the semaphore flag. This field sem_flag controls how AIX will behave during the manipulation of the semaphore. It may have one of four values: the predefined SEM_UNDO, SEM_ORDER, IPC_NOWAIT which will be explained later when we consider the system call semop(), or the value of zero which implies no special action.

## 11.3    Using and testing a semaphore

The system call used to achieve semaphore operations on an existing semaphore is

```
#include <sys/types.h>
#include <sys/ipc.h>
#include <sys/sem.h>
#include <sys/mode.h>
int    semop(SemaphoreId,SemaphoreSet,SemaNo)
int             SemaphoreId ;
struct sembuf *SemaphoreSet;
unsigned int   SemaNo;
```

The parameter SemaphoreId is the system identifier for the semaphore on which the operation is to act, and is the value returned from the system call semget().

The parameter SemaphoreSet is a pointer to an array of structures of the type sembuf as described in sem.h, each element of which describes a single semaphore in the semaphore set to which the operation is to be applied.

The parameter SemaNo is the number of semaphores in the set on which the operation is to be performed.

The return value of the system call semop() is 0 for a successful completion and (−1) for an unsuccessful completion. However, if the predefined SEM_ORDER flag is set in the sem_flg field of the first semaphore of the semaphore set, the failing operation will return the predefined SEM_ERR code. The global variable error can be interrogated for further error information.

## 11.4    How do semaphore operations work?

The semop() operation is guaranteed to be an atomic action with respect to all of the actions that may be performed on the semaphore set, provided that the flag

SEM_ORDER has not been specified in the sem_flg field of the first semaphore in the set. If this is the case each semaphore in the set is treated as if it were a separate entity and any operations on the set are *not* atomic.

Provided that the SEM_ORDER flag is not present, for each semaphore in the set of semaphores the following operation takes place:

- If the value of sem_op is 0 then test the value of the semaphore for the value of 0; if the semaphore has a non-zero value, block the process until the semaphore has a zero value. This occurs if the sem_flg does not contain the value of IPC_NOWAIT which causes the semop() system call to return to its calling process with an error code and not to block the process.

*Or*

- Examine the value of the semaphore and the value of the sem_op field which will be added to the semaphore value to give the new value. If this will cause the semaphore value to become less than 0, then undo the changes made to any other semaphores in the set up to this point and begin the whole set of semaphore operations again. If the flag IPC_NOWAIT is specified, the changes to all previous semaphores are undone and the semop() returns to the calling process with an error code.

The result of this operation is that if the system call semop() returns to the call process without an error, then all operations to all semaphores have been successful.

The flag SEM_UNDO is often specified in the sem_flg field of a semaphore. This protects our system from processes which terminate without releasing the semaphores they hold. Any changes to a semaphore containing this flag by a process are recorded by the system, and if the process terminates without releasing the semaphore all of the operations made by that process on that semaphore are reversed. This can be very important as a semaphore left lying around could cause a disaster.

## 11.5    Deleting, modifying and examining semaphores

The system call used to provide general control functions over a semaphore is

```
#include <sys/types.h>
#include <sys/ipc.h>
#include <sys/sem.h>
#include <sys/mode.h>
int semctl(SemaphoreId,SemaNum,cmd,Value)
or
int semctl(SemaphoreId,SemaNum,cmd,Buffer)
or
int semctl(SemaphoreId,SemaNum,cmd,Array)
```

```
int SemaphoreId;
int SemaNum;
int cmd;
int Value;
struct semid_ds *Buffer;
unsigned short Array[];
```

The first parameter `SemaphoreId` is the system identifier for the semaphore that was returned by the system call `semget()`.

The second parameter `SemaNum` is the semaphore number within the semaphore set on which the control action is to take place. This takes the values of 0 to `NoSem-1` where `NoSem` was used in the `semget()` system call that created the semaphore set.

The third parameter `cmd` is one of the following commands, and its value determines the data type of the fourth parameter.

The following values of `cmd` have a fourth parameter of type integer like the definition of the parameter `Value`.

| *Value of* cmd | *Action* |
|---|---|

GETVAL

Returns as the return value of `semctl()` the current value of the semaphore whose number is found in `semno`, the field `semval` in the structure `sem` as defined in `sem.h`.

SETVAL

Sets the value of the field `semval` to the value of the parameter `value`, for the semaphore specified in the parameter `SemaNum`. If this command is successful the value of `sem_op` for the semaphore is cleared in all processes.

GETPID

Returns as the return value of `semctl()` the value of `sempid` in the structure `sem` as defined in `sem.h`. This is the process ID of the last process that performed an operation on the semaphore.

GETNCNT

Returns as the return value of `semctl()` the value of `semncnt` in the structure `sem` as defined in `sem.h`. This is the number of processes that are waiting for the semaphore value to become larger than it is now.

GETZCNT

Returns as the return value of `semctl()` the value of `semzcnt` in the structure `sem` as defined in `sem.h`. This is the number of processes waiting for the semaphore to have a value of 0.

The following values of `cmd` have a fourth parameter of type array of unsigned short integers like the definition of the parameter `Array`.

*Value of* cmd                                     *Action*

GETALL

Stores all of the semvals in the structure sem, for the semaphore set into the elements of the fourth parameter Array. The returned value of semctl() is 0.

SETALL

Sets all of the values of semvals from the fourth parameter Array. When this command is successfully executed the sem_op field for each semaphore is cleared for all processes.

The following values of cmd have a fourth parameter of type pointer to the structure semid_ds as defined in sem.h, like the definition of the parameter Buffer.

*Value of* cmd                                     *Action*

IPC_STAT

Obtains a copy of the structure semid_ds as defined in sem.h and places it into the structure pointed to by the fourth parameter.

IPC_SET

Allows the user to set the values of the semaphore's owner, owner's group and access permissions. The values to set are taken from the values in the structure pointed to by the fourth parameter, and the fields defined in the structure sem_perm are defined within the structure semid_ds. The fields sem_perm.uid, sem_perm.gid and sem_perm.mode are the owner's user ID, owner's user group ID and access permissions respectively. In order to change any of these fields the calling process must have user ID zero, have group ID zero (i.e. root user), or have the same effective uid as the current value of sem_perm.uid, i.e. the current owner of the semaphore.

IPC_RMID

Removes the semaphore set identified by the semaphore identifier SemaphoreId. The command can only be executed by a process with uid zero or group ID zero (i.e. root user) or a process with the effective user ID the same as the current value of sem_perm.uid, i.e. the current owner of the semaphore. It is not recommended to remove semaphores on which processes are waiting; using the GETNCNT and GETZCNT functions to determine if any processes are waiting before removing a semaphore is good practice.

The return value of the semctl() system call is (−1) on failure, and for the cmd values which take a fourth parameter of type Value the value of any requested parameter is returned.

## 11.6    Application of semaphores

The primary use of semaphores is to provide mutually exclusive access to a shared resource, whether that resource is an interprocess communication data structure or any other shared resource. For example, we may have a simple application that has two processes each working on the same shared file. One process may update the file's records and the other process may display enquiries on the data contained within the file, but will not update the file. We may have any number of each of these processes trying to update and/or read from the file at what appears to them to be the same time. Our problem is simple: how do we prevent multiple processes trying to update the file at the same time and any number of processes trying to display incomplete data from the file while it is being updated?

In our example we may choose to take a very simplistic approach and use *file locking*. This ensures that during the time when a process is updating the file, no other process may either update or read it. However, while there is no process updating the file then any number of processes may read the file. For this locking strategy to work we require two types of file lock. The first type is an *exclusive lock*, which exclusively locks the file for the process that obtains the lock and excludes all other operations on the file while that process holds the lock. The second type of lock is called a *shared lock*, and it allows any number of processes to obtain the lock provided that no process holds an exclusive lock. Both of these locks must be mutually exclusive; in other words we cannot have a situation where one process holds an exclusive lock and another process holds a shared or an exclusive lock.

In order to use semaphores to achieve this we will define four semaphore sets as follows:

```
#include <sys/types.h>
#include <sys/ipc.h>
#include <sys/sem.h>
#include <sys/mode.h>
#define SEMA_READ        0
#define SEMA_WRITE       1
#define WAIT_EQUAL_ZERO      0
#define INC_BY_ONE           1
#define DEC_BY_ONE          -1
#define NOFLAGS              0
struct sembuf
          excl_lock[] = { SEMA_READ,WAIT_EQUAL_ZERO,NOFLAG,
                          SEMA_WRITE,WAIT_EQUAL_ZERO,NOFLAG,
                          SEMA_WRITE,INC_BY_ONE,SEM_UNDO };
struct sembuf
          shared_lock[] = { SEMA_WRITE,WAIT_EQUAL_ZERO,NOFLAG,
                            SEMA_READ,INC_BY_ONE,SEM_UNDO };
struct sembuf
          unlock_excl[] = { SEMA_WRITE,DEC_BY_ONE,SEM_UNDO };
```

```
struct sembuf
              unlock_shared[] = { SEMA_READ,DEC_BY_ONE,SEM_UNDO};
```

The semaphores SEMA_READ and SEMA_WRITE count the number of processes that are accessing the file for read and write access respectively. These semaphores are used to define the four semaphore sets above which perform the following functions, using the semop() system call.

The excl_lock semaphore set causes the calling process to block if any processes are currently accessing the file for read or write. This is achieved by the first two semaphore operations defined in the set, where both SEMA_READ and SEMA_WRITE are tested for equality to zero. Once both semaphores are zero, the semaphore set's next operation is to increment the semaphore SEMA_WRITE by 1, thus obtaining exclusive access to the file.

The shared_lock semaphore set causes the calling process to block if any processes currently have the file open for write access, but it ignores processes that have the file open for read access. This is achieved by the first semaphore operation where SEMA_WRITE is tested for equality to zero. Once the SEMA_WRITE is zero, the next operation in the set increments the number of processes which have the file open for read access by 1, by incrementing the semaphore SEMA_READ.

The two semaphore sets unlock_excl and unlock_shared are used to release the locks placed on the file by the excl_lock and shared_lock semaphore sets. They achieve this by decrementing by 1 either SEMA_WRITE for unlock_excl or SEMA_READ for unlock_shared. It is important that these operations are called only after the lock operations have been applied to the file, as they will cause the calling process to block if either of the semaphores is already zero.

Using these semaphores in our application is quite simple. Our program which updates the file requires an exclusive lock on the file and it therefore uses the semaphore sets excl_lock and unlock_excl. Any process wishing to read the file need only lock the file in a shared way, which excludes exclusive locks from being obtained. This can be done using the semaphore sets share_lock and unlock_shared.

Our example programs might look like this:

```
/* ******************************************************** */
/* Program to add data to shared file                      */
/* ******************************************************** */
#include "locks.h"
#define SEMA_KEY              ( key_t ) 0x405
#define ANYNUMBER          0
#define MAX_DATA_LENGTH  255
#define NOFLAGS (int) 0
main()
    {
        int lock_semaphore;
```

```
        char data_buffer[MAX_DATA_LENGTH];
        lock_semaphore=semget(SEMA_KEY,ANYNUMBER,NOFLAGS);
        Get_new_data(data_buffer);
        semop(lock_semaphore,&excl_lock,3);
        update_data(data_buffer);
        semop(lock_semaphore,&unlock_excl,1);
    }
/* ***************************************************** */
/* Program to read data items from shared file          */
/* ***************************************************** */
#include "locks.h"
#define SEMA_KEY          ( key_t ) 0x405
#define ANYNUMBER         0
#define MAX_DATA_LENGTH   255
#define NOFLAGS (int) 0
main()
    {
        int lock_semaphore;
        char data_buffer[MAX_DATA_LENGTH];
        lock_semaphore=semget(SEMA_KEY,ANYNUMBER,NOFLAGS);
        semop(lock_semaphore,&shared_lock,2);
        Read_data_from_file(data_buffer);
        semop(lock_semaphore,&unlock_shared,1);
        Display_data(data_buffer);
    }
/* ***************************************************** */
/* Program to initially create semaphore                */
/* ***************************************************** */
#include <stdio.h>
#include <sys/types.h>
#include <sys/ipc.h>
#include <sys/sem.h>
#include <sys/mode.h>
#define SEMA_KEY          ( key_t ) 0x405
#define SEMNO             3
#define SEM_FAIL          -1
main()
    {
        int lock_semaphore;
lock_semaphore=semget(SEMA_KEY,SEMNO,IPC_CREAT | IPC_EXCL |
                        S_IRUSR | S_IWUSR |
                        S_IROTH | S_IWOTH );
    if ( lock_semaphore == SEM_FAIL )
        {
            fprintf(stderr,"Semaphore create failed\n");
            fflush(stderr);
            exit(1);
        }
    exit(0);
    }
```

```
/* ********************************************************** */
/* Program to remove semaphore from system                  */
/* ********************************************************** */
#include <stdio.h>
#include <sys/types.h>
#include <sys/ipc.h>
#include <sys/sem.h>
#include <sys/mode.h>
#define SEMA_KEY            ( key_t ) 0x405
#define ALL_SEMAS          0
#define SEM_FAIL           -1
#define ANYNUMBER          0
#define NOFLAGS            (int) 0
main()
    {
        int lock_semaphore;
        struct semid_ds semaphore;
        lock_semaphore=semget(SEMA_KEY,ANYNUMBER,NOFLAGS);
        if ( lock_semaphore == SEM_FAIL )
            {
                fprintf(stderr, "Semaphore does not exist\n");
                fflush(stderr);
                exit(1);
            }
        semctl(lock_semaphore,ALL_SEMAS,IPC_RMID,&semaphore);
        exit(0);
    }
```

Three of the above programs that assume the definitions of the semaphore sets excl_lock, shared_lock, unlock_excl and unlock_shared are defined in a file called locks.h.

The first program above shows the program for obtaining exclusive access to the file for update purposes. The program first obtains the system semaphore identifier by calling semget(), then it prompts the user for new data by calling the function Get_new_data(). After obtaining new data it uses the system call semop() to obtain an exclusive lock on the file, using the semaphore set excl_lock which has three semaphores. Once the lock is obtained the new data is written to the file using the function update_data(). Finally, the program releases its exclusive lock on the file using the semop() system call and the semaphore set unlock_excl.

The second program is used to obtain read access to the file and uses very similar techniques to those used by the first program, only it uses the semaphore sets share_lock and unlock_shared.

The third program is of the utmost importance; it is used once and once only to create the semaphore. This is necessary because neither of the programs in our simple example will create the semaphore. Additional program code should be added to both the read and the update programs to test for the failure of the initial call made to semget(), which would of course fail if the semaphore did not exist.

The final program removes the semaphore from the system after the read and update programs have finished with it. It uses semget() to obtain the system semaphore identifier of the set of semaphores with the key SEMA_KEY and then uses the system call semctl() to remove all semaphores in the set from the system.

The above example is very simplistic, and most real semaphore operations are much more complex. For example, they usually do not require external programs to initially create semaphore sets and to destroy them after use. There are some important considerations which must be taken into account when allowing any general process to create and destroy semaphore sets, but these are outside the scope of this book.

# 12
# Information exchange between processes

The primary reason for the existence of any interprocess communication mechanism is to enable one or more processes to exchange information. Semaphores are not very useful for exchanging information: they are used primarily to enable synchronization of processes, not for information exchange. A semaphore is merely a flag, as its name suggests, and is never used to pass parameters between processes. Fortunately for us there are other mechanisms that allow one or more processes to share a common machine resource and thus pass parameter information between them.

As previously mentioned, under AIX 3.x as in UNIX each process is created with what amounts to its own private set of machine resources. For example, a process will have its own 'address space', an area of memory (RAM or virtual memory) to which it has exclusive access. The exclusion by a process of all other processes from accessing its machine resources presents the systems programmer with a problem. However, there are several interprocess communications mechanisms that allow access to privately owned machine resources, under operating system control. All these mechanisms depend on the operating system providing a common area of resource which is under its control, and access is then granted to one or more processes.

There are three major interprocess communication mechanisms which behave in this way under AIX 3.x: shared memory, message queues and FIFO pipes. Each of these mechanisms is illustrated below.

## 12.1    Interprocess communications with shared memory

The concept of shared memory segments under UNIX and AIX is far from new and the principle of its implementation is similar to that of semaphores. In general terms an area of memory within the kernel's address space is allocated as a shared memory segment. This segment is then mapped, using the memory management functions of the operating system, to the private address space of one or more

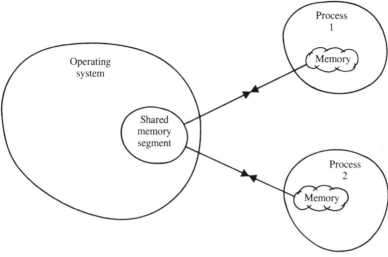

Figure 12.1. Shared memory segment mapping.

processes. Thus the processes have access to the shared memory segment, apparently within their own address space, so the normal operating system rules concerning addressing machine resources are not compromised.

Diagrammatically shared memory may be represented as in Fig. 12.1.

### 12.1.1 *Shared memory under AIX 3.x*

Shared memory is implemented under AIX 3.x using the familiar system call interface with the four functions, shmget(), shmdt(), shmctl() and shmat().These system calls provide the following primitive functions for shared memory management:

- create a shared memory segment
- attach or map a shared memory segment to a process's address space
- detach or unmap a shared memory segment from a process's address space
- change/destroy and examine characteristics of a shared memory segment

Shared memory segments are created and accessed in a similar way to semaphores. They each have two identifiers, one which is created by the creating process and another by which the operating system refers to a shared memory segment. This is the same arrangement as that found in the semaphore functions.

### 12.1.2 *Creation of a shared memory segment*

The system call shmget() which is analogous to the semaphore system call semget() is used to create and obtain access to a shared memory segment:

```
#include <sys/types.h>
#include <sys/ipc.h>
#include <sys/shm.h>
#include <sys/mode.h>
int shmget(shmkey,shmsize,shmflags)
key_t shmkey;
int   shmsize;
int   shmflags;
```

The first parameter `shmkey` is of the predefined system type `key_t` and is the same type as that used in the `semget()` system call. This parameter defines the user identifier for the shared memory segment, and must be unique within the system. It is possible, however, for the same key to be used for a semaphore, a message queue and a shared memory segment within a system at the same time; each will be considered unique within its abstraction type. As with semaphores a predefined key `IPC_PRIVATE` is defined for the creation of a shared memory segment that will be known only to the creating process, and will not be accessible to any other processes using the same value of `shmkey`.

The second parameter, `shmsize`, is the size in bytes of the shared memory segment required. Its value is determined in the C programming language using the `sizeof()` function. This causes the system call `shmget()` to reserve an area of shared memory either equal to or slightly larger than the value of `shmsize` in bytes, depending on the memory allocation algorithm used.

The third parameter `shmflags` is used to control the behaviour of the `shmget()` system call. The flags used are the same as those used by the `semget()` system call as defined in `sys/mode.h`.

The return value of the system call `shmget()` is $(-1)$ to signify the failure of the system call, in which case the global variable `errno` will be set to the error code as defined in the file `sys/errno.h`, or the system identifier for the shared memory segment which will be required for all other operations on the shared memory segment.

The same rules apply to the system call `shmget()` as to the system call `semget()` when used by a co-process to obtain the system identifier of a shared memory segment, particularly with respect to the flag `IPC_EXCL`.

For example, here is a simple program to create a shared memory segment using the `shmget()` system call.

```
 #include <stdio.h>
#include <sys/types.h>
#include <sys/ipc.h>
#include <sys/shm.h>
#include <sys/mode.h>
/* ********************************************* */
/*   random shared memory key ?                 */
/* ********************************************* */
#define SHARE_KEY  (key_t) 0x405
```

```
/* ********************************************* */
/* shmget() returns this on                      */
/* failure                                       */
/* ********************************************* */
#define SHARE_FAIL  (int) -1
/* ********************************************* */
/* Data structure for which shared memory is     */
/* required to hold and size of shared memory    */
/* segment                                       */
/* ********************************************* */
struct shared_structure {
                          int x;
                          int y;
                          int z;
                        };
#define SHMSIZE sizeof(struct shared_structure)
main()
  {
      int sharedmemId;
    /* ************************************************* */
    /* Create a shared memory segment of size SHMSIZE    */
    /* to hold the structure shared_structure with       */
    /* key value of SHARE_KEY and having read/write      */
    /* permissions for both the owner process and other  */
    /* processes                                         */
    /*                                                   */
    /* place the system shared memory identifier in the  */
    /* variable sharememId                               */
    /* ************************************************* */
    sharememId=shmget(SHARE_KEY,SHMSIZE,IPC_CREATE | IPC_EXCL |
                              S_IRUSR | S_IWUSR |
                              S_IROTH | S_IWOTH );
    if ( sharememId == SHARE_FAIL )
      {
        fprintf(stderr,"ERROR creating shared memory\n");
        fflush(stderr);
        exit(1);
      }
    printf("shared memory segment created ok\n");
    fflush(stdout);
    exit(0);
}
```

The program above may be one of many programs wishing to access the shared memory segment with the user identifier of SHARE_KEY. Other programs must be able to obtain the system identifier for the shared memory segment, in order to perform any functions on the shared memory segment. Other processes may access the system identifier for a shared memory segment, providing they have been given the access permissions, using the shmget() system call in the same way as semget() was used for semaphores.

### 12.1.3 *Attaching a shared memory segment to a process's address space*

As Fig. 12.1 indicated, the shared memory segment is created in the kernel's address space and therefore needs to be mapped to an area of memory located within the process's address space before it is accessible to any process including the process which created it.

Under AIX 3.x, shared memory segments may include file handles of files opened by the system call openx(). These files are then mapped into memory and all file input and output is taken care of by the memory management system. In this instance the reader may consider the file input/output buffer as being the shared memory segment, so accessing the buffer causes changes to the file.

The mechanism for mapping shared memory segments into a process's address space is primarily the concern of the memory management system within the operating system, and is transparent to the process. The process accesses memory within its address space and is unaware of the mappings. Thus all processes still obey the resource mutual exclusion rule as discussed before.

The system call used to attach a created shared memory segment to a process's address space is

```
#include <sys/types.h>
#include <sys/ipc.h>
#include <sys/shm.h>
#include <sys/mode.h>
char *shmat(sharememId, shareAdd, shareflags)
int sharememId;
char * shareAdd;
int shareflags;
```

The first parameter sharememId is the system identifier for the shared memory segment obtained from the system call shmget().

Alternatively, this may be the file handle of an open file opened by the system call openx(); this will then be mapped provided that the flag SHM_MAP is included in the shareflags parameter.

The second parameter shareAdd may be used to specify the address at which the shared memory segment is to be attached within the process's address space. This may take one of three valid values:

- If the value of shareAdd is 0 then the shared memory segment will be attached at the first available address as selected by the system.
- If the value of shareAdd is not equal to 0 and the flag SHM_RND is present in the shareflags parameter, the shared memory segment is mapped at the next lower segment boundary to the address given in shareAdd.
- If the value of shareAdd is not 0 and the flag SHM_RND is not set in the shareflags parameter, then the shared memory segment is mapped to the

address given by the value of `shareAdd`. However, if this address is not on a segment boundary then the system call fails returning a value of $(-1)$, setting the global variable `errno` to the value of `EINVAL` for an invalid value. Shared memory addresses must be aligned on segment boundaries.

The third parameter `shareflags` may have several values. It changes how the system call will attach the shared memory segment. These flags can be separated into two categories, one set which acts on mapped file handles and others which act generally on file handles and shared memory segments alike. The value of this flag used by default is zero. All of the flags are defined in the file `sys/shm.h`.

### *Flags used on mapped files*

*Flag* *Functionality*

`SHM_COPY`

Changes the file to deferred update mode. This has the same effect as using the `O_DEFER` flag with the system call `openx()` and is included only for compatibility with AIX 2.x. In deferred update mode changes to the mapped segment do not affect the file on the filesystem until a call to the system call `fsync()` is made on the file handle. Any new programs should use the `O_DEFER` option with `openx()`.

`SHM_MAP`

Used to signify that the system identifier supplied in the parameter `sharememId` is a file handle opened with `openx()` and not a shared memory identifier. Any file size can be mapped to a shared memory segment provided that there is the user address space.

### *Flags that apply to both shared memory segments and mapped files*

*Flag* *Functionality*

`SHM_RDONLY`

Overrides the access permissions given to the shared memory segment during its creation with `shmget()`. If it is specified the shared memory segment may be accessed for read operations only by the calling process.

`SHM_RND`

Causes the system call `shmat()` to round the address given by the parameter `ShareAdd` to the next lower memory segment boundary, if required, to cause the address to be segment boundary aligned.

Using shared memory segments to map files into memory may have some unexpected effects on the file. For instance, if a mapped file is accessed beyond the end-of-file, and the file is mapped with write permissions, then the file will be extended in increments of memory page size.

The return result of the system call shmat() is either (−1) for failure of the call, in which case the variable errno will contain the error code, or the start address of the attached shared memory segment or mapped file segment. For example, here is a program showing the mapping of a shared memory segment.

```c
/* ********************************************* */
/* attach shared memory segment to process      */
/* ********************************************* */
#include <stdio.h>
#include <sys/types.h>
#include <sys/ipc.h>
#include <sys/shm.h>
#include <sys/mode.h>
/* ********************************************* */
/*   random shared memory key ?                  */
/* ********************************************* */
#define SHARE_KEY   ( key_t) 0x405
/* ********************************************* */
/* shmget() returns this on                      */
/* failure                                       */
/* ********************************************* */
#define SHARE_FAIL  (int) −1
/* ********************************************* */
/* Data structure for which shared memory is     */
/* required to hold and size of shared memory    */
/* segment                                       */
/* ********************************************* */
struct shared_structure {
                          int x;
                          int y;
                          int z;
                        };
#define SHMSIZE sizeof(struct shared_structure)
/* ********************************************* */
/* defined ANYADDRESS to allow the system        */
/* to choose the segment address for the         */
/* attached shared memory                        */
/* ********************************************* */
#define ANYADDRESS  (char * ) 0
/* ********************************************* */
/* define NOFLAGS for defaults  flags for        */
/* shmat() and shmget()                          */
/* ********************************************* */
#define NOFLAGS (int) 0
main()
  {
      int sharedmemId;
      struct shared_structure *sharedsegment;
```

```
/* ************************************************** */
/* Obtain shared memory segment system identifier    */
/* for the user identifier SHARE_KEY                 */
/* ************************************************** */
sharememId=shmget(SHARE_KEY,SHMSIZE,NOFLAGS );
if ( sharememId == SHARE_FAIL )
   {
      fprintf(stderr,"ERROR obtaining shared memory id\n");
      fflush(stderr);
      exit(1);
   }
/* ************************************************** */
/* attach shared memory segment and assign           */
/* segment address to the pointer sharedsegment      */
/* ************************************************** */
sharedsegment=(struct shared_structure *) shmat(sharedmemId,
                                                 ANYADDRESS,
                                                 NOFLAGS);
if ( ((int) sharedsegment)  == SHARE_FAIL )
   {
      fprintf(stderr,"ERROR: attach shared memory failed\n");
      fflush(stderr);
      exit(2);
   }
  printf("shared memory segment attached ok\n");
  fflush(stdout);
/* ****************************************** */
/* update data in shared memory segment      */
/* ****************************************** */
   sharedsegment->x=(int) 10;
   sharedsegment->y=(int) 45;
   sharedsegment->z=(int) 67;
/* ****************************************** */
/* detach shared memory segment from process */
/* (see next section), always go to detach   */
/* before process terminates                 */
/* ****************************************** */
   shmdt(sharedsegment);
   exit(0);
}
```

## 12.1.4 *Detaching shared memory segments*

The system call used to detach a shared memory segment from the process address space is shmdt(). This does not destroy the shared memory segment, it simply detaches it from the current process's address space. Mapped files memory segments are automatically detached when the file is closed by the system call close(), but the user may use the system call shmdt() to detach mapped file segments at any time:

```
#include <sys/types.h>
#include <sys/ipc.h>
#include <sys/shm.h>
#include <sys/mode.h>
int shmdt(shareAdd)
char * shareAdd;
```

The parameter to this system call is the returned value of the system call shmat(). This value must have been returned by the system call shmdt(), or an error will occur.

The returned value of the system call shmdt() is either 0 for successful completion or (−1) for unsuccessful completion. If the system call is unsuccessful the value of errno will be set to the error code and the shared memory segment will not be detached.

### 12.1.5 Changing, destroying and examining the characteristics of a shared memory segment

The system call that provides control operations over a shared memory segment is shmctl(), which has a similar set of functions to the system call semctl() used with semaphores.

```
#include <sys/types.h>
#include <sys/ipc.h>
#include <sys/shm.h>
#include <sys/mode.h>
int shmctl(sharedmemId,cmd,buffer)
int sharedmemId;
int cmd
struct shmid_ds *buffer;
```

The first parameter sharedmemId is the system shared memory identifier as returned by the system call shmget().

The second parameter cmd controls the operations performed by the system call shmctl(). These functions are defined in the files sys/ipc.h and sys/shm.h and are listed below.

*Parameter function*                     *Functionality*

IPC_STAT

> Causes the shmctl() system call to obtain the status information for the shared memory segment identified by the first parameter sharedmemId and place the result in the structure, of type shmid_ds, pointed to by the third parameter.

IPC_SET

> Using the shared memory segment identified by the first parameter and the values specified in the third parameter, this command enables a

process which is either the owner of the shared memory segment or has effective uid of 0 and effective gid of 0, i.e. root user, to change the owner, the owner's group and the access permissions of the shared memory segment. The new values are taken from the values found within the third parameter.

IPC_RMID

Used to destroy the shared memory structure identified by the first parameter. It is not a good idea to destroy a shared memory segment while other processes still have it attached to their address spaces, but using the command IPC_STAT a process may determine if any processes still have the segment attached. In order for this command to succeed the process must have an effective uid of the owner of the shared memory segment or be root user.

SHM_SIZE

Enables the size of a created shared memory segment to be increased or decreased depending on the values found in the third parameter. In order for this to succeed the process needs to be the owner of the shared memory segment or root user. There may be a limit on the maximum segment size allowed; this is system dependent.

The third parameter buffer provides a pointer to a structure of type shmid_ds. This structure is defined in the file sys/shm.h, as follows.

```
struct shmid_ds {
                 struct ipc_perm  shm_perm;
                 int              shm_segsz;
                 pid_t            shm_lpid;
                 pid_t            shm_cpid;
                 unsigned short   shm_nattach;
                 unsigned short   shm_cnattach;
                 time_t           shm_atime;
                 time_t           shm_dtime;
                 time_t           shm_ctime;
                 vmhandle_t       shm_handle;
                 };
```

The fields are defined below and will be filled with information taken from the system's shared memory segment structure during any enquiry operation and values taken from this structure when operations are required to update the system's shared memory segment structure.

*Field*                                             *Definition*

shm_perm

A structure ipc_perm which in turn is defined in the file sys/ipc.h. This structure contains all of the access permissions for the owner, owner's group and other users to the shared memory segment. The set of valid

| *Field* | *Definition* |
|---|---|

values is defined in the file `sys/mode.h`. There are three main
fields within this structure, `shm_perm.uid`, `shm_perm.gid` and
`shm_perm.mode`, which are the user ID, the group ID of the owner of the
shared memory segment and the access permissions respectively.

`shm_segsz`

The size of the shared memory segment in bytes.

`shm_lpid`

The process ID of the process which last performed any shared memory
operation on the shared memory segment.

`shm_cpid`

The process ID of the process that created the shared memory segment.

`shm_nattach`

A count of the number of processes that currently have the shared
memory segment attached to their address space.

`shm_cnattach`

A count of the number of processes currently in memory that have the
shared memory segment attached to their address spaces.

`shm_atime`

Contains the time in a form defined in `sys/time.h` of the last `shmat()`
system call on the shared memory segment.

`shm_dtime`

Contains the time in a form defined in `sys/time.h` of the last `shmdt()`
system call on the shared memory segment.

`shm_ctime`

Contains the time in a form defined in `sys/time.h` of the last change
made to the shared memory segment.

`shm_handle`

The shared memory segment identifier.

The returned value of the `shmctl()` system call is either 0 for a successful
operation or (−1) for an unsuccessful operation, in which case the variable `errno`
will be set to the error code return by the system call.

For example, here is a simple program to destroy a shared memory segment
using the `shmctl()` system call.

```
#include <stdio.h>
#include <sys/types.h>
#include <sys/ipc.h>
#include <sys/shm.h>
#include <sys/mode.h>
/* ******************************************** */
/*   random shared memory key ?                 */
/* ******************************************** */
```

```
#define SHARE_KEY  ( key_t) 0x405
/* ******************************************** */
/* shmget() returns this on                    */
/* failure                                     */
/* ******************************************** */
#define SHARE_FAIL  (int) −1
/* ******************************************** */
/* Data structure for which shared memory is   */
/* required to hold and size of shared memory  */
/* segment                                     */
/* ******************************************** */
struct shared_structure {
                          int x;
                          int y;
                          int z;
                        };
#define SHMSIZE sizeof(struct shared_structure)
/* ********************************************** */
/* define NOFLAGS for defaults  flags for        */
/* shmat() and shmget()                          */
/* ********************************************** */
#define NOFLAGS (int) 0
main()
  {
     int sharedmemId;
     struct shmid_ds buffer;
     int result;
     /* ************************************************** */
     /* obtain the system identifier for the shared       */
     /* memory segment identified by the user id in       */
     /* SHARE_KEY                                          */
     /* ************************************************** */
     sharememId=shmget(SHARE_KEY,SHMSIZE,NOFLAGS);
     if ( sharememId == SHARE_FAIL )
       {
         fprintf(stderr,"ERROR obtaining shared memory\n");
         fflush(stderr);
         exit(1);
       }
     /* ********************************************** */
     /* remove shared memory segment, identified by   */
     /* the system identifier sharememId              */
     /* ********************************************** */
     result=shmctl(sharememId, IPC_RMID, &buffer);
     if ( result == SHARE_FAIL )
       {
         fprintf(stderr,"ERROR: failed to remove shared
                                                 memory\n");
         fflush(stderr);
         exit(2);
```

```
        }
exit(0);
}
```

The shared memory interprocess communication mechanism requires that processes that are updating shared memory segments are mutually excluded from doing so simultaneously. This may be achieved using a semaphore as shown in Chapter 11.3.

Shared memory segments are often used by client/server database applications to share common data between clients and servers.

## 12.2    Interprocess communications with message queues

The message queue under UNIX system V.x and AIX 3.x is a mechanism whereby data in the form of a message can be placed in a queue, which may be read or written to by any process having the permissions. Message queues can be considered as a pool of message datagrams.

There is a significant difference between a message queue and a shared memory segment. The operations provided to send and receive messages are atomic system calls, so there is no need for the user process to implement a mechanism for mutual exclusion. Message queues may therefore be written and read by many processes apparently simultaneously without any loss of data, which is a greater level of abstraction, than that found in the shared memory functions.

A message queue is created by a process in much the same way as a semaphore or a shared memory segment, and is allocated in the operating system's address space. Access to the message queue is limited to the system call interface.

Diagrammatically a message queue may be shown as in Fig. 12.2.

Although conceptually the message queue may be considered as a pool of

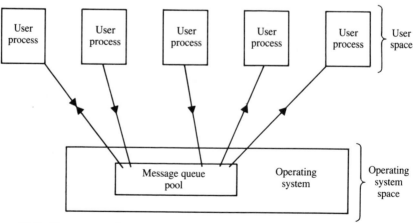

Figure 12.2.  Processes and message queue access.

messages which may be written to and read from at any time, under AIX 3.x message queues are implemented using the system calls msgctl(), msgget(), msgrcv() and msgsnd(). An extended system call for receiving messages, msgxrcv(), is provided under AIX 3.x.

## 12.2.1 Message queues under AIX 3.x

Under AIX 3.x message queues are implemented in a similar way to both semaphores and shared memory, in that they share common defined constants and have a similar system call interface. There are primarily four message queue functions:

- Creating a message queue
- Sending and receiving messages from the queue
- Deleting a message queue
- Changing or examining the characteristics of a message queue

## 12.2.2 Creating a message queue under AIX 3.x

Creating a message queue under AIX 3.x is very similar to the other interprocess communications abstractions previously presented. To create a message queue under AIX 3.x, the user uses the following system call interface:

```
#include <sys/types.h>
#include <sys/ipc.h>
#include <sys/msg.h>
#include <sys/mode.h>
int msgget(Msgkey, MsgFlag)
key_t Msgkey;
int   MsgFlag;
```

The system call interface msgget() will create a new message queue for the user identifier found in Msgkey depending on the flags used in the MsgFlag field. The user will notice that no size is implied when the message queue is created. A message queue may be considered as having no fixed size, but a system limit exists.

The first parameter Msgkey is the user identifier, and is used by the system to generate a system identifier for the message queue. This identifier may be generated by any algorithm but must be carefully chosen not to clash with other message queues already in existence. The same user identifier may be used for a semaphore, shared memory segment and a message queue within the same system at the same time; they will be considered as unique. The first parameter may have the value of IPC_PRIVATE as defined in the file sys/ipc.h. This value ensures that no other process will be able to obtain the system identifier of the message queue using the msgget() system call.

The second parameter MsgFlag is a set of flags identical to those used in semaphore and shared memory creation. These flags determine the function of the system call `msgget()`. If the `IPC_EXCL` flag is missing from the set of flags then, if the message queue exists with the user identifier of `Msgkey`, the system identifier is returned to the user.

If the flags `IPC_EXCL` and `IPC_CREAT` are both present the system call will attempt to create a new message queue with the user identifier given. If the message queue already exists then the system call will fail and return an error code in the global variable `errno`. If the message queue does not already exist the system call will create a new one and give it the access permissions specified in the `MsgFlag` field (see the sections on shared memory and semaphores, Section 11.2).

'Message queue' is a poor choice of terminology, because it is not a FIFO queue at all. Any number of processes may read and write messages to and from the queue at any time, and the queue's internal integrity is assured by AIX 3.x and not via semaphores as with shared memory segments.

An example program to create a message queue is as follows:

```
   #include <stdio.h>
#include <sys/types.h>
#include <sys/ipc.h>
#include <sys/msg.h>
#include <sys/mode.h>
/* ******************************************** */
/* random message queue key ?                   */
/* ******************************************** */
#define MESSG_KEY (key_t) 0x405
/* ******************************************** */
/* msgget() returns this on                     */
/* failure                                      */
/* ******************************************** */
#define MESSG_FAIL (int) -1
main()
  {
     int Messid;
     /* ********************************************** */
     /* Create a message queue with user identifier    */
     /* contained in MESSG_KEY, giving read/write       */
     /* permissions to the queue's owner and to others  */
     /* placing the system identifier in the variable   */
     /* Messid                                          */
     /* ********************************************** */
     Messid=msgget(MESSG_KEY,IPC_CREATE | IPC_EXCL |
                             S_IRUSR | S_IWUSR |
                             S_IROTH | S_IWOTH);
     if ( Messid == MESSG_FAIL )
       {
         fprintf(stderr,"ERROR creating Message queue\n");
         fflush(stderr);
         exit(1);
       }
```

```
        printf("Message Queue created ok\n");
        fflush(stdout);
        exit(0);
}
```

## 12.2.3  Sending and receiving messages using message queues

The two system call interfaces that are used to send and receive messages to and from message queues are msgrcv() and msgsnd() respectively. These system call interfaces allow any message of a generic form to be sent and received from the queue. The form of a message is that defined in the file sys/msg.h and is a structure called msgbuf, which acts as a template for all message structures.

```
struct msgbuf {
            mtyp_t mtype;
            char mtext[1];
        };
```

All messages sent and received from message queues will have this general structure. The first field is the message type, which is user definable and may take any value except zero. It can be used to enable processes to exchange messages of different lengths in the same message queue. The second field is the starting byte of the message text, which in reality is always longer than one character. A better way to define the structure would be as follows:

```
struct msgbuf {
            mtyp_t mtype;
            char mtext[MSGLENGTH];
        };
```

where the constant MSGLENGTH is the length in bytes of the message. The structure msgbuf acts only as a template from which user programs can construct their own message structures.

## 12.2.4  Receiving messages from a message queue

The system call used to receive messages from a message queue under AIX is either msgrcv() or the AIX extended message receiver call msgxrcv(). The standard call, however, has the following parameters:

```
#include <sys/types.h>
#include <sys/ipc.h>
#include <sys/msg.h>
int msgrcv(MsgqueueId,Msg,MsgSize,
            MsgType,MsgFlag)
int       MsgqueueId;
```

```
void    * Msg;
size_t    MsgSize;
long      MsgType;
int       MsgFlag;
```

The first parameter MsgqueueId is the system message queue identifier returned by the system call msgget(). This may also have the value of IPC_PRIVATE, as can semaphores and shared memory segments.

The second parameter Msg is a pointer to a generic structure of the general type specified above. Similarly to the structure msgbuf, this will be used as a storage area for the incoming message.

The third parameter MsgSize specifies the size of the mtext field of the structure msgbuf in bytes and is often defined as

```
sizeof(struct msgbuf)-sizeof(mtyp_t).
```

Any received message will be truncated to the size of MsgSize if the flag MSG_NOERROR is present in the parameter MsgFlag. Unless this flag is present, any message that will not fit in the area provided will cause the msgrcv() system call to return an error.

This parameter is of predefined system type size_t and may have any value from zero to a predefined system limit.

The fourth parameter is the message type to be received. A value of zero means any message will be received. A value greater than zero will cause the first message with that value as a type to be received. A value less than zero will cause a message of type less than or equal to the absolute value of this parameter to be received.

The fifth parameter is a set of flags, which may be formed by logically ORing the following flags together. The value that represents no flags is zero.

| *Flag* | *Functionality* |
|---|---|
| MSG_NOERROR | Causes any messages that will not fit into the field mtext to be truncated without an error message, to the size specified in the parameter MsgSize. |
| IPC_NOWAIT | Changes the standard behaviour of the system call msgrcv() when no message of the specified type is present in the queue. If this flag is present, then the system call will return a value of $(-1)$ and an error code in the global variable errno. However, if this flag is not present the system call msgrcv() will block the calling process until either |

- A message of the type required is placed in the queue.
- The message queue is removed from the system, in which case the

system call will return $(-1)$ and an error code in the global variable errno.

- The calling process receives a signal which is to be caught, in which case the message is not received and the process continues with the action specified in the sigaction subroutine (see Section 13.2).

The returned value of the system call msgrcv() will be either $(-1)$ for failure, in which case the global variable errno will contain the error code, or the number of bytes stored in the mtext field of the structure pointed to by Msg.

## 12.2.5 Sending messages to a message queue

The system call used in AIX 3.x to send messages to message queues is msgsnd() which has the following parameters:

```
#include <sys/types.h>
#include <sys/ipc.h>
#include <sys/msg.h>
int msgsnd(MsgqueueId,Msg,MsgSize,
           MsgFlag)
int      MsgqueueId;
void   * Msg;
size_t   MsgSize;
int      MsgFlag;
```

All of the parameters have the same functionality as those in the system call msgrcv(), but there are some subtle differences:

- There is no MsgType parameter, because the message type of the message being sent is defined with the message structure itself in the field mtype and it is therefore unnecessary to have the type of the message as a parameter.
- The MsgFlag parameter does not have the same number of flags, in fact the only meaningful flags allowed are noflags, which is a value of 0, or the flag IPC_NOWAIT in which case if the message cannot be sent the system call will return to the calling process with a value of $(-1)$ and an error code in the variable errno. However, if this flag is not present the calling process will be blocked until the message can be sent.
- There are two reasons why a msgsnd() system call may fail to send a message: either the number of bytes already in the queue is equal to the maximum allowed, msg_qbytes, or the number of messages present in the queue is equal to the system-imposed limit.
- A blocked process which is sending a message will be unblocked by the same events that unblocked the msgrcv() system call, that is one of the above limiting constraints being removed.
- The return value of the system call msgsnd() is either $(-1)$ for failure, in

which case the variable `errno` will contain the error code or 0 for successful completion.

### 12.2.6  Special receive system call

Under AIX there is an additional system call that may be used for receiving messages from and to message queues. The only difference between this system call and the standard system call is the definition of the template message structure `msgbuf`. The structure template `msgxbuf` is used in place of the structure template `msgbuf` in this system call. The structure of the template `msgxbuf` is as follows:

```
struct msgxbuf {
                time_t mtime;
                uid_t  muid;
                gid_t  mgid;
                pid_t  mpid;
                mtyp_t mtype;
                char   mtext[1];
            };
```

These additional fields in the message header could of course be incorporated using the standard `msgsnd()` and `msgrcv()` system calls, as the internal structure of the `mtext` field is user definable. However, when using this message structure template these fields have the following meanings:

| Field | Meaning |
|---|---|
| `mtime` | The time and date the message was sent, as defined in `sys/time.h`. |
| `muid` | The sender's effective user ID. |
| `mgid` | The sender's effective group ID. |
| `mpid` | The sender's process ID. |
| `mtype` | The message type of the message. |
| `mtext[1]` | The first byte of the message text. |

This additional information can be quite useful in certain instances.

### 12.2.7  Deleting a message queue and examining or changing its characteristics

Deleting a message queue from the system is achieved using the general message control system call `msgctl()`. This is analogous to the `semctl()` and `shmctl()` system calls but has the following parameters:

```
#include <sys/types.h>
#include <sys/ipc.h>
#include <sys/msg.h>
int msgctl(MsgqueueId,cmd,Buffer)
int        MsgqueueId;
int        cmd;
struct msqid_ds *Buffer;
```

The structure msqid_ds is defined in sys/msg.h and has the following structure:

```
struct msqid_ds {
                struct ipc_perm msg_perm;
                struct msg      *msg_first;
                struct msg      *msg_last;
                unsigned short  msg_cbytes;
                unsigned short  msg_qnum;
                unsigned short  msg_qbytes;
                pid_t           msg_lspid;
                pid_t           msg_lrpid;
                time_t          msg_stime;
                time_t          msg_rtime;
                time_t          msg_ctime;
                int             msg_rwait;
                int             msg_wwait;
                };
```

The definition of each of the fields is given below.

*Field*                                    *Definition*

msg_perm

> A structure containing the access permissions to the message queue. It
> has the same form as that defined in semid_ds and shmid_ds.

msg_first

> A pointer to an internal structure msg defined in the file sys/msg.h which
> contains the message queue abstraction. This is a pointer to the first
> message in the queue.

msg_last

> Analogous to msg_first, but this points to the last message in the
> message queue.

msg_cbytes

> The current number of bytes present in the queue.

msg_qnum

> The current number of messages in the queue awaiting retrieval.

msg_qbytes

> The current maximum number of bytes that may be present in the queue.

*Field*                                              *Definition*

`msg_lspid`

The process ID of the last process to access the queue using the system call `msgsnd()`.

`msg_lrpid`

The process ID of the last process to access the queue using the system call `msgrcv()` or `msgxrcv()`.

`msg_stime`

The time at which the last `msgsnd()` system call was used on the queue.

`msg_rtime`

The time at which the last `msgrcv()` or `msgxrcv()` system call was used on the queue.

`msg_ctime`

The time at which the last change was made to this structure with a `msgctl()` system call.

`msg_rwait`

The number of processes blocked waiting to receive a message.

`msg_wwait`

The number of processes blocked waiting to send a message.

The first parameter `MsgqueueId` is the system identifier for the message queue as returned by the system call `msgget()`. The second parameter cmd is the control command which will take place on the message queue specified by the first parameter, and may have the values listed below.

*Parameter value*                        *Functionality*

`IPC_STAT`

Returns the structure members from the structure `msqid_ds` for the queue specified, and places them in the structure pointed to by the third parameter `Buffer`. In order for this operation to be successful the calling process must have read permissions on the message queue.

`IPC_SET`

Allows certain message queue characteristics to be changed, provided that the calling process has write permission on the message queue, or is root user. The fields which may be changed are, `msg_perm.uid`, `msg_perm.gid`, `msg_perm.mode` and `msg_qbytes` which are the owners of the message queue's user ID, the owner's group ID and the permission set for the owner, owner's group and others. The field `msg_qbytes` is the maximum number of bytes allowed in the message queue, and may only be increased by the calling process having an effective user ID of zero, and group ID of zero, i.e. root user. The new values of these fields are taken from the values found in the structure pointed to by the third parameter.

IPC_RMID

> Allows a message queue to be removed from the system. In order for this operation to succeed the calling process must be the owner of the message queue or be the root user.

The return value of the system call `msgctl()` is $(-1)$ for failure in which case the global variable `errno` will contain the error code, or 0 for success.

## 12.2.8 Usage of message queues

Message queues are a much more flexible interprocess communication mechanism than semaphores and shared memory, lending themselves to client/server applications very much more easily than either of the previous mechanisms. Message queues may be used to enable a single server process to communicate with one or more client processes.

The first problem with a message queue client/server is that all processes have to agree on the format and types of messages used. In our simple example the server will accept requests from the clients and service them, returning the results back to the clients in the message queue. Our client/server application is very simple: the server accepts requests from one or more clients to read and write records to a shared file. The agreed message format is as follows:

```
struct message {
                mtyp_t mtype;
                mess[MESSLEN];
              };
```

The field `mtype` will be used to identify the intended recipient of the message. The server process will be identified as identifier 0001, and each client will use its own process ID as its identifier. Thus the server may wait on messages which appear on the queue for it, simply by waiting for a message with type 0001, and each client may also receive messages simply by waiting for messages with its own process ID as the message type.

The second field will be the message text which will be defined by the following. The message string will be divided into fields of the following sizes, using a structure as the `mess` field:

```
struct mestext {
                int cmd;
                mtyp_t org;
                char name[30];
                char age[10];
              }
```

Thus the message structure used in our examples will be

```
struct message {
                mtyp_t mtype;
                struct mestext mess;
                }
```

Thus allowing each of the field to be individually accessible within the mess field.

The first field of the structure mestext is an integer called cmd. This field will be used in two ways: first, for the clients to instruct the server which of the three operations to do, using the data provided within the message.

- The READ operation will cause the server to search the file for the name that matches the name specified in the name field of mess. If found the age will be returned in the age field of the returned message from the server.
- WRITE, which causes the server to append both the name and age fields to the end of the file, the returned message will contain the same data unaltered.
- EXIT, which causes the server to terminate, and destroy the message queue. This will not return a message.

The second use of this field is in the returned message sent back from the server after each operation (except the EXIT operation). The value of the cmd field will either be 0 for OK or 3 for FAIL, which signifies the result of the server operation.

The second field in the structure mestext is a field of type mtyp_t called org, which contains the identifier of the originator of the message. This field is used by the server to determine the value of the field mtype to be used in the returned message such that the process that sent the original message receives the correct reply.

The third field in the structure mestext is a character array called name, which is used to hold the name field contained within the message data. This name will be written or read by the server to or from the file to which it has access.

The last field in the structure mestext is a character array called age, which is the string representation of the age associated with the name field. It is written or read by the server to or from the file to which it has access.

Using the client/server relationship and message queues it is possible to have several clients apparently updating the same file simultaneously. However, this is never really the case because all file access is directed to the server, and the server services only one request at a time. The example which follows is a very primitive example of a client/server program and makes a lot of assumptions about the behaviour of both the client and the server programs. It is intended only as an illustration of the properties of message queues, and is not an ideal way to implement client/server applications.

Both the client(s) and the server program include a header file which contains certain defined constants. This file is called clserv.h and contains the following text:

```
/* *************************** */
/* Message queue identifier    */
/* *************************** */
```

```
#define MESSG_KEY ( key_t ) 0x405
/* ************************** */
/* Message queue system call   */
/* failure code                */
/* ************************** */
#define MESSG_FAIL ( int ) -1
/* **************************** */
/* Message error codes returned  */
/* in the cmd field of           */
/* mestext                       */
/* **************************** */
#define FAIL 3
#define OK   0
/* **************************** */
/* Message commands sent in the  */
/* cmd field                     */
/* **************************** */
#define READ   ( mtyp_t ) 1
#define WRITE  ( mtyp_t ) 2
#define EXIT   ( mtyp_t ) 3
/* **************************** */
/* message type for message to be */
/* sent to the server            */
/* **************************** */
#define FORSERVER ( mtyp_t ) 1
/* **************************** */
/* Flags used when noflags are   */
/* required                      */
/* **************************** */
#define NOFLAGS ( int ) 0
/* ***************************** */
/* Message text size constants    */
/* ***************************** */
#define SNAME  30
#define SAGE   10
#define MESSLEN (int) sizeof(struct mestext)
/* ***************************** */
/* structure mestext for message  */
/* information                    */
/* ***************************** */
struct mestext {
                int    cmd;
                mtyp_t org;
                char   name[SNAME];
                char   age[SAGE];
               };
  /* ***************************** */
  /* message structure used in system */
  /* calls                            */
  /* ***************************** */
```

```
struct message {
                mtyp_t              mtype;
                struct mestext mess;
            };
```

The server program in our example is coded as follows:

```
 #include <stdio.h>
#include <sys/types.h>
#include <sys/ipc.h>
#include <sys/msg.h>
#include <sys/mode.h>
#include "clserv.h"
/* **************************** */
/* constant identifier for this  */
/* process, for the server it is */
/* defined as                    */
/* **************************** */
#define THISPROCESS ( mtyp_t ) 1
main()
 {
    int messid;            /* message id returned from
                                            msgget() */
    int res;               /* return result from msgrcv()   */
    FILE *Datafile;        /* handle for server's data file */
    struct message buffer  /* input message buffer          */
    struct message obuffer /* output message buffer          */
    struct msqid_ds data;  /* message queue control data
                                            buffer */
    int error;             /* returned error codes          */
     /* ****************************************** */
     /* let server create message queue on startup */
     /* giving read/write permissions to owner and */
     /* others                                      */
     /* ****************************************** */
     messid=msgget(MESSG_KEY,IPC_CREAT | IPC_EXCL | S_IRUSR |
                 S_IWUSR | S_IROTH | S_IWOTH);
     if (messid == MESSG_FAIL)
        {
           fprintf(stderr,"Server failed to create queue\n");
           fflush(stderr);
           exit(1);
        }
 /* ********************************** */
 /* body of server is infinite loop   */
 /* ********************************** */
 while ( TRUE )
```

```
{
    /* ***************************************** */
    /* get any message in queue for the server */
    /* ***************************************** */
    res=msgrcv(messid,(void *) &buffer,MESSLEN,FORSERVER,
              NOFLAGS);
    /* ***************************************** */
    /* if error on message queue terminate      */
    /* server removing the message queue from   */
    /* the system, using msgctl()               */
    /* ***************************************** */
    if ( res == MESSG_FAIL )
      {
        fprintf(stderr,"Server failed on message read\n");
        fflush(stderr);
        msgctl(messid,IPC_RMID,&data);
        exit(2);
      }
    /* ***************************************** */
    /* act upon the command in the cmd field */
    /* ***************************************** */
    switch ( buffer.mess.cmd )
      {
        case READ:
                {
                    /* *************************** */
                    /* open datafile for readonly  */
                    /* *************************** */
                    Datafile=fopen("test.txt","r");
                    if ( Datafile == (FILE *) NULL)
                      {
                          error=FAIL;
                      }
                    else
                      {
                      /* ************************** */
                      /* search for name in file    */
                      /* ************************** */
                    error=searchfile(Datafile,(char *)
                                              &buffer);
                  fclose(Datafile);
                      }
                    /* ************************** */
                    /* format reply message       */
                    /* ************************** */
                formatmess((char *) &obuffer,
                                      buffer.mess.name,
                            buffer.mess.age,
                                      buffer.mess.org,
                          error);
```

```
                        /* ************************** */
                        /* send reply message         */
                        /* ************************** */
                  msgsnd(messid,(void *) &obuffer,MESSLEN,
                              NOFLAGS);
                        break;
                        }
            case WRITE:
                        {
                        /* ************************** */
                        /* open file for append        */
                        /* ************************** */
                        Datafile=fopen("test.txt,"a+");
                        if ( Datafile == (FILE *) NULL )
                          {
                              error=FAIL;
                          }
                        else
                          {
                          /* ********************** */
                          /* update file from message */
                          /* ********************** */
                  error=update(Datafile,(char *)
                                          &buffer);
                  fclose(Datafile);
                        }
                        /* **************************** */
                        /* format reply message         */
                        /* **************************** */
                  formatmess((char *)
                                 &obuffer,buffer.mess.name,
                              buffer.mess.age,buffer.mess.org,
                                 error);
                        /* **************************** */
                        /* send reply message           */
                        /* **************************** */
                  msgsnd(messid,(void *) &obuffer,MESSLEN,
                              NOFLAGS);
                        break;
                        }
            case EXIT :
                        {
                        /* ********************************** */
                        /* destroy message queue and terminate */
                        /* ********************************** */
                        msgctl(messid,IPC_RMID,&data);
                        exit(0);
                        }
            }
```

```
        }
    }
int formatmess(buf,tname,tage,torg,err)
char *buf;
mtyp_t org;
char *tname;
char *tage;
int err;
{
    struct message *ptr;  /* pointer to a message structure */
    /* ******************************** */
    /* make message structure accessible */
    /* ******************************** */
    ptr1=(struct message *) buf;
    /* ***************************** */
    /* set message type to originator */
    /* ***************************** */
    ptr1->mtype=torg;
    /* *************************** */
    /* set cmd field to returned error */
    /* *************************** */
    ptr1->mess.cmd=err;
    /* ******************************** */
    /* set the originator field in the id */
    /* of THISPROCESS                   */
    / ******************************** */
    ptr1->mess.org=THISPROCESS;
    /* ******************************** */
    /* copy values to tname and tage into */
    /* name and age fields               */
    /* ******************************** */
    strcpy(ptr1->mess.name,tname);
    strcpy(ptr1->mess.age,tage);
    }
int searchfile(f,buf)
FILE *f;
char *buf;
 {
    char name[SNAME+1];
    char age[SAGE+1];
    struct message *ptr1;
    /* ******************************** */
    /* make message buffer accessible    */
    /* ******************************** */
    ptr1=(struct message * ) buf;
    /* ********************************** */
    /* read a line at a time from the file  */
    /* into the variables name and age     */
    /* ********************************** */
     while ( fscanf(f,"%29s%9s",name,age) != -1 )
```

```
        {
        /* **************************** */
        /* if name found copy age into    */
        /* message buffer return OK        */
        /* **************************** */
            if ( strcmp(name,ptr1->mess.name) == 0)
              {
                strcpy(ptr1->mess.age,age);
                return(OK);
              }
        }
      /* ***************************** */
      /* no match found return FAIL       */
      /* ***************************** */
        return(FAIL);
    }
int updatefile(f,buf)
FILE *f;
char *buf;
{
    struct message *ptr1;
    int res;
    /* ***************************** */
    /* make message buffer accessible    */
    /* ***************************** */
      ptr1=(struct message *) buf;
    /* ****************************** */
    /* write name and age to file        */
    /* ****************************** */
    res=fprintf(f,"%29s %9s",ptr1->mess.name,
                  ptr1->mess.age);
    fflush(f);
    if ( res == 2 )
      {
        return(OK);
      }
    else
      {
        return(FAIL);
      }
    }
```

And the client process may be coded like this

```
   #include <stdio.h>
#include <sys/types.h>
#include <sys/ipc.h>
#include <sys/msg.h>
#include <sys/mode.h>
#include "clserv.h"
```

```
/* ****************************** */
/* constant identifier for this  */
/* process, for the client it is */
/* defined as the process id      */
/* ****************************** */
#define THISPROCESS ( mtyp_t ) getpid()
main()
  {
  int messid;              /* message queue system identifier */
  struct message buffer   /* output message buffer           */
  struct message obuffer  /* input message buffer            */
  char tname[SNAME+1];    /* temporary strings for name,age  */
  char tage[SAGE+1];      /* and command name                */
  char tcmd[SNAME+1];
  /* **************************************** */
  /* open message queue                      */
  /* **************************************** */
   messid=msgget(MESSG_KEY,NOFLAGS);
  if ( messid == MESSG_FAIL )
    {
      /* *********************************** */
      /* client failed to open message queue */
      /* abort with error message           */
      /* *********************************** */
      fprintf(stderr,"client failed to open queue\n");
      fflush(stderr);
      exit(1);
    }
  /* **************************************** */
  /* prompt for command name, either READ,WRITE */
  /* or EXIT and the values of name and age  */
  /* **************************************** */
  printf("Enter command (READ,WRITE,EXIT) : ");
  fflush(stdout);
  gets(tcmd);
  printf("Enter name : ");
  fflush(stdout);
  gets(tname);
  printf("Enter age  : ");
  fflush(stdout);
  gets(tage);
  /* **************************************** */
  /* make simple check on string command and */
  /* make requests to the server            */
  /* **************************************** */
  /* ************************* */
  /* READ command maybe !!!     */
  /* ************************* */
   if ( strcmp(tcmd,"read") == 0 )
     {
```

```
/* ********************************** */
/* format message to be sent to server */
/* ********************************** */
formatmess((char *) &buffer,tname,tage,FORSERVER,
           READ);
/* ********************************** */
/* send message to server and get reply */
/* ********************************** */
msgsnd(messid,(void *) &buffer,MESSLEN,NOFLAGS);
msgrcv(messid,(void *) &obuffer,MESSLEN,THISPROCESS,
       NOFLAGS);
/* ********************************** */
/* print the results on screen       */
/* ********************************** */
printmess((char *) &obuffer);
}
/* ********************************** */
/* WRITE command maybe !!!           */
/* ********************************** */
if ( strcmp(tcmd,"write") == 0 )
  {
    /* ********************************** */
    /* format message to be sent to server */
    /* ********************************** */
    formatmess((char *) &buffer,tname,tage,FORSERVER,
               READ);
    /* ********************************** */
    /* send message to server and get reply */
    /* ********************************** */
    msgsnd(messid,(void *) &buffer,MESSLEN,NOFLAGS);
    msgrcv(messid,(void *) &obuffer,MESSLEN,THISPROCESS,
           NOFLAGS);
    /* ********************************** */
    /* print the results on screen       */
    /* ********************************** */
    printmess((char *) &obuffer);
  }
    /* ********************************** */
    /* EXIT command maybe !!!            */
    /* ********************************** */
    if ( strcmp(tcmd, "exit") == 0 )
      {
        /* ********************************** */
        /* format and send message to server */
        /* do not wait for reply as one is   */
        /* not expected                      */
        /* ********************************** */
        formatmess((char *) &buffer,tname,tage,FORSERVER,
                   EXIT);
        msgsnd(messid,(void *) &buffer,MESSLEN,NOFLAGS);
```

```
                }
   }
int printmess(str)
char *str;
{
   struct message *ptr1;
   /* ********************************** */
   /* make message text accessible         */
   /* ********************************** */
   ptr1=(struct message *) str;
   printf("------------------------------------\n\n");
   printf("Message type      [%ld]\n", (long) ptr1->mtype);
   printf("Message cmd/err   [%d]\n", ptr1->mess.cmd);
   printf("Message originator[%ld]\n", (long) ptr1->mess.org);
   printf("Message name      [%30s]\n", ptr1->mess.name);
   printf("Message age       [%10s]\n", ptr1->mess.age);
   printf("------------------------------------\n\n");
   fflush(stdout);
}
int formatmess(buf,tname,tage,torg,err)
char *buf;
mtyp_t org;
char *tname;
char *tage;
int err;
{
    struct message *ptr;   /* pointer to a message structure */
    /* ********************************** */
    /* make message structure accessible */
    /* ****************************** */
    ptr1=(struct message *) buf;
    /* ****************************** */
    /* set message type to originator */
    /* ****************************** */
    ptr1->mtype=torg;
    /* ****************************** */
    /* set cmd field to returned error */
    /* ****************************** */
    ptr1->mess.cmd=err;
    /* ****************************** */
    /* set the originator field to the id*/
    /* of thisprocess                  */
    / ****************************** */
    ptr1->mess.org=THISPROCESS;
    /* ****************************** */
    /* copy values to tname and tage into */
    /* name and age fields            */
    /* ****************************** */
    strcpy(ptr1->mess.name,tname);
    strcpy(ptr1->mess.age,tage);
}
```

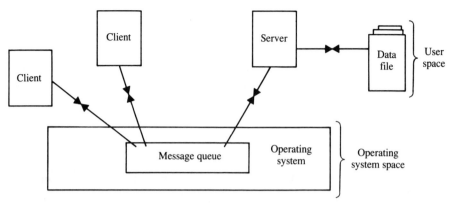

Figure 12.3.  Client–server use of message queues.

The client and server programs listed are illustrations of the use of message queues as a means of interprocess communication. The server program must be initiated at the AIX command line first, usually in background, for example

```
$ ./server &
```

It is very important that only one server process is initiated at any point in time. Any number of client processes may be initiated at any one point in time, and they will all communicate with the server process via the message queue.

Diagrammatically the relationship between client(s) and server can be represented as in Fig. 12.3.

## 12.3    Interprocess communication with FIFO pipes

The abbreviation FIFO stands for first in, first out. Under AIX 3.x and UNIX System V.x FIFO pipes can be used as an interprocess communication mechanism. FIFO pipes may be divided into two main categories. The *named* pipe resides as a special file on the filesystem and is created by the system call mkfifo(), and *unnamed* pipes often reside in main memory. These may be created by the system calls pipe() and popen(). Although the fundamental principles of the two categories are identical their application and flexibility are quite different.

### 12.3.1  *What is a FIFO pipe?*

A FIFO pipe is often opened by two processes simultaneously, one process for reading and the other process for update; it may be considered as a one-way tube down which information will pass from one process to another. If two processes wish to communicate together bidirectionally then they open two FIFO pipes, one for receiving input and the other for sending output. Unlike message queues it is not possible to use FIFO pipes as bidirectional message agents, because their very FIFO nature, which would require complete process synchronization on the part of the consumer and the producer of the data: this is often unobtainable or undesirable.

## 12.3.2 Creation of a named FIFO pipe

Under AIX named FIFO pipes may be created by one of two system calls, mknod() and mkfifo(). The system call mknod() is not exclusively used to create FIFO pipes; it is often used with root authority to create special files:

```
#include <sys/mode.h>
#include <sys/types.h>
int mknod(Pathname,ModeType,devno)
char *Pathname;
int   ModeType;
dev_t devno;
```

The first parameter Pathname is always used and is the full pathname of the named file (which in our case will be a FIFO pipe). This pathname may even extend over NFS filesystems to a remote node if NFS is configured. However, the use of a special file located at a remote node must be considered slightly dangerous, to say the least.

The second parameter ModeType is the parameter used to specify what type of special file the system call mknod will create and what user access permissions will be given to it. The values used are found in the file sys/mode.h and are logically ORed together.

The permissions used are those used for message queues, semaphores and shared memory system calls, but the identifier S_IFIFO must be present to cause mknod() to create a FIFO pipe.

The third parameter devno is not used when the parameter S_IFIFO is present in the ModeType field, and may therefore be safely given a value of zero. However, during the creation of special files, both block and character, its value must be the device ID for the device to be attached.

Thus when creating a named FIFO pipe using the system call chmod(), the following code fragment could be used:

```
 #include <sys/mode.h>
#include <sys/types.h>
#define NODEV (int) 0
main()
 {
```

```
/* ***************************************** */
/* create FIFO called /usr/fifo with         */
/* read / write permissions for everyone     */
/* ***************************************** */
mknod("/usr/fifo",S_IFIFO | S_IRUSR | S_IWUSR |
                  S_IRGRP | S_IWGRP | S_IROTH |
                  S_IWOTH, NODEV);
}
```

AIX 3.x provides another interface to create named FIFO pipes. This interface is called mkfifo(), and is defined as follows:

```
#include <sys/mode.h>
#include <sys/types.h>
int mkfifo(Pathname,Mode)
char *Pathname;
int   Mode;
```

The first parameter Pathname is the same as that defined for the system call mknod().

The second parameter Mode is slightly different from the second parameter of the system call mknod() in that there is no requirement for any file type parameter to be present in the Mode value. The value of S_IFIFO is assumed when using the system call mkfifo.

No special user privileges are required to use mkfifo(), but this is not the case for some of the uses of the system call mknod().

To create a named FIFO pipe using the system call mkfifo() the following code fragment could be used:

```
 #include <sys/mode.h>
#include <sys/types.h>
main()
 {
    /* ***************************************** */
    /* create FIFO called /usr/fifo with         */
    /* read/write permissions for everyone       */
    /* ***************************************** */
    mkfifo("/usr/fifo",S_IRUSR | S_IWUSR |
                       S_IRGRP | S_IWGRP | S_IROTH |
                       S_IWOTH);
}
```

Once created, the named FIFO pipe may be accessed via the standard file input/output system calls fopen() etc. and open() etc. It should be noted, however, that using buffered input/output system calls on a FIFO pipe may cause unpredictable results if the system call `fflush()` is not used to ensure file buffer flushing to the FIFO pipe.

### 12.3.3  *Creation of an unnamed FIFO pipe*

The creation of an unnamed or regular FIFO pipe can be achieved in two ways, with the system calls `pipe()` and `popen()`, but a full understanding of the mechanism used to implement `popen()` requires an explanation of the system call `pipe()`. This has the following definition:

```
int pipe(fd)
int fd[2];
```

The parameter `fd[2]` is an array of integers which will be used to hold two file descriptors.

The file descriptor in element `fd[0]` will be attached to a regular pipe and opened for reading, and the file descriptor in element `fd[1]` will be attached to the same regular pipe and opened for writing. Thus any output sent to the file descriptor held in `fd[1]` may be read by reading the file descriptor held in `fd[0]`. At first sight it may seem rather stupid to have a regular pipe attached to two different file descriptors within the same process. However, the reader should be aware of the properties of the system call `fork()` and the relationship between parent and child files and variables. If we accept that during a `fork()` system call the process is replicated in every way, including all open files and pipes then we may use this to our advantage.

Consider the following

```
 #include <stdio.h>
#include <sys/mode.h>
#include <sys/types.h>
#define PIPE_FAIL (int) -1
main()
  {
    int fd[2];        /* file descriptor array */
    /* ************************************** */
    /* create pipe with pipe() system call    */
    /* check return result and print message   */
    /* ************************************** */
    if ( pipe(fd) != PIPE_FAIL)
      {
        printf("Pipe created ok\n");
        fflush(stdout);
        exit(0);
      }
    printf("Pipe failed to be created\n");
```

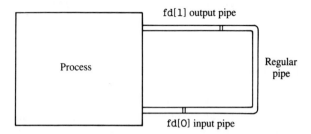

Figure 12.4.  Regular pipe creation state in a process.

```
        fflush(stdout);
        exit(1);
}
```

With this code fragment the pipe is created and the two file descriptors allocated, diagrammatically with respect to the process the result may look like Fig. 12.4. This in itself is not very useful, in that the process may use the write system call on the file descriptor held in fd[1] and use the read() system call on the file descriptor held in fd[0] to read back the same data. However, consider the AIX 3.x command line

```
$ pgm1 | pgm2
```

In this example the STDOUT file of pgm1 is attached to the STDIN of pgm2; it may be self-evident by now that the shell makes use of the pipe() system call to achieve this interprocess regular pipe connection.

Consider the following program:

```
include <stdio.h>
#include <sys/mode.h>
#include <sys/types.h>
#define PIPE_FAIL (int) -1   /* failure code from pipe()   */
#define STDINFD   (int) 0    /* stdin file descriptor      */
#define STDOUTFD  (int) 1    /* stdout file descriptor     */
#define CHILDPS   (int) 0    /* child return from fork()   */
#define PIPER     (int) 0    /* pipe read descriptor       */
#define PIPEW     (int) 0    /* pipe write descriptor      */
#ifndef EOF                  /* define EOF if not defined  */
#define EOF -1
#endif
main(argc,argv)
int argc;
char *argv[];
   {
     FILE *infile;   /
      * Buffered file descriptor for input file   */
```

```
FILE *outfile; /* Buffered file descriptor for
                                         output file */
int fd[2];      /* pipe file descriptors   */
int ch;         /* character read from file */
/* ***************************************** */
/* check for the correct number of parameters */
/* input filename should be given as first   */
/* parameter                                 */
/* ***************************************** */
if ( argc != 2 )
 {
   fprintf(stderr,"Usage: pgm1 filename\n);
   fflush(stderr);
   exit(1);
 }
/* ***************************************** */
/* open the file given as the first parameter */
/* for input within this process            */
/* ***************************************** */
 infile=fopen(argv[1],"r");
 if ( infile == (FILE *) NULL )
    {
      fprintf(stderr,"Can't open file %s\n",argv[1]);
      fflush(stderr);
      exit(2);
    }
/* ***************************************** */
/* create regular pipe within this process   */
/* ***************************************** */
 if ( pipe(fd) == PIPE_FAIL )
    {
      fprintf(stderr,"Can't create pipe\n");
      fflush(stderr);
      fclose(infile);
      exit(3);
    }
 /* ***************************************** */
 /* END OF STAGE 1                          */
 /* ***************************************** */
 /* ***************************************** */
 /* Use fork() system call to create child process */
 /* ***************************************** */
 if ( fork() == CHILDPS )
   {
 /* ***************************************** */
 /* END OF STAGE 2                          */
 /* ***************************************** */
 /* ***************************************** */
 /* This code will be executed by the child  */
 /* process                                 */
 /* ***************************************** */
```

```
        /* ***************************** */
        /* Close STDIN file descriptor    */
        /* ***************************** */
        close(STDINFD);
        /* ******************************** */
        /* duplicate pipe read to STDIN      */
        /* file descriptor                   */
        /* ie attach STDIN to read pipe      */
        /* descriptor                        */
        /* ******************************** */
         dup(fd[PIPER]);
         close(fd[PIPER]); /* discard old descriptor */
        /* ********************************** */
        /* Close write side of pipe descriptor */
        /* ********************************** */
        close(fd[PIPEW]);
        /* ********************************** */
        /* overwrite this process with the    */
        /* program /bin/wc                    */
        /* ********************************** */
        execlp("/bin/wc", "wc",NULL );
        /* ************************************* */
        /* END OF STAGE 3                         */
        /* ************************************* */
        /* ************************************* */
        /* if we get here the execlp() call      */
        /* failed                                */
        /* ************************************* */
        fprintf(stderr,"Can't exec /bin/wc\n");
        fflush(stderr);
        exit(4);
      }
  /* ****************************************** */
  /* This code will be executed by the parent   */
  /* process only                               */
  /* ****************************************** */
  /* ************************* */
  /* Close read side of pipe   */
  /* ************************* */
  close(fd[PIPER]);
  /* ******************************************* */
  /* create a buffered i/o file handle for write  */
  /* pipe descriptor                              */
  /* ******************************************* */
  outfile=fdopen(fd[PIPEW],"w");
  if ( outfile == (FILE *) NULL )
     {
        fprintf(stderr,"Can't buffer output descriptor\n");
        fflush(stderr);
        exit(5);
     }
```

```
/* ******************************************** */
/* END OF STAGE 4                               */
/* ******************************************** */
/* ********************************** */
/* read all characters from input file  */
/* and send them down the write pipe     */
/* descriptor                            */
/* ********************************** */
   while ( (ch=getc(infile)) != EOF )
      {
          putc(ch,outfile);
      }
/* ************************************ */
/* fflush and close both input and output  */
/* files                                    */
/* ************************************ */
   fflush(outfile);
   close(infile);
   close(outfile);
   exit(0);
}
```

The above program could be activated at the AIX 3.x command line as follows:

```
$ pgm1 /etc/passwd
```

This will cause the program to use /etc/passwd as its input file and initiate a copy of the program /bin/wc as a child process. The contents of /etc/passwd will be read by the program pgm1 and passed to the child process /bin/wc via the regular pipe which the parent process pgm1 created.

The relationship between the process while this is going on can be represented diagrammatically as in Fig. 12.5.

At the end of stage 5 the STDOUT of the process pgm1 is attached to the fd[1] file descriptor and the STDIN of the process /bin/wc is attached to the fd[0] file descriptor of the same regular pipe. Although it is not shown in the figure, the process /bin/wc also technically has the input file open, as it inherited the open file descriptor from its parent. However, we do not need to take account of this here as both processes do not access the file.

The above code is almost the code used to implement the final system call used to create an unnamed or regular pipe, the system call popen. This system call has the following definition:

```
#include <stdio.h>
FILE *popen(cmd,mode)
char *cmd;
char *mode;
```

The first parameter cmd is a pointer to a null terminated string which contains the shell command line to execute as a child process.

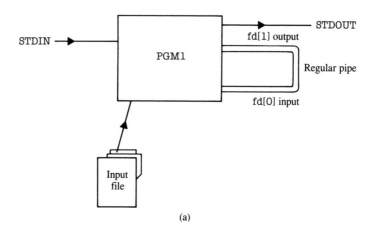

(a)

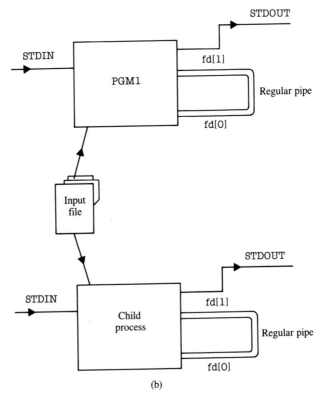

(b)

Figure 12.5. Standard file behaviour during an interprocess pipe creation. (*Continues.*)
        (a)  end of stage 1.
        (b)  end of stage 2.

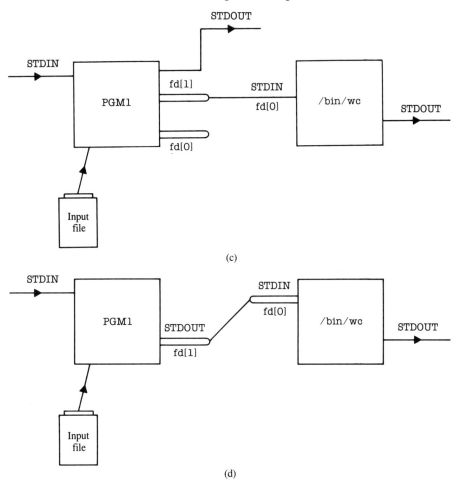

Figure 12.5.  Standard file behaviour during an interprocess pipe creation. *Concluded.*
          (c)  end of stage 3.
          (d)  end of stage 4.

The second parameter mode also points to a null terminated string which contains the type of access given to the returned stream on the STDIN or STDOUT of the child process. Valid values are:

r

   Allows the calling process to read from the returned stream; this stream will be attached to the STDOUT of the child process created and defined in the parameter cmd.

w

   Allows the calling process to write to the returned stream; this stream will be attached to the STDIN of the child process. This is the same as our example with the system call pipe().

The user may notice the similarity between the mode parameter used in the system call `fopen( )`. In fact the calls are very similar in usage, but it is not possible to open a FIFO for read and write using the same stream as it is for a file. This is an important point to note. The system call `popen( )` either returns a pointer to a stream on success or a NULL pointer on failure. The following is a simple code example of the use of the system call `popen( )`:

```c
 #include <stdio.h>
#ifndef EOF
#define EOF -1
#endif
#define POFAIL (FILE *) NULL
main(argc,argv)
int argc;
char *argv[];
   {
      FILE *infile;      /* Buffered file descriptor for input  */
      FILE *outfile;     /* Buffered file descriptor for output */
      int ch;            /* character from input file           */
      /* ************************************** */
      /* check arguments and open input file    */
      /* ************************************** */
      if ( argc != 2 )
          {
              fprintf(stderr,"Usage: pgm2 filename\n");
              fflush(stderr);
              exit(1);
          }
       infile=fopen(argv[1],"r");
       if ( infile == ( FILE *) NULL )
          {
              fprintf(stderr,"Can't open file %s\n",argv[1]);
              fflush(stderr);
              exit(2);
   }
       /* ******************************************* */
       /* Use popen() to initiate /bin/wc             */
       /* allow parent process to write to stream     */
       /* ******************************************* */
       outfile=popen("/bin/wc", "w");
       if ( outfile == POFAIL )
          {
             fprintf(stderr,"Can't open pipe\n");
             fflush(stderr);
             fclose(infile);
             exit(3);
          }
```

```
/* ******************************************* */
/* Copy contents of input file to pipe        */
/* and therefore to /bin/wc                   */
/* ******************************************* */
  while ( (ch=getc(infile)) != EOF )
     {
          putc(ch,outfile);
     }
/* ******************************************* */
/* fflush and close files                     */
/* ******************************************* */
  fflush(outfile);
  fclose(infile);
/* ******************************************* */
/* close pipe using pclose() system call      */
/* ******************************************* */
  pclose(outfile);
  exit(0);
}
```

The above program could be initiated at the AIX 3.x command line in the same way as the previous example. It performs exactly the same function, but using popen() instead of the code shown there.

The problem of two-way communication between processes using regular pipes is solved using two streams and two pipes. The code given in the first example on the use of the pipe() system call could be modified to provide two-way communication between two processes.

Using regular pipes as an interprocess communication mechanism is not ideal. The program often encounters problems using buffered streams with regular pipes attached, mainly owing to the asynchronous nature of the buffer flushing. This can be almost overcome with the correct use of the system call fflush() to ensure data is flushed to the pipe directly, but there may still be some problems.

In summary, it is wise to beware when using regular or named pipes as interprocess communication channels.

# 13
# Processes and signals

Signals as an interprocess communication mechanism in the strictest sense are not very useful; in many respects they have the same limitations as semaphores, in that a signal is either present or absent and carries no other useful information with it. However, signals are vital to the implementation of a multitasking operating system. They are used to inform a process or processes of the occurrence of an event: this event may be one of many different things, from a disk controller acknowledging the transfer of data to a disk, to a special key being pressed by the operator at the keyboard.

Under AIX 3.x as in UNIX System V.x signals are used as a high-level abstraction for interrupts, be they hardware generated or software generated. AIX 3.x has many advanced signal handling functions which are not found under UNIX System V.x or BSD 4.x, and these system calls will be presented after we have looked at the standard signal handling system calls.

## 13.1    Signal manipulation

Under UNIX system V.x and BSD 4.x there are two common system calls which enable processes to manipulate signals, the system call `signal()` and the system call `kill()`. These system calls are used to trap and send signals from one process to another.

AIX 3.x allows any process to use the system call `kill()` to send a signal to any other process, but the use of this system call is governed by a fixed set of security rules which state that although any process may signal another process, for the signal to be accepted the signalling process must either have root user authority or be owned by the same user who owns the signalled process. In short, except for the root user, you may only send signals to your own processes. There is one exception to this rule: the kernel may send signals to any process, and it will send signals with root user authority.

There is another simple rule, that if a process receives a signal which it has not trapped using the signal() or similar system call, it will cause the process to terminate. This is rather like an interrupt being present without an interrupt handler—not a pretty sight.

### 13.1.1 *Compatibility functions*

Consider the UNIX System V.x and BSD 4.x compatibility functions present in AIX 3.x.

*The system call* signal()

This is used by a process to trap a defined signal, and it has the following definition:

```
#include <signal.h>
void (*signal(Signalno,ActionFuc))()
int Signalno;
void (*ActionFuc)();
```

This rather strange-looking definition for a system call, may seem quite complex, but in fact most of its apparent complexity is due to the syntax of the C programming language rather than to the system call itself. The first parameter Signalno is an integer representation of the signal number to be trapped. A full list of all of the predefined signals available is defined in the file signal.h. These signal numbers will vary from machine to machine and from one version of UNIX to another, so it is not advisable to use numeric values that happened to work on the last machine you used. It is better practice to use the predefined values which take the form SIGxxx. There are two special signals that it is not possible to trap: not even a root user may trap the signals defined by SIGKILL and SIGSTOP, the 'sure kill' and 'stop' signals that may be sent to any process to terminate it. Without these special signals it would be possible to enable the kernel processes not to respond to a shutdown request, and this is not really desirable.

The second parameter ActionFuc is a pointer to a function that will be called when the specified signal is received by the calling process. This function must be defined within the calling process's address space. There are two standard definitions present in the file signal.h that can be used to cause the signal to be ignored or to have its default action, SIG_IGN and SIG_DFL.

The system call signal() returns a pointer to a function returning void type. This is a pointer to the signal handling function that was installed before the system call was made, and it gives the process the ability to dynamically change and restore signal handling functions by using the old signal trap pointer returned by signal().

Whenever a signal trap function is called the signal trap is restored to its default value, and therefore the signal trap function must use the signal() system call to reinstate the trap routine before it terminates. However, during the processing of the signal function, before the trap is reinstated, if another signal of the same type is received by the process, it will often cause the process to terminate because at this point the signal action has the value of SIG_DFL . This is why on a slow system it is possible to terminate the shell by typing ⟨CTRL-C⟩ (the SIGINT signal) very quickly.

The system call that is used to send a signal to a process is called kill() and has the following definition:

```
#include <signal.h>
#include <sys/types.h>
int kill(ProcessId,Signalno)
pid_t ProcessId;
int   Signalno;
```

The first parameter ProcessId specifies the process ID or process group ID to which the signal is to be sent. There are two special process IDs which have special meanings under AIX 3.x and UNIX; these processes have process IDs 0 and 1 respectively. These processes are often referred to as proc0 and proc1, and are treated in a special way by many of the calls to kill(). Sending a signal does not guarantee that it will be accepted, because of the standard security checks mentioned above.

Valid values of the parameter ProcessId are:

- A process ID of an active process that is greater than zero. This can include the process proc1, but this process is the /etc/init program and it would be catastrophic to issue a SIGKILL as root user against this process.
- A process ID of zero, in which case the signal is sent to all processes present in the system, excluding proc0 and proc1, whose process group ID is the same as that of the senders.
- A process ID of −1, in which case the signal is sent to all processes present in the system providing the sender has permissions to do so, again excluding processes proc0 and proc1.
- A process ID that is negative but not −1, in which case the signal is sent to all processes present in the system which have the same process group ID as the absolute value of the parameter specified.

### The system call interface killpg()

This is also supported by AIX 3.x as a compatibility feature with BSD 4.x. It can be emulated by the use of the system call kill() and is not presented here.

Let us look at the way a signal can be trapped using the system call signal() and sent using the system call kill(). The following program will catch the standard signal SIGINT which is sent to a process by the user typing a ⟨CRTL-C⟩ at the keyboard.

```c
#include <stdio.h>
#include <signal.h>
#define FOREVER ;;
void catchc();    /* function prototype of signal catch */
                  /* function                           */
main()
   {
      signal(SIGINT,catchc);    /* set trap to SIGINT      */
                                /* to call function        */
                                /* catchc()                */
      for ( FOREVER )           /* Send program into an    */
         ;                      /* infinite loop           */
   }
 void catchc()
   {
      /* ********************************* */
      /* issue warning  to the user       */
      /* ********************************* */
      printf("Don't press that key !!! \n");
      fflush(stdout);
      /* ********************************* */
      /* re install trap for SIGINT       */
      /* ********************************* */
      signal(SIGINT, catchc);
   }
```

A process may signal another process using the system call kill() as shown in the following example, but the AIX 3.x utility program kill uses the system call kill() to send signals to a process.

The following program shows the use of the system call kill() to implement a version of the AIX utility kill called xkill.

```c
#include <stdio.h>
#include <signal>
#include <sys/types.h>
#define KILL_FAIL (int) -1
main(argc, argv)
int argc;
char *argv[];
  {
     pid_t pid;    /* process id of signalled process */
     int sig;      /* signal number to be signalled   */
     int error;    /* returned error from kill()      */
     /* ************************************** */
     /* This program illustrates the use of the */
     /* system call kill by emulating the utility */
```

```
/* kill                                            */
/* ******************************************** */
/* ********************************* */
/* check out command line parameters    */
/* ********************************* */
  if ( argc != 3 )
    {
       fprintf(stderr,"Usage: xkill -sig pid\n");
       fflush(stderr);
       exit(1);
    }
  if ( argv[1][0] != '-' )
    {
       fprintf(stderr,"Invalid sig number\n");
       fflush(stderr);
       exit(2);
    }
    /* ********************************* */
    /* convert process id and sig to     */
    /* correct types for use with kill() */
    /* system call                       */
    /* ********************************* */
    pid=(pid_t) atoi(argv[2]);
    sig=(int) atoi(argv[1]);
    sig=(-sig);
    /* ********************************* */
    /* send system call and report error */
    /* ********************************* */
    error=kill(pid,sig)
    if ( error == KILL_FAIL )
      {
         fprintf(stderr,"Failed to send signal\n");
         fflush(stderr);
          exit(3);
      }
    exit(0);
}
```

There are three problems that arise for a program wishing to use signal processing:

- Firstly, signals may arrive at any time, even during the execution of a system call. What should this system call do in this case? Should it suspend its execution, service the signal handling routine and then resume, or should it abort, returning an error code, making sure any changes that it had made up to then are reversed and then service the trap? The answer is far from simple. Certain system calls must provide atomic actions, that is they will run to completion without interruption by other processes or signal handling routines. These system calls have no choice but to abort and return an error code. It is then up to the user process to check for this error code and restart the system call. Other system calls do not need to provide this type of guarantee and therefore they suspend execution, service the signal handling routine and resume the system call after its completion. We will see when we look at AIX 3.x extended signal handling system calls how the behaviour of these system calls may affect how we write programs.

- Secondly, there is a problem of what system calls can be safely used from within a signal handling routine, bearing in mind that the same system call may have been interrupted in order to service this signal handling routine. In short, only certain system calls are 'reentrant' and can be called without restriction from signal handling routines. Other system calls may have restrictions placed upon their use with signal handling routines. Again we will see the system calls involved in greater detail when we look at AIX 3.x extended signal handling.

- Thirdly, what is to stop another signal from occurring during the execution of a signal handling routine, and causing an interruption of that routine? The signal may conceivably be the same one that caused the current signal handling routine to be called. In the above examples it can be seen that the signal handling trap has to be reinstated by the signal processing routine. Thus a process may receive a signal for which it has no current signal handling routine, in which case program termination takes place, or it may call a signal handling routine in a reentrant manner. Whichever event pattern we choose, it is a problem.

### The system call sigvec()

This precursor of the extended POSIX 1003.1 signal handling system calls found in AIX 3.x allows greater control over the signal handling process, and has the following definition:

```
#include <signal.h>
int sigvec(Signalno,Newvec,Curvec)
int Signalno;
struct sigvec *Newvec;
struct sigvec *Curvec;
```

The first parameter Signalno is the signal number defined in the file signal.h on which the system call will act. The signals are defined as constants of the form SIGxxx. The second and third parameters are pointers to a structure sigvec. This structure has the following definition, and is found in signal.h:

```
struct sigvec
     {
        int (*sv_handler)();
        int sv_mask;
        int sv_flags;
     };
```

The first field of this structure is a pointer to the signal handling function associated with the signal specified in the system call. This is the same form as that used in the old system call `signal()`.

The second field in the structure is an integer which is used as a signal mask, allowing the signals in the range 1 . . . 31 to be masked while the signal handling routine is running. This is achieved by setting the nth bit of this field to mask the nth signal. This will go some way to solving the concurrent signal problem discussed above; however, AIX 3.x has 63 different signals so we may still experience some problems with this system call.

The third field in this structure is used to modify, if possible, the behaviour of system calls that are interrupted by a signal being delivered to a process. The behaviour of this flag is dependent on the library support code that is linked to the program code. The flag `SV_INTERRUPT` will cause any system call to interrupt its processing and return an error code to the calling process upon the delivery of a signal during a system call. This is the default value set whenever the standard library (`libc.a`) is selected, in which case the contents of this field are ignored. However, if the BSD library (`libbsd.a`) is linked, then the default action is for system calls to restart if possible and therefore the flag `SV_INTERRUPT` if present will cause the system calls to return an error code, the same as using the `libc.a` library.

The second parameter to the system call `sigvec()` is used to set the action taken on receipt of the signal specified by the process. The third parameter returns the current values of these parameters before the new values are set. This again is similar to the `signal()` system call returning a pointer to the old signal handling function.

Using the `sigvec()` system call instead of the `signal()` system call is quite simple. Let's rewrite our previous example with `signal()` in terms of `sigvec()`:

```
#include <stdio.h>
#include <signal.h>
#define FOREVER ;;
void catchc();    /* function prototype to signal catch */
                  /* function                           */
#define MASK_INT (int ) 0x0002 /* sv_mask flag for SIGINT    */
#define NOFLAGS  (int)  0      /* no flags for struct sigvec */
main()
    {
    struct sigvec newvec,curvec;
    /* ************************************* */
    /* setup newvec for signal handling     */
    /* values                               */
    /* ************************************* */
    newvec.sv_handler=catchc;   /* set function              */
    newvec.sv_mask=MASK_INT;    /* do not allow SIGINT       */
                                /* while running handler      */
    newvec.sv_flags=NOFLAGS;    /* standard lib no flags      */
```

```
    /* **************************************** */
    /* set new values                          */
    /* **************************************** */
       sigvec(SIGINT, &newvec, &curvec);
        for (FOREVER)          /* Send program into an */
            ;                  /* infinite loop        */
   }
void catchc()
   {
       struct sigvec newvec,curvec;
       /* ************************************** */
       /* issue warning  to the user            */
       /* ************************************** */
       printf("Don't press that key !!! \n");
       fflush(stdout);
       /* ************************************** */
       /* re install trap for SIGINT            */
       /* ************************************** */
    /* **************************************** */
    /* setup newvec for signal handling         */
    /* values                                   */
    /* **************************************** */
    newvec.sv_handler=catchc;   /* set function         */
    newvec.sv_mask=MASK_INT;    /* do not allow SIGINT  */
                                /* while running handler */
    newvec.sv_flags=NOFLAGS;    /* standard lib no flags */
    /* **************************************** */
    /* set new values                           */
    /* **************************************** */
       sigvec(SIGINT, &newvec, &curvec);
   }
```

As you can see, very little extra effort is required to use `sigvec()` instead of the older `signal()` system call. Under AIX 3.x it is possible to intermix the use of `signal()` and `sigvec()`, as they are really only interfaces to the extended system call set found under AIX 3.x. However, this practice should be avoided as it is not compatible with other systems. The system call `sigvec()` only provides some of the extra functionality required by an operating system to allow signals to be used safely and effectively within applications and systems software alike.

With this in mind, during the design of AIX 3.x IBM tried to incorporate some of the standards defined by the POSIX committee of which IBM is a founder member. POSIX, like all standards, has taken time to be accepted within the ever-changing computer industry, but as a bold step into the new world IBM implemented the POSIX standard for signal handling in addition to maintaining compatibility with the old-established standards.

IBM's foresight in including such extensions into AIX 3.x is one of the difficulties many AIX 3.x critics face when they make statements such as 'AIX is not really UNIX!'. This, as most people know by now, is rubbish.

## 13.2    Extended signal handling under AIX 3.x

The first function used to substitute for the system calls `signal()` or `sigvec()` is very similar to the system call `sigvec()`. It is called `sigaction()`, and is defined as follows:

```
#include <signal.h>
int sigaction(signalno,newaction,oldaction)
int signalno;
struct sigaction *newaction;
struct sigaction *oldaction;
```

The structure `sigaction` is similar to the structure `sigvec` except that the `sa_mask` field is not an integer, it is of predefined type called `sigset_t` which allows all of the signals to be masked. The structure is defined as follows:

```
struct sigaction
                  {
                       void       (*sa_handler) ();
                       sigset_t   sa_mask;
                       int        sa_flags;
         };
```

The field `sa_handler` is again a pointer to a signal handler function. It takes the same format as that used by the system call `signal()` for the simplest case.

The field `sa_mask` is defined as the system type `sigset_t` and may have several values, which govern the behaviour of the signal processing system during a signal handling routines execution. These values may be set by the system calls that manipulate signal sets (see page 246).

The field `sa_flags` may have any of the values listed below, or a value of zero for no value:

*Flag value*                              *Functionality*

SA_ONSTACK

     Cause the signal handler routine to run on the stack specified by the `sigstack()` system call. If this flag is not set the signal handler will run on the stack of the process to which the signal was delivered.

SA_OLDSTYLE

     Included for backward compatibility with `signal()`. If set it will cause the signal to be reset during the processing of a signal handler routine, and thus require reinstating by the routine. This will cause all of the problems discussed above and is not recommended.

SA_RESTART

     Causes system calls which are able to do so, to restart after being interrupted by a signal event. There are only a few system calls to which this applies: they are

```
read,readx,readv,readxv
write,writex,writev,writexv
ioctl,ioctlx
fcntl,lockf,flock
wait,wait3,waitpid
```

All other system calls will return an error code to the calling process.

The first parameter `signalno` specifies the signal number on which the `sigaction` will act. If the `newaction` field is not NULL and points to a `sigaction` structure, then the action specified in that structure will be set as the default action for that signal by that process. The old set of `sigaction` values will be returned in the field `oldaction`.

If the `newaction` field is NULL then the signal action is not changed, it is just returned in the structure `oldaction`. This may be quite useful for examining the current contents of the `sigaction` structure without changing the action.

The `newaction` and `oldaction` parameters described above have similar roles to the parameters in the system call `sigvec()`, the only difference being the structure definition.

## 13.3    Creating and manipulating signal masks

Signal masks are of the same type as the `sa_mask` field found in the structure `sigaction`, and this provides an object-orientated way of manipulating this mask. These functions work on objects defined within a process and not on the structure `sigaction` directly for any given signal. It is therefore necessary to use the additional functions provided to insert these values into the required structure.

*Exclude all signals from set*

```
#include <signal.h>
int sigemptyset(set)
sigset_t *set;
```

This function takes the set variable `set` and initializes the set of values so that all of the known signals will be excluded, except `SIGKILL` and `SIGSTOP`.

*Include all signals in set*

```
#include <signal.h>
int sigfillset(set)
sigset_t *set;
```

This function takes the set variable set and fills the set so that all of the known signals will be included, except SIGKILL and SIGSTOP.

It is important to note that each set variable of type sigset_t must be initialized by either sigemptyset() or sigfillset() before it may be used by any other set manipulation function.

### Add signal to set

```
#include <signal.h>
int sigaddset(set,signalno)
sigset_t *set;
int        signalno;
```

This function will take the set variable set and add the signal defined by signalno to the set. The variable signalno may be any of the defined signals in the file signal.h, except SIGKILL and SIGSTOP which may not be masked or trapped.

### Delete signal from set

```
 #include <signal.h>
int sigdelset(set,signalno)
sigset_t *set;
int        signalno;
```

This function will take the set variable set and exclude the signal defined by signalno from the set. The variable signalno may be any of the defined signals in the file signal.h, except SIGKILL and SIGSTOP which may not be part of this set.

### Test for membership of a set

```
#include <signal.h>
int sigismember(set,signalno)
sigset_t *set;
int        signalno;
```

This function will test the given set variable set for the presence of the signal defined by the parameter signalno. The function returns TRUE (1) if the signal is a member of the set, and FALSE (0) if the signal is not a member of the set.

The sets generated in this way may be used in conjunction with the structure sigaction or to set the current processes signal mask, using the support functions provided. See sigprocmask() on page 248.

The usage of the above functions is self-evident. They are used to create an object abstraction for the defined masks in the sa_mask field of the structure sigaction. A simple example of using two of these functions to build a set of masks for the sa_mask field is shown in the following code fragment.

```
#include <signal.h>
main()
    {
        sigset_t signalset;
        struct sigaction newsignal;
        sigemptyset(&signalset);        /* create an empty set */
        sigaddset(&signalset,SIGINT);   /* add SIGINT to set    */
        newsignal.sa_mask=signalset;    /* assign signal set    */
                                        /* to mask in sa_mask   */
    }
```

*Controlling system call interrupt behaviour*

```
#include <signal.h>
int siginterrupt(signalno,Flag)
int signalno;
int Flag;
```

If the SA_RESTART or SV_RESTART flags are present in the data structures of the system calls sigaction() or sigvec(), then the above subroutine call can be used to toggle between restart and error code return behaviour for any given signal. If the subroutine siginterrupt() is called during a signal handling routine then the change will take place during the next call to the signal handling routine and not instantaneously.

The two parameters are the parameter signalno which is the signal number as defined in signal.h for the signal to which the change is to take place, and the parameter Flag is a Boolean flag which takes the value of TRUE (1) for restart behaviour to be enabled and FALSE (0) for restart to be disabled. It should be noted that restart will not occur unless the necessary flag is present in the sigaction or sigvec data structures.

*Examining pending signals*

```
#include <signal.h>
int sigpending(pendingset)
sigset_t *pendingset;
```

This function will return in the parameter pendingset the set of signals that are blocked and pending for this process. These signals will be present in the sa_mask field of the sigaction structure. This set may be examined using the sigismember() routine.

*Examining and setting process signal masks*

```
#include <signal.h>
int sigprocmask(function,newset,oldset)
int function;
sigset_t *newset;
sigset_t *oldset;
```

The first parameter of this function is the function code required. This routine will set and return the process signal mask. The valid function codes are listed below.

*Function code*                    *Functionality*

SIG_BLOCK

Gives a set containing the *union* of the current set and the set pointed to by the `newset` parameter, causing the members of the `newset` parameter to be blocked for that process.

SIG_UNBLOCK

Gives a set containing the *intersection* of the current set and the set pointed to by the parameter `newset`, causing the members of the `newset` parameter to be unblocked for that process.

SIG_SETMASK

Results in the parameter `newset` becoming the current set.

The second parameter `newset` is a variable of the type `sigset_t` and is used to contain the signal set information used by the system call. With the function described above, however, if this parameter is NULL then no action is taken on the signal set, irrespective of the value of the parameter `function`. The only result is for the current signal set to be returned in the parameter `oldset`, thus giving a method of examining the current set of blocked signals.

The third parameter `oldset` is a pointer to a set used to contain the current value of the set before any operation takes place, so the old value of the set may be restored if required.

It is interesting to note that if there are any signals unblocked by a call to `sigprocmask()` then at least one of these signals will be received by the process before the `sigprocmask()` subroutine returns to the calling process.

*Enhanced signal management functions*

The following set of functions provide enhanced signal management on a subset of the signals available. It should be noted that the signal management routine `signal()` should not be used in conjunction with these functions on the same signal.

The following subroutines are available:

```
#include <signal.h>
void (*sigset(Signalno,Func))()
int Signalno;
void (*Func)();
int sighold(Signalno)
int Signalno;
int sigrelse(Signalno)
int Signalno;
int sigignore(Signalno)
int Signalno;
```

The first function sigset() provides identical functionality to the system call signal(). Its parameters are Signalno, which is the signal number on which the new action is to be placed, and Func, which is the function that will be activated up on receipt of the signal. The value of the parameter function may have any of the values listed below.

*Parameter function*                    *Functionality*

SIG_DFL

Set the default action for the signal, which is usually to terminate the process receiving the signal.

SIG_IGN

Ignore the signal within this process.

SIG_HOLD

Hold any signal of the type specified, only one signal will be held at any instant in time.

Function

The address of the function to be called when the signal is received by the process (see signal(), Section 13.1). This function will be called with the effective signal handling action set to SIG_HOLD, thus preventing any further recursive calls to the signal handling routine. During the normal return process from a signal processing routine the signal handling function will be restored to the value set by sigset(). If, however, a non-local jump is taken with the setjump() routine, the routine sigrelse() must be called to restore the signal handling function state.

The sighold() function when called with a signal number will cause the signal to be held until the function sigrelse() is called with the same signal number. This can be used to protect code for certain signals during critical sections.

The sigrelse() function restores the signal handling function to that specified by the system call sigset().

The sigignore() function sets the value of SIG_IGN for the signal handling function causing the signal to be ignored.

The above functions can only operate on the following subset of the signals available under AIX 3.x for portability:

| *Signal* | *Function* |
|---|---|

SIGHUP
>    Hangup signal.

SIGINT
>    Interrupt signal.

SIGQUIT
>    Quit signal.

SIGILL
>    Illegal instruction signal.

SIGTRAP
>    Trace trap signal.

SIGABRT
>    Abort signal.

SIGFPE
>    Floating point exception signal.

SIGSYS
>    Bad argument to routine signal.

SIGPIPE
>    Write on a pipe with only read permissions.

SIGALRM
>    Alarm signal.

SIGTERM
>    Software termination signal.

SIGUSR1
>    User definable signal number 1.

SIGUSR2
>    User definable signal number 2.

The use of these extended signal handling functions to ensure that certain sections of code are immune from signal interruption is quite a powerful tool. This cannot be achieved using the standard function `signal()` or the function `sigaction()`. This can be very useful to defer the receipt of a signal until certain code is complete, particularly with the inability of most of the system calls to restart automatically after a signal interruption.

What follows is a simple example to enable a program to complete a critical section without the possibility of interruption by the signal SIGQUIT but to abort if the signal is received at any other time.

```
#include <stdio.h>
#include <signal.h>
```

```
/* ************************************************ */
/* This program appends its current process id to  */
/* a file called pid.txt                           */
/* ************************************************ */
main()
  {
    FILE *outfile;      /* File handle of output file */
    int   pid;               /* current process id        */
    sigset(SIGQUIT,SIG_DFL);   /* set signal processing to */
                               /* default action          */
    pid=(int) getpid();        /* get current process id   */
    /* ***************************** */
    /* Enter critical  section so hold */
    /* signal now                     */
    /* ***************************** */
     sighold(SIGQUIT);
    /* ********************************** */
    /* open file for output                */
    /* exit releasing signal if open fails  */
    /* ********************************** */
     outfile=fopen("pid.txt","a");
     if ( outfile == (FILE *) NULL )
       {
           fprintf(stderr,"Failed to open pid.txt\n");
           fflush(stderr);
           sigrelse(SIGQUIT);
           exit(1);
       }
       /*************************************** */
       /* update file with current pid          */
       /* *********************************** */
       fprintf(outfile,"10%d\n", pid);
       fflush(outfile);
    /* *********************************** */
    /* close file                          */
    /* *********************************** */
     fclose(outfile);
    /* *********************************** */
    /* end of critical  section release signal*/
    /* *********************************** */
     sigrelse(SIGQUIT);
     exit(0);
  }
```

### Context jumps within signal handlers

A signal handling routine may optionally choose not to return to the procedure
that was interrupted but to restore the process context to another procedure. This
is achieved in much the same way as global jumps between functions are achieved

with the C programming language using the functions `setjump()` and `longjump()`. The two system calls used to enable signal handlers to achieve this are defined as follows:

```
#include <setjump.h>
int sigsetjump(SaveEnv,SaveMask)
sigjmp_buf SaveEnv;
int        SaveMask;
int siglongjmp(RestoreEnv,RetVal)
sigjmp_buf RestoreEnv;
int        RetVal;
```

The system call `sigsetjmp()` has two parameters. The parameter `SaveEnv` is defined by the system type `sigjmp_buf`, which is defined in the file `setjump.h`. This parameter will contain the current stack context when the system call `sigsetjmp()` is called. The second parameter `SaveMask` is a Boolean flag. If it is TRUE, i.e. non-zero, then the value of the process signal mask is also saved, but if the value of this parameter is FALSE, i.e. zero, then no signal mask is saved.

The system call `siglongjmp()` restores the stack context found in the parameter `RestoreEnv`. If the process signal mask was saved using the `sigsetjmp()` call, then it too will be restored. This will cause a context switch, and the program will jump unconditionally to the instruction that follows the `sigsetjmp()` system call.

The second parameter `Retval` is the return value used when returning from the system call `siglongjmp()`.

The returned values of the system call `sigsetjmp()` is always zero, but the returned value from the system call `siglongjmp()` as defined in the parameter `RetVal` must be non-zero.

The following example code shows the use of the `sigsetjmp()` and `siglongjmp()` system calls:

```
#include <stdio.h>
#include <setjmp.h>
#include <signal.h>
#ifndef TRUE
#define FALSE 0
#define TRUE ( ! FALSE )
#endif
#define FOREVER     ;;
#define DONOTHING   ;
#define QUIT (int) 1
#define INT  (int) 2
/* ************************************** */
/* define sigsetjmp() environment         */
/* ************************************** */
sigjmp_buf  SavedEnv;
```

```
/* ************************************** */
/* define signal handling routines for    */
/* SIGQUIT and SIGINT                      */
/* ************************************** */
int catchQuit();
int catchInt();
main()
   {
      /* ****************************************** */
      /* set sigsetjmp() environment()              */
      /* To jump to this function after the signal */
      /* handling has been called                   */
      /* ****************************************** */
      setenviron();
      /* ****************************************** */
      /* catch signals SIGQUIT and SIGINT           */
      /* ****************************************** */
       signal(SIGQUIT,catchQuit);
       signal(SIGINT,catchInt);
      /* ************************************** */
      /* infinite loop waiting for a signal     */
      /* ************************************** */
       for ( FOREVER )
          {
             DONOTHING
          }
   }
/* ****************************************** */
/* SIGQUIT signal handler which jumps to the  */
/* saved environment                          */
/* ****************************************** */
int catchQuit()
   {
       siglongjmp(SavedEnv,QUIT);
   }
/* ****************************************** */
/* SIGINT  signal handler which jumps to the  */
/* saved environment                          */
/* ****************************************** */
int catchInt()
   {
       siglongjmp(SavedEnv,INT);
   }
/* ******************************************* */
/* setenvorn function which is called once to set */
/* the environment and then the environment is    */
/* restored by the siglongjmp() system call        */
/* ******************************************* */
int setenviron()
```

```
{
    /* ***************************************** */
    /* save environment in SavedEnv and return  */
    /* as sigsetjmp() always returns zero       */
    /* ***************************************** */
    if ( sigsetjmp(SavedEnv,TRUE) != 0 )
        {
        /* ****************************************** */
        /* restored context by call to siglongjmp() */
        /* will be here !!!                          */
        /* ***************************************** */
        printf("Signal arrived program aborted\n");
        fflush(stdout);
        exit(1);
        }
}
```

It can be seen clearly from the above example that long jumps within signal handling routines are handled in a very similar way to long jumps within the standard C library definition.


*Process stack usage and signals*

Under normal circumstances, when a signal handling routine is called all of its stack requirements will be satisfied using the process stack. From time to time this may not be desirable or practical. AIX has a system call which enables the programmer to nominate a stack on which signal processing will take place. This is done using the system call sigstack() which is defined as follows:

```
#include <signal.h>
int sigstack(NewStack,OldStack)
struct sigstack *Newstack;
struct sigstack *OldStack;
```

The two parameters are both pointers to structures of the system-defined type sigstack. This type is defined in the file signal.h. The first parameter points to a structure defining the new stack frame, and the second parameter is used to store to current stack frame. If the first parameter is set to NULL then the value of the state frame is not changed, but the current stack frame is returned in the second parameter. The second parameter being set to NULL causes the current stack frame not to be returned.

The sigaction() or sigvec() system calls must have the SA_ONSTACK or SV_ONSTACK flag present in their SA_FLAGS and SV_FLAGS field parameters so that a given signal handler will use the alternative stack. However, it is very important that the new stack is defined using sigstack() before a signal event takes place.

The signal stack will not be automatically extended as a normal process stack is when required, so the size of the signal stack should be chosen carefully, as a stack overflow will cause unpredictable results.

The structure `sigstack` is defined as follows:

```
struct sigstack
                {
                    char *ss_sp;
                    int ss_onstack;
                };
```

The first field is a pointer to a new stack frame. Note that stacks grow from high addresses toward low addresses, so this pointer should point, initially at least, to the highest location available in the new stack frame.

The second parameter defines the state of the stack with respect to other processes, usually the interrupted process, and if this field has a value of 1 then the stack is currently being used by another process, and if the value is 0 the stack is free of process activity.

When a signal occurs the stack status is examined. If a process is already running on the stack then the signal handler continues to run on the stack after the signal handler returns. However, if the stack is free of process activity then the signal handler will return on the current stack and restore the original stack state.

The system call `sigstack()` returns 0 for success and –1 for failure, in which case the error code is found in the global variable called `errno`. The system call will fail if either of its parameters points to addresses outside the process's address space.

The usage of `sigstack()` is a specialized function, more often in conjunction with `sigsetjmp()` and `siglongjmp()` to preserve the stack frame. What follows is a simple example of using the `sigstack()` system call to implement a signal stack.

```
#include <stdio.h>
#include <signal.h>
#include <malloc.h>
#define FOREVER ;;
void catchc();    /* function prototype to signal catch */
                  /* function                           */
#define MASK_INT (int ) 0x0002 /* sv_mask flag for SIGINT    */
#define STACK_SIZE (int) (1000 /* sizeof(char))
#define EXCL_STACK   (int) 0   /* constants for exclusive use */
#define SHARED_STACK (int) 1   /* of the stack and not
                                            exclusive*/
                               /* use by the signal handler  */
#define STACK_OK     (int) 0   /* ok returned from sigstack() */
main()
    {
       struct sigvec newvec, curvec;
```

```
    char *new_stack_ptr;
    struct sigstack NewStack, OldStack;
    /* ************************************** */
    /* Use malloc() to allocate new stack    */
    /* area                                  */
    /* ************************************** */
    new_stack_ptr=(char *) malloc( STACK_SIZE );
    if ( new_stack_ptr == ( char *) NULL )
        {
            fprintf(stderr,"can't allocate new stack\n");
            fflush(stderr);
            exit(1);
        }
    /* *************************************** */
    /* setup new stack frame structure sigstack */
    /* for exclusive use for the signal handler */
    /* *************************************** */
    NewStack.ss_sp=new_stack_ptr;
    NewStack.ss_onstack=EXCL_STACK;
    /* *************************************** */
    /* setup new signal stack                  */
    /* *************************************** */
    if ( sigstack(&NewStack,&OldStack) != STACK_OK )
        {
            fprintf(stderr, "Can't set new stack\n");
            fflush(stderr);
            exit(2);
        }
    /* *************************************** */
    /* setup newvec for signal handling        */
    /* values                                  */
    /* Allowing it to use the new signal       */
    /* stack.                                  */
    /* *************************************** */
    newvec.sv_handler=catchc;   /* set function         */
    newvec.sv_mask=MASK_INT;    /* do not allow SIGINT  */
                                /* while running handler */
    newvec.sv_flags=SV_ONSTACK; /* run on signal stack  */
    /* *************************************** */
    /* set new values                          */
    /* *************************************** */
    sigvec(SIGINT,&newvec,&curvec);
    for ( FOREVER )           /* Send program into an */
        ;                     /* infinite loop        */
}
void catchc()
    {
    struct sigvec newvec,curvec;
```

```
/* ********************************* */
/* issue warning  to the user          */
/* ********************************* */
printf("Don't press that key !!! \n");
fflush(stdout);
/* ********************************** */
/* re install trap for SIGINT          */
/* ********************************** */
/* ********************************** */
/* setup newvec for signal handling    */
/* values                              */
/* ********************************** */
newvec.sv_handler=catchc;    /* set function */
newvec.sv_mask=MASK_INT;     /* do not allow SIGINT   */
                             /* while running handler */
newvec.sv_flags=SV_ONSTACK; /*Run on signal stack   */
/* ********************************** */
/* set new values                      */
/* ********************************** */
  sigvec(SIGINT,&newvec,&curvec);
}
```

Each time the signal handler is called it runs exclusively on the signal stack, returning to the process stack after the signal handler returns.

### Blocking a process waiting for a signal

In order to block a process waiting for a specific signal, at first sight it may seem that we could use the system call sigprocmask() to set the process's signal mask, and then use the system call pause() to cause the process to suspend awaiting a signal. However, this is not a perfect solution as it is possible for a signal to arrive in the finite time between the calls to the system call sigprocmask() and pause(), and any such signal would be lost. AIX 3.x provides an atomic method of achieving the above requirement using the system calls sigsuspend() and sigpause() which are defined as follows.

```
#include <signal.h>
int sigsuspend(Signalmask)
sigset_t *Signalmask;
int sigpause(Signalmask)
int SignalMask;
```

The system calls sigsuspend() and sigpause() provide the same functionality. However, the same limitations apply to the Signalmask using the system call sigpause() as to the system call sigvec(). All signals except SIGKILL and SIGSTOP may be masked using the functions.

The system call sigsuspend() will not affect the calling of the signal handling routine. If a signal handling routine is defined for the signal, or the signal causes the process to terminate, the system call sigsuspend() will not return. If the signal process returns then sigsuspend() will return, restoring the original process signal mask. The process will always return after the system call sigsuspend() and will not retry the system call. The return value of the system call is −1 and the error code in the variable errno is EINTR, signifying that the process was interrupted by a signal's arrival.

# Part Four
# AIX 3.x development utilities

# 14
# The XL C compiler

Software development is, as one would expect, very similar under AIX 3.x and other UNIX offerings from other manufacturers. However, AIX 3.x does have a number of distinctive features which often ease software development without necessarily sacrificing its portability.

AIX 3.x is a unified UNIX environment with support for BSD 4.x, System V.x and POSIX. Combining all of these standards or emerging standards into one environment has been no easy task, and not without its problems. Unification often means compromise, and compromise means differences in implementation and often definition of library functions and, to a lesser degree, system calls. IBM have generally tried very hard not to change the definition of system calls and library functions found on machines that conform to any of the standards that were incorporated into AIX 3.x, although the implementation detail of these system calls and libraries may have changed. This is usually of little consequence to the application developer who is only concerned with the applications interface to the operating system at the highest level. However, the systems programmer may find some features which have been combined with others into a unified standard interface, and also additional features.

It has been said, often by AIX opponents, that AIX 3.x is IBM's first open proprietary system. This of course is quite untrue, as good object-orientated design of software always ensures that a high level of abstraction is maintained between the application and the operating system, which is certainly enough to insulate any application from any implementation specifics of AIX 3.x. It should however be pointed out that AIX 3.x does have features not found in any other UNIX implementation. These features are often transparent to the application user, but a systems programmer using them must be aware that portability is almost certainly lost.

This part of the book is dedicated to the description of the command line and programming options of development utilities found under AIX 3.x. It is not, however, a complete reference to all of these utilities, which may be found within the `man` or `info` pages provided under AIX 3.x. It provides an introduction and some examples. The utilities covered here and in the three following chapters are:

- `cc`     the XL C compiler
- `ld`     the XCOFF object linker
- `ar`     the library archive program
- `make`   the System V.x `make` utility

Under AIX 3.x, as under UNIX, the programming language which is most appropriate is often C. Although the debate about the merits and pitfalls of the C language is set to continue for some time to come, the use of C under UNIX by far exceeds the usage of any other third-generation programming language.

The more recent addition of the object-orientated C++ has given a new dimension to programming in what could loosely be called C. C++, like its predecessor, is an acquired taste, and many of the derogatory remarks levelled at the C programming language unfortunately still apply to C++.

It has been said that C was developed to be the closest third-generation programming language to assembler without being an assembler. This is, in fairness, only partly true. Whatever the reader's views on the merits or otherwise of the C programming language, AIX 3.x and UNIX are linked very closely with it. A good 95% of the AIX 3.x kernel and all of the utility programs are written in C, so it is easy to see (no pun intended) why it is the natural choice for systems programmers and, if execution speed is required, applications programs too.

The XL C compiler produced by IBM and present under AIX 3.x is unique in that it generates code which is link-compatible with other XL compilers such as FORTRAN and Pascal. This enables the software developer to make use of the best features of all three of these languages and combine them together into one heterogeneous program. The XL compiler series were designed as state-of-the-art optimizing compilers producing code which is optimized for the environment on which they run. This level of optimization is achieved without sacrificing the high-level portability of the compiler suite.

It is interesting to note that the performance of the RISC System/6000 and AIX 3.x is greatly affected by the ability of the compiler to optimize code. This optimization takes into account the POWER architecture and its ability to dispatch multiple instructions in one clock cycle. This was dramatically demonstrated during upgrades of early releases of AIX 3.x, during which a performance increase of some 15–25% was recorded. This was due solely to improvements made in the XL C compiler.

## 14.1   Installation

The XL C compiler, like all other program products under AIX 3.x, may be installed using SMIT (System Management Interface Tool) or using the utility `installp` from the shell. In order to install any program product successfully, the installation should be performed while the user is logged in as root user or superuser.

The files installed are listed below. In the following paths the variable %LANG is the natural language directory selected during the installation of the AIX 3.x operating system, which is often En_US by default.

*File*                                   *Description*

`/usr/lpp/xlc/bin/xlcentry`
        XL C compiler module code used by xlc, cc and c89
`/usr/lpp/xlc/DOC/README.xlc`
        Text file explaining the environment variables required to the compiler
        suite to execute
`/usr/lpp/msg/%LANG/xlcsmsg.cat`
        File containing all common language compile-time messages
`/usr/lpp/msg/%LANG/xlcmsg.cat`
        XL C compiler compile-time message file
`/usr/lpp/msg/%LANG/xlcdmsg.cat`
        XL C compiler command line message file
`/usr/lpp/msg/%LANG/xlc.help`
        XL C help file
`/bin/xlc`
`/bin/cc`
`/bin/c89`
        XL C command line invocation for invoking xlcentry
`/etc/xlc.cfg`
        XL C configuration file

## 14.2   Compiler environment

There are two environment variables that must be set before the XL C compiler can be used. These variables are concerned with the natural language support provided by AIX 3.x and its utilities, and the XL C compiler will require the appropriate language catalog (.cat) files to be installed for the language selected before it will execute. The natural language is selected by default to be the same as that chosen during the installation of AIX 3.x, but this may not be appropriate for each installation. The environment variables LANG and NLSPATH define the natural language to use and the path used to search for the natural language catalog files respectively.

These variables will have default values which the user may examine using the following commands at the Bourne or Korn shell:

```
$ echo $LANG
En_US
$ echo $NLSPATH
/usr/lpp/msg/En_US
```

These variables may be appropriate to the use you wish to make of them, but if you wish to change their values the following lines may be placed in either /etc/profile or each user's .profile:

```
$ LANG=En_US
$ NLSPATH=/usr/lpp/msg/%L/%N:/usr/lpp/msg/En_US/%N
$ export LANG NLSPATH
```

The values of %L and %N are defined during AIX 3.x installation and are used to locate the current natural language being used.


## 14.3    Compiler configuration

The XL C compiler xlcentry uses a default configuration file found in /etc/xlc.cfg. This file determines default options for both the compiler and the linkage editor. The XL C compiler xlcentry has by default three symbolic links, to cc, xlc and c89. These links each have a stanza within the configuration file, and the default configuration for each link will be taken from this file. The user may create any number of symbolic links to xlcentry and then create stanzas for this link with the default configuration file.

A typical example of the structure of this configuration file is as follows:

- **standard C compiler**

```
xlc:    use         =    DEFLT
        crt         =    /lib/crt0.o
        mcrt        =    /lib/mcrt0.o
        gcrt        =    /lib/gcrt0.o
        libraries2  =    -lc
        proflibs    =    -lc_p
        options     =    -H512 -T512 -D_ANSI_C_SOURCE
```

- **standard C compiler aliased as cc**

```
cc:     use         =    DEFLT
        crt         =    /lib/crt0.o
        mcrt        =    /lib/mcrt0.o
        gcrt        =    /lib/gcrt0.o
        libraries2  =    -lc
        proflibs    =    -lc_p
        options     =    -H512 -T512 -qlanglvl=extended
```

- **standard C compiler aliased as** c89

| c89: | use | = | DEFLT |
|---|---|---|---|
| | crt | = | /lib/crt0.o |
| | mcrt | = | /lib/mcrt0.o |
| | gcrt | = | /lib/gcrt0.o |
| | libraries2 | = | -lc |
| | proflibs | = | -lc_p |
| | options | = | -H512 -T512 -D_ANSI_C_SOURCE |

- **common definitions**

| DEFLT: | xlc | = | /usr/lpp/xlc/bin/xlcentry |
|---|---|---|---|
| | as | = | /bin/as |
| | ld | = | /bin/ld |
| | options | = | -estart, -D_IBMR2, -D_AIX, -bhalt:4 |
| | ldopt | = | "b:o:e:u:R:H:Y:Z:L:T:A:V:k:j:" |

The options shown in the configuration file apply to each symbolic link to the XL C compiler xlcentry. A full list of options follows.

*Option*                                            *Description*

as

This defines the pathname used for the assembler. The default is /bin/as

asopt

List of options that if found on the command line are directed to the assembler and not the compiler. The options are specified in the getopt() format as shown in the ldopt found in the configuration file above. These flags overwrite all normal processing by xlcentry and are passed to as.

crt

The pathname of the C run-time object passed as the first parameter to the linkage editor. This parameter is the default if no -p or -pg options are found on the command line. The default is /lib/crt0.o.

csuffix

The default suffix used in C source programs. The default is c.

gcrt

Alternative C run-time object used if the -pg option is found on the command line. The default is /lib/gcrt0.o.

ld

Defines the pathname for the linkage editor. The default is /bin/ld.

ldopt

Similar to asopt, but these options are passed to the linkage editor (see example configuration file, Section 14.3).

libraries

Flags separated by commas that the XL C compiler passes as the last

| *Option* | *Description* |

parameters to the linkage editor. These parameters specify the parameters the linkage editor is to use for both profiling and non-profiling linkage. The defaults are -lrts and -lc.

libraries2

Similar to parameters specified in libraries, but each parameter specified in this stanza must have a profiled version existing in the stanza proflibs.

mcrt

Alternative C run-time object used if the -p option is found on the command line. The default is /lib/mcrt0.o.

options

Processes by the XL C compiler as if they were entered on the command line.

osuffix

The default suffix used for object files. The default is o.

proflibs

These parameters, separated by commas, specify profiled versions of the libraries specified in the stanza libraries2 to be used when profiling is required.

ssuffix

The default suffix used for assembler files. The default is s.

use

Use options values specified after the stanza name which follows. Any options separated by commas are added to the options specified in this stanza, options without commas apply only if no value for that stanza is specified locally in this stanza.

xlc

The pathname used to locate the XL C compiler. The default is /usr/lpp/xlc/bin/xlcentry.

xlcopt

These options are similar to ldopt and asopt but are directed to the XL C compiler only when seen on the command line.

## 14.4 Compiler options

Compiler options can change any of the XL C compilers default option settings, and these options may be specified in three ways:

- In the configuration file /etc/xlc.cfg.
- On the command line of the XL C compiler.
- In the source file itself with a special preprocessor option.

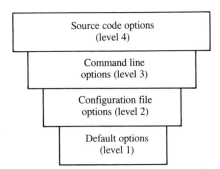

Figure 14.1. Order of precedence of configuration options of the XL C compiler.

If there are any conflicts between compiler options the compiler will resolve them using the rules shown in Fig. 14.1. Options present at higher levels within this block diagram will overwrite options at lower levels.

A detailed list of compiler options available for the XL C compiler follows.

### 14.4.1 *Language level*

This option specifies which of the four C language levels is used by the XL C compiler. The levels available are listed below.

*Language level*                        *Functionality*

`ansi`

Forces the compiler to conform to ANSI standard. This is the default option when the compiler is invoked using `xlc` or `c89`.

`saal2`

Forces the compiler to conform to IBM's SAA level 2 standard.

`saa`

Forces the compiler to conform to the current IBM SAA standard.

`extended`

Causes the compiler to provide backward compatibility with the RT compiler under AIX 2.x. This is the default level when the compiler is invoked using the `cc` command.

These options are used on the command line using the command

```
$ cc -qlanglvl=lang file.c
```

where `lang` is any one of the above four options or may be set within the source file using the preprocessor directive

```
#pragma langlvl=lang
```

where again `lang` is any of the above four options.

### 14.4.2 Configuration file specification

The default configuration file is /etc/xlc.cfg and the stanza to use with this file is defined by the name of the symbolic link used to invoke the XL C compiler xlcentry, either xlc, c89 or cc by default. Using the command line options as follows it is possible to invoke the XL C compiler giving it the full path of a configuration file to use instead of the default and the stanza to use for the compiler environment. For example,

```
$ cc -F/tmp/new.cfg:xxc file.c
```

will cause the cc compiler link to use the configuration file /tmp/new.cfg instead of /etc/xlc.cfg and to use the stanza xxc instead of cc by default.
    There is no source file definition for this option.

### 14.4.3 Include file directory path

This option specifies the include search path for include files used in C source programs. It may appear many times, and if so, the directories specified are searched in the order in which they appear. This option may be specified on the command line using the command

```
$ cc -I/tmp/include file.c
```

This -I option causes the compiler to search /tmp/include directories for include files, instead of the standard include directories.
    There is no source file definition for this option.

### 14.4.4 Character type sign convention

This option causes the compiler to treat variables defined as character type to be signed or unsigned. The default is unsigned for all character variables. On the command line the option used is

```
$ cc -qchars=signtype file.c
```

where `signtype` is either signed or unsigned. This option may also be specified within the source file using

```
#pragma options chars=signtype
```

where `signtype` is defined as above.

## 14.4.5  Code optimization

The code optimizer present in the compiler suite is activated only if this flag is present on the command line. There is no source file definition for this flag. It should however be noted that the use of this flag with the `-g` flag for the dbx symbolic debugger is not recommended as optimized code is not always directly attributable to the source code from which it was generated.

The flag is used as follows:

```
$ cc -O file.c
```

## 14.4.6  Literal storage allocation

The compiler can place literals found in C source code in either read-write or read-only storage. This option instructs the compiler to place literals in either read-only or read-write storage. The default is read-only.

This option may be specified on the command line or within the C source by two flags, which are defined as follows:

```
ro      Place literals in read-only storage.
noro    Place literals in read-write storage.
```

On the command line these may be specified as:

```
$ cc -qro file.c        /*place in read-only storage */
$ cc -qnoro file.c      /*place in read-write storage */
```

With the C source the directive

```
#pragma options storagetype
```

where `storagetype` is either of the flags defined above, has the same effect as the command line options.

## 14.4.7  Sub-routine in-lining

It is often more efficient for program execution speed to have the code generated by small sub-routines in-line, instead of generating branch calls to one copy of the code. This increases the size of an executable program, but may improve its execution speed.

This option may only be specified on the command line, and the default state is not to place sub-routines in-line. The only sub-routines that will be considered to be placed in-line with this option are those that generate less than 100 intermediate code instructions.

On the command line the option is specified as

```
$ cc -Q file.c
```

### 14.4.8 Floating-point rounding and evaluations

This option specifies the method used to round floating-point constants at compile time. The valid values are:

n     Round to nearest representable number.
m     Round towards minus infinity.
p     Round towards plus infinity.
z     Round towards zero.

The option may only be specified on the command line, and its default value is n. It is specified on the command line as follows:

```
$ cc -yroundm file.c
```

where roundm may be any of the values defined above.

Another option prevents floating-point optimizations that are incompatible with run-time rounding to plus and minus infinity modes. The default option norrm generates code which is compatible with run-time n and z. It is therefore necessary to specify this option if either the m or the n option is to be used in the option above, so that run-time and compile-time floating-point rounding is consistent.

The valid values are:

rrm

        Prevent optimization which is incompatible with run-time rounding to plus or minus infinity.

norrm

        Do not prevent the above optimization (default case).

The option may only be specified on the command line and is specified as follows:

```
cc -qoption  file.c
```

where option is either of the two options specified above.

Another option performs calculations on all single-precision floating-point expressions in double-precision and then rounds the results back to single-precision.

The default is to leave the result in double-precision format. This could result in faster code, however the final result may not adhere to the IEEE standard and it is therefore recommended to use this flag on code where this is a requirement. The flag may only be specified on the command line, and if absent will cause the default action to be taken. In order to adhere to the IEEE standard the following command line should be used:

```
$ cc -qrndsngl file.c
```

Another option specifies that constant floating-point expressions are not to be evaluated at compile-time. The default action is that they are. This option has two flags:

fold

        Evaluate floating-point expressions at compile-time (default).

nofold

        Do not evaluate floating-point expressions at compile-time.

This option may only be specified on the command line, as follows.

```
$ cc -qoption file.c
```

where option is either of the two options specified above.

    The floating-point option is concerned with the use of specific instructions. The special multiply–add instruction may or may not be used by the compiler if this option is present. This will affect the precision of floating-point intermediate results. The possible options are as follows:

nomaf

        Do not use the multiply–add instruction.

maf

        Use the multiply–add instruction (default case).

The option may be specified only on the command line, with the following command:

```
$ cc -qoption file.c
```

where option is either of the two options specified above.

    The floating-point option used to force the detection of overflow in rounding floating-point intermediate results to single-precision is as follows. The default value is that detection will not be made, and this option should always be used when the -qrndsngl is used.

    The option can only be specified on the command line and is specified as follows:

```
$ cc -qxflag=dd24 file.c
```

### 14.4.9 Debugger information

In order for the symbolic debugger dbx to be usable with code produced by the compiler, this option must be present on the command line during compilation. It should also be noted that the optimization option -O should not be used if the debug option is selected. Code produced using this option is also likely to be very much larger than code produced without it.

By default the option is not switched on, and no debug information is inserted into the code. In order to switch the debug information on, the following command line should be used. This option cannot be specified within the source code:

```
$ cc -g file.c
```

Another option used in conjunction with the dbx debugger is an option which causes the program to trap when a run-time exception occurs. This enables the debugger dbx to determine the cause of the exception. This option is specified on the command line as follows:

```
$ cc -qexcopt file.c
```

where the value of excopt can take either of the following options:

check
> Enable exception checking in object file.

nocheck
> Disable exception checking in object file. The default option.

### 14.4.10 Bind-time checking for modules

AIX 3.x and the XL C compiler provide a number of intermodule procedure calls and parameter checking. This option allows extra bind-time checking to be performed by inserting bind-time checking information into the object code.

This option is specified on the command line as follows:

```
$ cc -qbindoption file.c
```

where bindoption is either of the following:

extchk
> Enable extra bind-time checking to be performed.

noextchk
> No extra bind-time checking is to be performed. This is the default value.

This option may not be specified in the source code.

## 14.4.11  Preprocess and compile only

This option causes the compiler only to preprocess and compile the source files provided. The compiler will not pass the object files produced to the linker, as is its default action. Each file produced will be placed in files with the suffix .o for each file given with the suffix .c.

This option will be overridden by either of the options -E or -P and will in turn override the -o option.

An example of its usage is as follows. To generate object files for library generation with the ar command the following command line could be used:

```
$ cc -c module1.c module2.c module3.c
```

This will produce output files module1.o, module2.o and module3.o which may be used to produce a library using the ar command. It should be noted that without the -c option an executable file a.out would have been produced containing the linked code contained within the three modules. The production of this executable file might of course have failed due to unresolvable references within the object code.

## 14.4.12  Preprocess only

This option will cause the compiler to preprocess the source files and output the result to the current standard output device. No further action will take place. This option may be very useful for debugging as the expansion of macros by the preprocessor is often not as one might expect. This option will be specified on the command line and will override the -P, -c and -o options. The option is specified as follows:

```
$ cc -E file.c
```

Another option which causes the compiler only to preprocess the source files given is -P, but this option writes the output to a file with a suffix of .i for each file with a suffix of .c supplied on the command line. This option is overridden by the above -E option but in turn overrides the -c and -o options.

In both of the above cases comments found in the source files are not written to the output, but if the -C option is used in conjunction with either -E or -P then comments will be written to the output. The -C option must be used in conjunction with either -E or -P, it has no effect alone.

Examples of the usage of the above options are as follows:

```
$ cc -P file.c   /* preprocess to file.i */
$   cc -P -C file.c /* preprocess to file.i + comments */
$   cc -E -C file.c /* preprocess to STDOUT + comments */
```

### 14.4.13  Compiler listing production

The XL C compiler can produce a variety of helpful listings which may aid the debugging processes of a C program. The production of these listings is controlled by the following options. By default the option is not to suppress any listing that is specified, but no listings will be produced without being requested. The command line option to suppress all listings is

```
$ cc -qnoprint file.c
```

This option will suppress all listings that may be specified either on the same command line or within the source file itself.

The option to produce a compiler listing with source code during the compilation is as follows. The option may be specified within the source code and may act as a switch, in that it may be selectively turned on and off to generated source listing of selected sections of the code. This option is overridden by the option -qnoprint and the default is the option nosource which will produce no source listing.

The option is specified in the command line with the option:

```
cc -qsourceopt file.c
```

where the value of sourceopt may be either of the following:

source
      Produce source listing during compilation.
nosource
      Do not produce source listing during compilation.

Within the source file the option may be specified as follows:

```
#pragma options source /* switch on source listing */
#pragma options nosource /* switch off source listing */
```

The command line option that produces a compiler listing which includes a cross-reference listing is

```
$ cc -qxrefoption file.c
```

where xrefoption is one of the following:

xref
      Produce cross-reference report of identifiers used within the source program.

```
xref=full
```
Produce full cross-reference listing including all identifiers, with unused identifiers.
```
noxref
```
Produce no cross-reference listing. The default option.

The option to produce an attribute listing with the compiler listing is specified as follows on the command line:

```
$ cc -qattroption file.c
```

where `attroption` is any one of the following options:

```
attr
```
Produce attribute listing for used identifiers within the program.
```
attr=full
```
Produce attribute listing for all identifiers within the program including identifiers not used.
```
noattr
```
Produce no attribute listing. This is the default option.

The compiler option to produce a compiler listing which includes an object listing is specified on the command line as

```
$ cc -qcomoption file.c
```

where `comoption` is one of the following options:

```
list
```
Produce compiler listing including an object listing.
```
nolist
```
Do not produce compiler listing with object listing. This is the default option.

The compiler option, which includes a listing of all of the current options in effect within the compiler listing, is specified on the command line as

```
$ cc -qoptlist file.c
```

where `optlist` is any one of the following options:

```
listopt
```
Produce listing of all options in effect within the compiler listing.
```
nolistopt
```
Do not produce listing of options with compiler listing. This is the default option.

The compiler option to produce a compiler listing with compiler statistics included is specified on the command line as

```
cc -qstatopt file.c
```

where `statopt` is one of the following options:

`stat`
> Produce compiler listing that includes compiler statistics.

`nostat`
> Do not produce compiler listing that includes compiler statistics. This is the default option.

### 14.4.14  Compiler error reporting

Several command line options may be given to the XL C compiler to restrict its reporting of errors, both to the terminal and to the compiler listing file, if used. Errors encountered by the compiler may be classified into groups, each group being given a flag option which may be used with the compiler options. The groups are defined as follows:

| *Flag ID* | *Group* |
|---|---|
| I | |
| | Informational error. |
| W | |
| | Warning error. |
| E | |
| | Syntax error, etc. |
| S | |
| | Severe error. |
| U | |
| | Unrecoverable error. |

The first of the options which may be specified on the command line specifies the minimum level of error reporting produced by the compiler. The levels of error reporting produced on both the terminal and in the compiler listing can be controlled separately, and are specified using the command line option

```
$ cc -qflag=sev1:sev2
```

where `sev1` is the minimum level of error reporting given on the compiler listing and `sev2` is the minimum level of error reporting given on the terminal. Both `sev1` and `sev2` can take any one of the group ID flags specified above.

The default minimum error reporting level is -qflag=w:w, which specifies that warning errors and others are reported to the terminal and the listing file.

Another command line option specifies the error level at which the compiler should stop upon encountering an error of this severity and above. This option is specified on the command line as

```
$ cc -qhalt=serv file.c
```

where serv is any one of the group ID flags specified above. The default setting for this option is -qhalt=s, which specifies that the compiler should terminate upon encountering a severe error message.

There is another option which instructs the compiler to suppress reporting of warning messages. This option is specified using the command line option

```
cc -w file.c
```

This is the same as specifying the option -qflag=e:e; the default option is -qflag=w:w, so that warning errors are not suppressed by default.

## 14.4.15 *Compile-time debugging options*

Debugging of XL C programs is often done using the symbolic debugger dbx, but at compile-time certain options control how much debug information is reported. These options report only additional information with respect to the compilation.

The first option causes the compiler to report the time taken for the total compilation together with timings for each phase of the compilation. This option is specified on the command line as

```
$ cc -qtimeopt file.c
```

where timeopt is one of the following options:

phsinfo
> Enable reporting of times for both total compilation and each phase.

nophsinfo
> Disable reporting of times for compilation and each phase. This is the default option.

Another option will cause the compiler to enter verbose mode, in which it will output information on the progress of the compilation together with timing for phases and the command lines used for each phase of the compilation.

This option can be overridden by the option -#. The default option is no verbose output. To specify verbose output the command line option

```
$ cc -v file.c
```

is used. The final option is trace compilation, which displays all the command lines of all the compilation phases and options used on the linker command line if the cc command was issued with the options specified. The compilation does not take place as none of the phases or the linker are executed. This option overrides the -v option.

An example of the trace compilation is

```
cc -# -O -ophil -qlist phil.c
```

The -# option causes the compiler trace option to be activated, and the compilation options specified subsequently are then passed to the command lines of the subsequent phases of the compilation.

### 14.4.16 Execution profiling

Two profiling options are specified for use with the XL C compiler. These options provide execution profiling for object code produced with the options specified. They cause the linkage editor to link special versions of the library code to the executable code. These options are -p and -pg. The only difference is that the -pg option provides more information than the -p option. They are specified on the command line as follows:

```
$ cc -ophil -p phil.c
$ cc -ophil -pg phil.c
```

The default option is for no execution profiling to be done.

### 14.4.17 Preprocessor options

There are two command line preprocessor options, both of which may be used at the source code level. These two option allow the user to define and undefine macro values within the source code. At the source code level a macro value may be defined as

```
#define NAME value
```

where NAME is the identifier to be defined and value is the value to be assigned to it. If no value is assigned then a default value of 1 or TRUE is assigned. On the command line the same macro may be defined as

```
cc -DNAME=value file.c
```

This will cause the identifier NAME to be assigned the value of value before the compilation begins. Again the default value is 1 or TRUE if no value is given, as in

```
$ cc -DNAME file.c
```

In order to undefine an identifier with a source file the following option may be used at the source level:

```
#undef NAME
```

This will cause the value of NAME to be undefined from this line in the source onwards.

On the command line this is achieved with the command

```
$ cc -UNAME file.c
```

where the value of the identifier NAME will be undefined within the source file file.c.

## 14.4.18 Options passed to the linker

In order to specify the filename for the object file produced by the linkage editor, the following command line option is used. The default object filename used by the linker is a.out:

```
cc -oobjectname file.c
```

where objectname is the name of the file in which the object code is to be placed, for example above this may be the string 'file'.

This option may be overridden by one of the options -E, -P or -c, in which case no object file is produced.

During the linkage phase the linker ld searches for unresolved references in the standard libraries specified in the directory /lib, each of which has the naming convention /lib/libxxxx.a, where xxxx is the name of the library. In order to instruct the linkage editor to search a specific library for unresolved references, the following command line option should be specified:

```
cc -llibname -ofile file.c
```

where libname is the name of the library, such that libname is equal to xxxx of the full path /lib/libxxxx.a.

By default the linkage editor will only search the standard library directory /lib for library files specified using the -l option. However, the following option which may appear more than once on the command line specifies alternative directories which should be searched in an attempt to find the library file specified using the -l option. This option is specified as

```
$ cc -L/usr/lib -lfred -ofile file.c
```

This will cause the linkage editor to search both /lib and /usr/lib for the library file libfred.a.

# 15
# The linkage editor or binder

The linkage editor under AIX 3.x combines object files, import lists and libraries to form either executable files or a file which may in turn be used as a file parameter to `ld`. The `ld` (linkage editor or binder) under AIX 3.x is very different from the command of the same name found under other implementations of UNIX. The first major difference between AIX 3.x and other vendors' versions of UNIX is that the object format used under AIX 3.x is Extended Common Object File Format (XCOFF) instead of the usual COFF format used by most versions of UNIX. There is little difference between COFF and XCOFF, except that XCOFF has been extended to support dynamic load-time and run-time linking. This object file format difference is almost always transparent to the application and systems programmer.

Invoking the linker can be done via the `ld` command on the AIX command line or via the `cc` command during a compilation.

## 15.1   Flags and options

The object linker has a large number of flags which may be supplied on the command line and affect the behaviour of the linker. In this chapter we will look at some of the flags and options which affect the behaviour of the linkage editor. A number of flags may be specified on the command line of the linkage editor, but these are ignored for the moment. These flags are to be used for future expansion, and are therefore not discussed here.

The order in which flags are specified does not affect their function. Unless specifically stated in the text, specified flags that conflict with each other are processed from left to right by the `ld` command and the latest flag specified (i.e. the one on the far right) will take precedence.

Some flags may be specified with optional parameters, which may be entered with or without a space between them and the flag option.

Numeric values of parameters may be specified in one of the following: decimal, octal, or hexadecimal format. Octal has a leading zero and hexadecimal has a leading 0x or 0X, as defined in the C programming language.

Under AIX 3.x object files are created with reserved symbols listed below present with their symbol tables. C programmers must be careful not to use these symbols within their programs, because this will cause an error at linkage time.

| *Flag* | *Description* |
| --- | --- |

`_text`

A pointer to the first location of the program segment.

`_data`

A pointer to the first location of the data segment of the program.

`_etext`

A pointer to the first location above the program segment.

`_edata`

A pointer to the first location above the data segment.

`_end` and `end`

A pointer to the first location above all data including initialized and dynamic data.

`-D arg`

Makes the value of `arg` the starting address for the data segment. The value of `_data` is affected by this option. The default value for this option, if not specified, is for the `_data` segment to begin at location zero.

`-e label`

Makes `label` the entry point to the executable code in the output object file. The default label is `start`.

`-H arg`

Takes the value of `arg`, which is usually the output file block size, and using pad sections where necessary ensures that the `_test`, `_data` and `_loader` sections are aligned within the object file to the block size specified. This can have performance benefits for the final executable code. The default action is for no alignment to be done on any of the sections within the output file.

`-K`

`-z`

Cause the linker to pad all segments to lie on page boundaries. This may be used later with memory mapped files to permit demand paging. This can improve the efficiency of file access, although it may increase the size of the object file.

`-S arg`

Specifies the maximum size to which the user stack will be allowed to grow, in bytes. The value of `arg` specifies the number of bytes allowed and must be greater than zero. The default value for this option is the system limit.

`-T arg`

> Makes the value of `arg` the starting address for the text segment. The value of `_text` is affected by this option. The default value for this option if not specified is for the `_text` segment to begin at location zero.

`-l name`

> Provides addition libraries to be linked to the object file. These libraries will be located either in the standard directories which are `/lib` or `/usr/lib` or in a directory specified by the `-L` option. This option may be repeated as often as necessary. It should be noted that the linker does not have any left to right dependence which may be found using other linkers. The first definition of a symbol always takes precedence over any further definition. The order in which libraries are processed is as follows: first all standard libraries, then all files specified by the `-f` option, then finally the libraries specified by the `-l` option in the order which they are specified on the command line. The parameter `name` specified with the `-l` option will cause the linker to look for a library of the name `libname.a`.

`-L dirname`

> Provides the linker with additional directories to search for library files when linking object files. This option may be repeated as many times as is necessary. It also causes the linker to include the directory name `dirname` in the loader section of the object file, to make any libraries available for run-time dynamic linking.

`-M`

`-m`

> Causes the linker to produce a loadmap output file which contains a list of all files and object members that were used to create the output object file.

`-o outputname`

> Causes the linker to place the object output in the file with the name `outputname`. The default for this option is `a.out`.

`-r`

> Allows the linker to produce an output file which contains unresolved references. The default option is that the linker will not produce such a file. This file would then be included on the contain line of another linker call to resolve any unresolved references.

`-s`

> Causes the linker to strip all symbol table information from the output object file. It is the same as the utility strip. This produces object files which are generally smaller, but very difficult to debug using the debugging tools because no symbol information is present.

`-v`

> Causes the linker to provide additional diagnostic information. The default option is for the linker not to provide this information.

| *Flag* | *Description* |
|---|---|
| -x | |

Causes the linker to enter only external symbols in the object files symbol table. This option will save some space in the object file.

| -Q | |
|---|---|

Causes the linker to enter all symbols in the object symbol table and overrides the -x option. This is the default option.

**-Z prefix**

This option prefixes the directories searched by the linker during linking with the value of prefix. This prefix is applied to all libraries specified with the -l option. Thus if the option

```
ld -Z/rs600 -lusers
```

was specified then the libraries searched would be /rs600/lib/libusers.a and /rs6000/usr/lib/libusers.a and not the standard directories /usr/lib and /lib. This option is very useful for cross-compilation and the use of alternate standard libraries.

**-b options**

The linker has many binder options which are specified on the command line using the above option, which may be repeated many times. These options will affect the behaviour of the kernel binder when it loads the object file produced. Each of the following options is specified on the command line using -b option as above:

**asis**

The binder will treat all external symbols as mixed-case asis, so for example the symbol _Percent will be different from the symbol _percent. The binder will treat symbols as mixed case by default.

**autoimp**
**so**

Causes the binder to import symbols contained in shared objects at load-time or run-time and not to be statically bound to the output file. This is the default option for the binder.

**binder:pgm**

Gives the linker the full path of the binder. The default is /usr/lib/bind, but this option may specify a pathname for this program. For example

```
ld -bbinder:/usr/bin/newbind
```

would make the binder /usr/bin/newbind instead of the default /usr/lib/bind.

**bindcmds:file**

Causes the binder commands passed to the binder by ld to be written to the file called file. This file may be used as the command input for the binder so that the binder program may be run interactively for debugging purposes. The default option is that no file of these commands is produced.

`bindopts:file`

Causes the linker to write the command line options passed to the binder to the file called `file`. This file may be used to invoke the binder interactively for debugging purposes. The default option is for no file to be produced.

`calls:file`
`C:file`

Causes the binder to write a calls symbol cross-reference to the file called `file`. The default option is for no such file to be produced.

`caps`

Causes the binder to treat all external symbols in upper case, so that the symbols `_percent` and `_Percent` would be identical. The default option is `asis`, where these symbols are case sensitive.

`erok`

Allows the binder to produce an output file even if unresolved external symbols are still present. The default option is `ernotok`, which will not allow the binder to produce an object file with unresolved symbols in it.

`ernotok`
`f`

The binder will not produce an output file with unresolved external symbols present in it. This is the default action.

`errmsg`

The binder writes error messages to the standard error file, usually the terminal if the error code is greater than that specified by the `halt` option. This option overrides the `quiet` option. The default option is `noerrmsg`.

`noerrmsg`

The binder will not write error messages to the standard error file if the `quiet` option is set. This is the default action.

`glink:file`

Specifies the file containing the global linkage prototype code used by the binder to bind all imported external functions and data items. The default is `/lib/glink.o`.

`halt:errlevel`
`h:errlevel`

Specifies the maximum error level in the parameter `errlevel` that will be tolerated for binder processing to continue. If any

*Flag*                                    *Description*

binder command returns an error code greater than `errlevel` then binder processing terminates. The default value of `errlevel` is 2.

`loadmap:file`

`l:file`

>  Causes the binder to write the results of each command to the file called `file`. This may help debugging binder problems. The default action is that no file is produced.

`map:file`

`R:file`

>  Causes the binder to produce a symbol table and write it to the file called `file`. The default option is that no symbol table is produced.

`modtype:type`

`M:type`

>  This option sets both the module type field and the shared object flag within the output object file. In order to set the object type one of the following options may be set:

- `1L`   A single-use module which requires a private copy of its data section for each load. The default option.
- `RE`   A reusable module which requires a separate copy of the data section for each process dependent on the module.
- `RO`   A read-only module which requires one copy of the data section that may be used by many processes at once.

>  If any of the above options is prefixed by an `S`, then the shared flag will also be set within the object file.

`noautoimp`

`nso`

>  Causes the binder to bind all shared objects as part of the output object file. This is static binding of object code. The default option is `autoimp`.

`nobind`

>  Causes `ld` not to call the binder, thus no output file will be produced. The default is for `ld` to call the binder.

`noglink`

>  The binder will not insert global linkage code into the output object. The default option is `glink` to insert global linkage code.

`noloadmap`

`nl`

>  The binder will not produce a `loadmap` file. The default option.

`noquiet`

>  The binder will write the results of each command to the

standard output file. The default option is `quiet` where no results are written.

`quiet`

The binder will not write the results of each command to the standard output file. The default option.

`rename:Symname:Newname`

This causes the binder to rename the external symbol `Symname` to the new name `Newname`.

`typchk`

Causes the binder to do parameter type checking between external function calls. This check will be performed on all functions for which no parameter check information was provided by the compiler. The external parameter check between different languages is a key feature of the XL compiler series. This is the default action.

`notypchk`

The binder does not perform function parameter checking between external function calls.

`export:file`
`E:file`

The binder will export all symbols specified in the export file called `file`. See below for description of export file format.

`import:file`
`I:file`

The binder imports external symbols specified in the import file called `file`. See below for description of import file format.

## 15.2 Import and export files

The binder included in the XCOFF object files produces information for the kernel loader concerning the location of shared objects required for the successful execution of the executable code. This information is given to the binder at link-time, using one or two files.

In simple terms, any object file may export symbols to be used by any other object file. However, if these symbols are to be used then an *export file* must be produced, which defines which symbols are to be exported. This file is then used during the linking of the object file which is required to export these symbols.

For any object file which requires to import symbols, there must be an *import file* which defines which object file is exporting these symbols and which symbols the object file wishes to import.

Diagrammatically the relationship between the object file importing symbols, the object file exporting symbols and the import and export files is represented in Fig. 15.1.

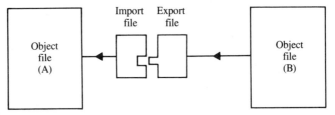

Figure 15.1. Import/export files and the lock and key to dynamic object linking.

---

The object file A has an associated import file which has defined in its contents the symbols which are required to be imported. The object file B defines a set of symbols which it will export. This export file may contain more symbols than object file A requires to import, but it is not a requirement for all symbols exported to be imported.

Within these two import/export files common symbols will be defined, and at load-time or run-time these symbols will be resolved by the kernel loader. The object file A will become the executable object and the object file B the shared object.

### 15.2.1 The structure of import/export files

Import and export files are text files which define the following:

- **Object path**   the full path of the object file or shared library object.
- **Object filename**   the filename of the shared object or library.
- **Object members**   the members of the shared object to which either the import or export is to take place.
- **Shared symbols**   the symbols within object members which will to required as either imports or exports.

An import file and an export file are very similar in structure, and the general structure of an import/export file is as follows:

```
*
* comments are ignored
*
#! path/filename (member)
symbol1
symbol2
symboln
```

There is one single special symbol, #!, which denotes the beginning of the definition of the import object path. All lines beginning with * are ignored as comments. The key difference between an import file and an export file is that with an export file the line that begins with #! is not required and should not be present. Thus an export file is only a list of exported symbols.

The import file is slightly more complicated, in that imported objects may be imported from shared object files or shared libraries and the syntax of the import file is slightly different for shared object file imports and shared library imports.

Both shared objects and shared libraries require at least a filename to be specified, to identify to the kernel loader which object file contains the symbols to be imported. The path is optional, but if included it should be absolute and not relative.

The member section is required only for shared library objects as these libraries may contain both shared and non-shared objects. The name of the shared object must be specified in the member set to uniquely identify any shared symbols. For example, consider the shared object `phil.obj` which contains the symbols `func1()`, `func2()` and `func3()` as a shared object file. An import file may look like this:

```
  #! phil.obj
func1
func2
func3
```

But consider what happens if this object file `phil.obj` is combined with `screen.obj` and `key.obj` into a shared library called `libutil.a` using the ar utility. Then the shared library import file will look like this:

```
  #! libutil.a (phil.obj)
func1
func2
func3
```

The member set identifying that the symbols will be found in the shared object `phil.obj` within the shared library `libutil.a`.

Chapter 8 of this book contains a discussion of the use of shared objects and libraries.

## 15.3   Linker usage

The linker is normally invoked by the cc command, relatively transparently to the user. However, there are times when invoking the linker from the command line is required. We now consider some simple examples of the use of the linker.

*Linking separate objects together to produce an output file*

This is the simplest use of the linker. An example is

```
$ ld -T512 -estart -lc /lib/crt0.o -opgm \
  pgm.o mod1.o mod2.o
```

This rather complex-looking command line links the object modules `pgm.o`, `mod1.o` and `mod2.o` together with any library support from the standard library `libc.a` (`-lc`) to form an output file `pgm`. The file `/lib/crt0.o` is the run-time support object used by all C object code.

The other options are relatively standard. The `-T512` option specifies that the text segment `_text` must start at location 512 and not zero which would be the default. The option `-estart` makes the label `start` the entry point to the text segment at location 512.

### *Linking different libraries with object code*

Normally only the libraries and object code specified on the linker command line are linked with the object code to form the output file. The standard libraries are located in the directories `/lib` and `/usr/lib`, so if the user wishes to specify an additional library or an additional library search path to be included it may be done as follows

```
$ ld -T512 -estart -lc /lib/crt0.o -lxlib \
    -L/usr/libs \
    -opgm pgm.o mod1.o mod2.o
```

The above link command would also generate an output file `pgm` using the objects `pgm.o`, `mod1.o` and `mod2.o` but would include the library `libxlib.a` and the library search path `/usr/libs`.

### *Generating shared objects with the linker*

Assume we have two object files, `mod1.o` and `mod2.o`, containing the symbols `func1`, `func2` and `func3` and we wish to make a reusable shared object file called `shared.o` which exports all of these symbols. Then we would need to generate an export file for `shared.o`, called for example, `shared.exp`, with the following contents:

```
* export file for shared.o
func1
func2
func3
```

Then using the linker we can generate `shared.o` as follows:

```
$ ld -T512 -H512 -bM:SRE -lc -bE:shared.exp \
    -o shared.o mod1.o mod2.o
```

The additional option `-H512` causes the linker to align the segments of 512 byte page boundaries. The option `-bM:SRE` defines a shared reusable object to be generated. The option `-bE:shared.exp` gives the binder the export file for exported objects from this shared object. This file is called `shared.exp`, and its contents are defined above.

### Linking a shared object to an object file

This is achieved using an import file. If for example we wish to link `shared.o` to a program object call `pgm.o` which imports the symbols `func1`, `func2` and `func3`, then we need an import file defined as follows:

```
  * import file for pgm.o from shared.o
*
* define object where symbols are located
*
#! shared.o
func1
func2
func3
```

This file may be called `pgm.imp`, for example; then the linker command line to link `shared.o` to `pgm.o` and produce an output file `pgm` would be

```
$ ld -T512 -H512 -lc -o pgm \
      -bI:pgm.imp pgm.o -L ":"
```

The `-L ":"` tells the linker to include the current directory in the library search path and the `-bI` option tells the binder the location of the import file which defines the symbols imported from the shared object `shared.o`.

# 16
# Library archive maintenance

Many modern programming languages allow the separate compilation of modules into separate object files, which may at some later time be combined by the linkage editor to produce an executable object.

The process of combining a large number of separately compiled object files into a single executable object is prone to errors, because often 20 or 30 objects may be required even for a simple program. The solution is to combine many related object modules into an archive, or library as it is commonly known, then to use the library as the source for the objects. Using this method significantly reduces the number of command line parameters that have to be passed to the linker, and thus the number of possible typing errors.

Under AIX 3.x, as with UNIX, the utility ar is used to maintain these archive files. The only difference under AIX 3.x is that the archive files may contain objects which are shared load-time or run-time linkable, as well as the normal statically linked objects.

The ar command provides the mechanism for creating and maintaining library archives. It has a number of command line options. The general form of an ar command line is

```
ar options [option parameters] library_name \
        object_name
```

All of the options must be specified together without spaces. An optional minus sign – may be placed at the beginning of the option list to maintain consistency with other utilities.

| *Options* | *Description* |
|---|---|
| s | |
| | Causes the ar command to regenerate the symbol table for the archive |

specified. For example, to regenerate the symbol table for the library
`xlib.a` the command `$ ar s xlib.a` could be used.

q

Causes the `ar` command to unconditionally add the `object_name` to the
`library_name` supplied. It will make no check to determine if the object
already exists within the library, and may even add the object to the
library more than once. For example, if we wish to add the object
`strings.o` to the library `str.a` then we can use the command

```
ar q str.a strings.o
```

d

Causes the `ar` command to remove the `object_name` from the library
named `library_name`. For example, if we wanted to remove `string.o`
from the library `str.a` we could do so with the command

```
$ ar d str.a strings.o
```

-r

Causes the `ar` command to replace the object specified on the command
line with the previous object of the same name already in the library
specified. This option may be used in conjunction with the u option,
which will cause `ar` to replace the object only if it has changed since the
archived object was placed into the library. For example, to replace
unconditionally the object `strings.o` in the library `str.a` the command
`$ ar -r str.a strings.o` could be used.

u

May be used in conjunction with the r option above and will cause `ar` to
replace the object in the archive only if it has changed since the object
already in the library was archived. For example, we may want to update
the library `str.a` with the object `strings.o` but only if the object
`strings.o` has changed. We could do this with the command

```
$ ar -ru str.a strings.o
```

If the named object is not already in the library the `ar` will add it to the
library, normally at the end. There are some positioning options which
will affect the positioning of the object within the library.

-m

Moves a named object from one position to another with the named
library. Normally it moves the named object to the end of the library, but
the positioning options if present will affect the new position of the
object. For example, if we want to ensure that the object `strings.o` is
positioned at the end of the library `str.a` then the following command
could be used:

*Options*                          *Description*

```
$ ar -m str.a string.o
```

This command assumes that the object does exist with the library specified.

a Pos_name

If used in conjunction with the m option this will cause the object specified to be moved to a position within the library after the position of the object named by `Pos_name`. For example, if we wish to ensure that the object `strings.o` in the library `str.a` is archived at a position after the object `key.o`, then the following command could be used:

```
$ ar -ma key.o str.a strings.o
```

This will cause ar to move the object `strings.o` to a position after `key.o` within the library `str.a`.

b Pos_name

i Pos_name

Similar to the a option but causes ar to position the object specified before the object specified by `Pos_name`.

o

Causes ar to sequentially order and remove any free space from the library file caused by the deletion or replacement of objects. This option will rebuild the library with all possible ordering and space saving. For example to rebuild the library `str.a` the following command could be used:

```
$ ar o str.a
```

l

Causes the ar command to use the current directory for any temporary files it may need to create instead of the default directory `/tmp`. An example of an ar command with this option is

```
$ ar lo str.a
```

This command will reorder the library `str.a` using the current directory for its temporary files.

t

Produces a table of contents for the `library_name` specified. If any `object_names` are specified then the table of contents will contain only those names, but without any `object_name` all objects within the library are included. The table of contents is output to standard output. An example of this command is

```
 $ ar t str.a
$ ar t str.a strings.o key.o
```

The two commands above will produce first a full table of contents of the library `str.a`, and second a table of contents showing only the objects `strings.o` and `key.o`.

**h**

Causes `ar` to modify the time/date stamp in the headers of the `object_names` specified within the library to the current time/date. This function is similar to the utility touch for object files and affect the `r` option. If no object names are specified, all objects within the library are assumed. An example of the use of this command is

```
$ ar h str.a string.o
$ ar h str.a
```

The first command will modify the header of the object `string.o` to be the current time/date. The second command will modify all objects within the library to have the current time/date.

**p**

Causes `ar` to output to standard output the contents of the object named from the library. If no object name is supplied, all objects within the library will be output. For example, to output the contents of `string.o` from the library `str.a` the following command would be used:

```
$ ar p str.a string.o > string.out
```

This will output the contents of the object `string.o` from the library `str.a` and redirect this output to a file called `string.out`. This process does not change the contents of the library.

**x**

Causes `ar` to extract into the current directory the objects specified from the library. The objects will be extracted into the same filenames as they were archived from. If no object name is specified, all objects will be extracted. This process does not change the contents of the library. For example, to extract the object `key.o` from the library `str.a` the following command could be used:

```
$ ar x str.a key.o
```

To extract all objects from the library `str.a` this command could be used:

```
$ ar x str.a
```

**w**

Causes the `ar` command to display the symbol table of the library specified. Each symbol is displayed with the name of the object in which the symbol is defined. For example, to display the symbol table for the library `str.a` the following command could be used:

```
$ ar w str.a
```

| *Options* | *Description* |
|---|---|
| c | |
| | Causes ar to suppress the normal messages that are generated whenever a library is created. |
| v | |
| | This verbose option will cause the ar command to output additional information to standard output during the course of certain commands. The commands affected by this option are t, x, h and the creation of a library archive. |

# 17
# The make utility

An applications or systems program developed under AIX 3.x and UNIX, will inevitably contain a large number of related modules. These modules are often contained in separately compiled objects and/or libraries. The procedure used to build the final application becomes more and more complex, as a direct result of the modular construction of the program itself. This procedure may involve several compilations and invocations of the linkage editor and the library archiver before the final executable object is obtained. It can become quite difficult to determine which modules and which parts of the overall procedure of construction have to be executed when only a single module changes.

AIX 3.x and UNIX provide a utility called make. This enables the program developer to control the construction of programs which may be built from many different modules, ensuring that the correct construction procedures are executed when a module is changed in order to rebuild an up-to-date version of the final target program.

The make utility alone does not provide a mechanism for total control of a software development project. This requires the use of another utility SCCS (Source Code Control system). However, in combination with other AIX utilities make provides an environment in which software development projects can be controlled.

## 17.1   What does make do?

The make utility is not intelligent, in that it needs to be told what modules are dependent on what other modules to produce the final target program, and what procedures are to be used to reconstruct each module. This information is supplied to the make utility within a description file which describes the following information:

- The target filename   This is the name used for the target output, which is produced from the dependency filenames and the rule sets or procedures specified.
- The dependent filename(s)   These filename(s) are used to construct the target filename using the set of procedures specified.
- Procedures or commands used for construction   These procedures are used to reconstruct the target filename from the list of dependent filenames.

In general terms these three pieces of information, which may be repeated many times, are the key elements of any description file, or *makefile* as it is often termed. However, make does allow three further types of information to be present within the description file:

- Macro definitions   The make utility allows macros to be defined and used within the description file. These macros may be quite complex and are often the source of great flexibility within the description file and the make utility's functionality.
- User-defined rules for the creation of target filenames   The make utility has a default set of standard rules which it uses to convert one type of object into another. For example, the make utility will know by default that to convert a C source file into an object file the use of the C compiler cc will be required. However, from time to time it is very useful and often mandatory for new rules to be added to this list. The make utility allows these to be added to the description file, together with the other information specified above.
- Comments   These may be placed in the make description file simply by making # the first character of the line. All characters up to a new line are then ignored by make.

The description file has a defined format and syntax that the make utility expects. The following entries may appear in a make description file in any order and with any frequency.

### A macro definition

A macro definition (Fig. 17.1) may be a null definition where the macro is not assigned. For example, to define the macro LIBS as having no value we could use the line

```
LIBS=
```

Alternatively, a macro may consist of any number in any combination of constant identifiers of references to previously defined macros. For example, to assign the macros LIBS the value of libc.a the line

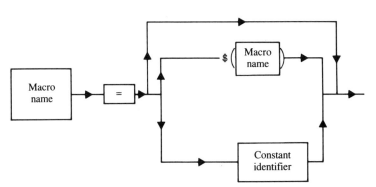

Figure 17.1. Make utility macro syntax.

---

```
LIBS=libc.a
```

could be used, which assigns the constant identifier `libc.a` to the macro `LIBS`. However, it is possible to assign a combination of macro references and constant identifiers to a macro. Consider the lines

```
LIBOPT= -lc
COMPOPT= -c
CCDEF   = $(COMPOPT) $(LIBOPT) -O
```

This would result in the definition of three macros, `LIBOPT`, `COMPOPT` and `CCDEF`. The value of `CCDEF` would be `-c -lc -O`, the values of the previously defined macros `COMPOPT` and `LIBOPT` being de-referenced using the `$()` operator to provide an identifier used in the new macro.

### General definition line

The general definition (Fig. 17.2) defines the dependencies between the target name and the list of dependent files which are used to construct the target. It also defines the procedures used to construct the target from the dependencies.

The simplest form of a general definition for the construction of a module is

```
pgm            :       pgm.o
                       cc -opgm pgm.o
pgm.o          :       pgm.c
                       cc-c pgm.c
```

These two rules are quite simple. The first one defines how to create the target `pgm` from the object `pgm.o` using the command `cc`, and the second one defines how to create the object file from the source file `pgm.c` using the command `cc`. Thus if the

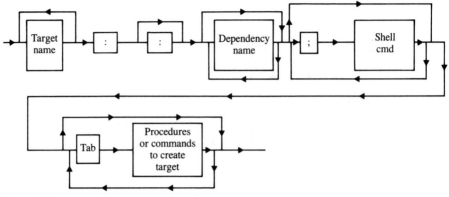

Figure 17.2. Make utility command line syntax.

source file pgm.c is changed both rules will be executed by make to regenerate the executable file pgm.

It is important to notice that each dependency file has a defined rule which allows make to construct it, if required. In certain cases this may not be appropriate, as with a header file; if these files are found to be missing by the make utility and no rule exists to create them, make will abort with an error message. Thus the following file would fail to create the pgm executable if the file pgm.o was not present, as the rule for creating the pgm.o object file is not defined:

```
pgm        :       pgm.o
                   cc -opgm pgm.o
```

The order in which these rules appear within the make file is important. They should appear so that the dependencies used in previous rules have the rules used to create them defined after their first use, as above when the rule to define pgm.o is defined after its use as a dependency in the rule line to define pgm. It should be noted that it is not necessary for all files used as dependencies to have rules enabling their creation to be defined, but in this case these files must exist for make to complete its function.

The example above is far too simple to illustrate the usefulness of the make utility. Its real advantage to the developer is realized when several separate source files are combined to generate one or more final objects. The example below shows the use of make to combine three C source files and three header files to make a final object:

```
pgm           :         pgm.o xlib.o ylib.o
                        cc -opgm pgm.o xlib.o ylib.o
pgm.o         :         pgm.c pgm.h
                          cc -c pgm.c
```

```
xlib.o        :        xlib.c xlib.h
                       cc -c xlib.c
ylib.o        :        ylib.c ylib.h
                       cc -c ylib.c
```

This makefile defines the rules and dependencies for the creation of three object files from three source files, these source files being also dependent on three header files. The final executable object is the combination of all three object files. It should be noted that the rules for the creation of the header files are not defined, although they are used as dependencies for the creation of each object. This means that if one or more of these files is not present the make utility will abort its operation with an error message, as it has no way of creating them. This situation is of course not true with any of the object files, as the rules used to create or re-create these are defined.

## 17.2    Macros and their use

As described above, with the makefile macros may be defined. These macros will often make the makefile easier to maintain and often more flexible. The simplest way in which a macro may be used is as follows:

```
COMPILER = cc
LOPTION = -o
COPTION = -c
  pgm                   :          pgm.o xlib.o ylib.o
                        $(COMPILER) $(LOPTION) pgm pgm.o xlib.o ylib.o
  pgm.o      :       pgm.c pgm.h
                     $(COMPILER) $(COPTION) pgm.c
  xlib.o     :       xlib.c xlib.h
                     $(COMPILER) $(COPTION) xlib.c
  ylib.o     :       ylib.c ylib.h
                     $(COMPILER) $(COPTION) ylib.c
```

The macro COMPILER defines the name of the program which will be used as the C compiler, and the two macros LOPTION and COPTION define the options used for linking the objects and for compiling the source respectively. In this very simple example changing any of these values is very simple. They need only be changed in one place within the source of the makefile, and this is analogous to the preprocessor directives for macros within the C language.

Macros are de-referenced by using $(macroname) or ${macroname}, which substitutes this string with the current value of the macroname. This macro substitution may be recursive, so the following definition is legal:

```
COMPILER = cc
COMMACRO = COMPILER
```

Then the expression

```
$( $(COMMACRO) )
```

has the value of cc. Conceptually the macro is expanded recursively using strict rules which ensure that all macros are expanded from the lowest level to the highest level. Thus to cause this macro expansion to produce the value of cc, first the macro $(COMMACRO) is expanded to its value of COMPILER, which then leaves the string $(COMPILER) to be expanded. This expansion takes place in the normal way, and the value of cc is produced. Macros may be nested in this way up to 10 levels deep, but in the author's view this level of nesting is difficult to debug and even more difficult to maintain. Nesting should be limited to a maximum of three levels, if possible.

Macros may be defined as shown above within the makefile, or alternatively on the command line of the make utility as follows:

```
$ make "COMPILER = xlc"
```

This will define the value of the macro COMPILER as xlc, but any definition present within the makefile source will be re-defined by this macro. It should be noticed that the double quotes are used by the AIX shell to enclose the string "COMPILER = xlc". This is so that the make utility receives the string as a single parameter and not as three separate parameters, which is what would happen without the quotes.

In addition to the user-defined macros the make utility has some useful internal or pre-defined macros which cannot be redefined by the user. These are as follows:

*Macro*                                *Functionality*

$@

Expanded to the name of the current target file. For example, this macro is used in the following makefile extract:

```
pgm        :        pgm.o
                    cc -o $@ pgm.o
```

The macro $@ is expanded to the current target name pgm, and used as the output filename given to the C compiler.

$$@

Expanded to the label name on the dependency line. For example, the following makefile uses this macro:

```
FILES = pgm xlib ylib
$(FILES) : $$@.c
            echo $@
```

This example uses macros to define the list of targets and the two internal macros to cause make to echo the filenames to the targets that are out of date. The macro $$@.c is expanded to pgm.c, xlib.x or ylib.c depending on which file is out of date. The value of $@ is the value of pgm, xlib or ylib which corresponds to the expanded macro value given by $$@.c, for example if $$@.c is pgm.c then $@ is pgm. This macro may also have an extension whereby $$(@F) is expanded to the file part only of the current target, which can be very useful if the targets are prefixed by a directory path.

$?

Expanded to the names of all of the files that have changed more recently than the current target file. An example of this would be the following makefile fragment:

```
FILES = pgm xlib ylib
$(FILES) : $$@.c
            cc $? -o $@
```

This example will cause all the executable programs pgm, xlib and ylib to be compiled if their source files pgm.c, xlib.c and ylib.c are out of date via the macro $$@.c. For each file the name of the file that has changed more recently than the current target will be generated via the macro $?, and this target name will be used as the final destination for the executable object via the macro $@.

$<

Expanded to the name of the dependency file that caused the target file to be re-generated by make. The following makefile fragment demonstrates the use of this macro:

```
pgm        :       pgm.c
                   cc -o pgm $<
```

This will replace the macro $< with pgm.c if the command line is executed by make. This macro may also have two further extensions which allow the use of the file part and/or the directory part of the dependency file which was used in the expansion. The macro $(<F) will expand to the file part only of the dependency file, and $(<D) will expand to the directory path only of the dependency file.

Consider the following extract from a makefile:

```
pgm        :       /usr/source/pgm.c
                   cc -o $(<D)/pgm $<
```

This will compile the source /usr/source/pgm.c into /usr/source/pgm. The macro $(<D) will expand to /usr/source,

which will be used in the creation of the output filename
/usr/source/pgm. The macro $< will expand to /usr/source/pgm.c.

$*

The name of the current dependency file without suffix, which may be
used in the following way:

```
pgm    :      /usr/source/pgm.c
              cc -o $* $<
```

The macro $* will expand to /usr/source/pgm and the macro $< will
expand to /usr/source/pgm.c. This macro can also make use of the D
and F extensions to obtain the directory path and filename respectively.
Thus the macro $(*D) is the directory path, and $(*F) is the filename
without extension.

$%

Will expand to the name of the archive library member specified in the
current target file. An example of its use is

```
xlib(phil.o) :      $%
                    ar uv xlib.a $%
phil.o       :      phil.c
                    cc -c -ophil phil.c
```

The macro $% will expand to the name phil.o which will cause the library
xlib.a to be updated by the ar command if phil.o is out of date. The
file phil.o will be created by the cc command from phil.c.

### 17.2.1 Macro assignments

Macros can be assigned values either during the definition of a macro or during its
evaluation. The method of assigning values to a macro during its definition has
been defined above, but it is often useful to change all or part of a macro during the
evaluation of the macro itself. This can be done using the general form

```
$(Macro_name:oldstring=newstring)
```

During the evaluation of this macro, the macro specified by macro_name is
searched for the occurrence of the string oldstring, which is then replaced with
the string defined by newstring. For example, consider

```
TARGETS = cmd.o xlib.o ylib.o
cmd      :          $(TARGETS:ylib.o=zlib.o)
              cc -ocmd $(TARGETS)
```

This example has quite an interesting side effect. The macro
$(TARGET:ylib.o=zlib.o) produces a macro for TARGET which has the value

cmd.o xlib.o zlib.o, thus making zlib.o a dependency for the file cmd. However, it is important to notice that this substitution is only done during the reading of the macro, and thus the command macro $(TARGETS) remains unchanged with the value cmd.o xlib.o ylib.o. This assignment to macros is effective for that evaluation of the macro only.

### 17.2.2 Predefined macros

The file /etc/make.cfg contains certain rules and predefined macros which may be used by the make utility. This file may contain many macros, but macros defined with the makefile source or on the command line of the make utility will redefine these macros, which may be useful from time to time. The most useful of them are listed below:

*Macro*                          *Functionality*

CC
     Defines the C compiler command used by default rules using $(CC).

AS
     Defines the assembler used by the rules using $(AS).

YACC
     Defines the yacc compiler used by the rules using $(YACC).

LEX
     Defines the lex utility used by the rules using $(LEX).

CFLAGS
     Defines the default flags sent to the $(CC) command.

YFLAGS
     Defines the default flags sent to the $(YACC) command.

LFLAGS
     Defines the default flags used by the $(LEX) command.

In order to change the default CFLAGS used by the C compiler the make command line may be used to redefine the macro CFLAGS and allow the default rule to create the target from the C source:

```
make "CFLAGS = -O" phil
```

This ensures that the optimizer is run on the object file produced from phil.c.

## 17.3    Rules and their definitions

As shown above, the make utility has a complex syntactic structure which defines targets, dependencies and the rules which allow targets to be constructed from a list of dependencies.

The syntax described above, although complex, is really quite easy to understand. In simple terms there are three parts to a definition within a makefile. They are the target, the dependency list and the rules which define how the dependencies shown are to create the target. A simple example is

```
pgm    :        pgm.c
                cc -opgm pgm.c
```

In this case the rule string cc -opgm pgm.c is executed only if the target pgm is out of date with the dependency pgm.c. This is a very simple rule, and several dependencies for any given target may be given by using the double : syntax described (see page 300). Then the rule for each dependency line will be executed if any of the dependencies are out of date with the target. In this case, however, dependencies may not appear in both dependency lines. Here is an example of a make file with two definitions for the same target:

```
pgm    :        pgm.c
                cc -opgm pgm.c
pgm           ::        pgm.h
                cc -opgm pgm.c
```

This will cause the target pgm to be constructed if either the file pgm.c or the file pgm.h is out of date with the target. This example is very simple, in that the result could have been achieved in a more basic way. However, the rules defined with each dependency's line need not be the same as they are in this case, and this gives great flexibility. As mentioned earlier, it is illegal to have the same dependency string in both definitions. Thus in this case pgm.c and pgm.h may appear only once within the dependency strings of the above definitions.

The rules defined for each makefile definition are usually defined within the makefile source. However, the make utility has several internal command rules which will assume that certain commands are required depending on the suffix applied to the target file. These rules are defined in a file called /etc/make.cfg and apply to several types of file that make may have defined within a makefile source. The standard suffixes that are defined are listed below.

*Suffix*                                    *File type*

.c

          C program source files

.a

          archive library file

.f

          FORTRAN source file

.h

          C header file

.l

> Lex source file

.o

> Object file

.s

> Assembler source file

.sh

> Shell command source

.y

> YACC-c source grammar

Each of these suffixes may be suffixed by a tilde (˜) to signify that the file of the type described above is an SCCS file containing this type of file. Thus a file with the suffix .c˜ is an SCCS file containing C source files. The user of the make utility may use these default rules to simplify the definition of a makefile; for example, the default rule for any target ending in .c is:

```
.c.o        :        $(CC) $((CFLAGS) -c $<
```

This definition uses the predefined macros CC and CFLAGS used in /etc/make.cfg to define the default C compiler and the flags used by that compiler. The definition above applies whenever no rule is defined. When the target ends in .o and the dependency ends in .c the macro $< is expanded to the full dependency name as described above. Thus the makefile with the definition

```
pgm.o        :        pgm.c
```

will be interpreted as the following definition by make:

```
pgm.o        :        pgm.c
                 $(CC) $(CFLAGS) -c $<
```

because the default rule for the conversion of .c file to .o files is defined in /etc/make.cfg as described above. Several of these default rules are defined for all the suffixes listed above. It is a good idea to examine /etc/make.cfg in order to ensure that you are aware of all of these rules before using make.

### 17.3.1 *Adding new default rules and suffixes*

The user of make may add new default rules or suffixes to the set described above. New default rules could of course be added to /etc/make.cfg, but this is not recommended because these files are often updated during operating system updates and thus changes made may be lost. It is far safer to insert any default rules and new suffixes required into the makefile source itself.

Consider how we would add a default rule to create target files with a suffix of .k from a dependency file with a suffix of .t using the C compiler. First we need to add the suffixes to the default list of recognized suffixes. This can be done using the fake target .SUFFIXES: with the makefile source. The order in which the suffixes are inserted into this list is important. They should be inserted in target dependency order from left to right, so in our case .k will be inserted before .t. The use of the .SUFFIXES: fake target should be carefully considered. Normally any use of this fake target will add additional suffixes to the standard list, but a .SUFFIXES: directive without a suffix list following will erase the complete suffix list, which may give your makefile a nasty shock. To add new suffixes to our standard list we can insert the following line in our makefile source:

```
.SUFFIXES:    .k .t
```

Note that we insert these suffixes in a defined order.

Next we have to define the default rule that will apply to the creation of a file with a .k suffix from a dependency with a .t suffix. By convention this is done by defining a definition line within the makefile source which has the dependency .t.k:; this states that when .k files are created from .t files this rule should be used.

We could use the following definition within our makefile source:

```
.t.k:
      $(CC)  $(CFLAGS) -c  $<
```

This will instruct the make utility to use the C compiler to compile files with the .t suffix from files with the .k suffix. Thus the final makefile we use may look like this:

```
.SUFFIXES:    .k .t
.t.k:
      $(CC)  $(CFLAGS) -c  $<
phil.k       :        phil.t
```

Then the file phil.t will be compiled using the rule specified above.

### Single-suffix rules

Certain file suffixes have default rules defined: they are .c, .sh and their associated .c¯ and .sh¯ suffixes. Thus the command

```
make phil
```

will try to locate phil.c or phil.sh and if such files exist will use the defined rules to create the targets.

*The default action to create a target*

If make cannot find a predefined rule and no rule exists within the makefile source which gives instructions of how to create a target, make will execute the set of rules defined after the fake target .DEFAULT:. Thus using this target you can define error recovery procedures with your makefile source. For example,

```
.DEFAULT:
        echo "Can't make target no rules"
```

will cause the shell command echo to echo the error message if this condition exists.

*Including text with a makefile source*

Within a makefile source you may include text from other files by including the following statement within the source text:

```
include   text_filename(s)
```

Thus to include the text of the file /usr/text/mydefs into a makefile source file, the following line would be inserted:

```
include   /usr/text/mydefs
```

It is advisable to use such a file within your makefile(s) to include your predefined rules and suffixes, rather than modifying /etc/make.cfg. The included text may be nested, but a maximum of 16 levels of nesting is supported by make.

*Fake targets used by make*

The make utility has a number of so-called fake targets used to change the configuration of the make utility. Some of these fake targets have been mentioned above, and a full list follows:

*Fake target*                          *Functionality*
.DEFAULT
        Defines the action of make. If no rules can be found for the creation of any
        target, make will search the current makefile and the default rule set
        before using these rules.
.IGNORE
        Instructs the make utility not to stop when an error occurs with a
        command rule executed from a makefile source. The default action is to
        abort with an error message.

*Fake target*             *Functionality*

.PRECIOUS
> Causes files specified on the same line to be preserved if `make` is interrupted. Under normal conditions these files will be removed.

.SILENT
> Causes `make` not to send the command strings it is executing to the STDOUT file handle. Usually, `make` echos all commands to STDOUT.

.SUFFIXES
> Used to add new suffixes to the standard list that `make` will recognize.

## 17.4   `make`: the environment

Using the `make` utility macros may be defined at several levels and in several places. Macros defined at higher levels redefine macros defined at lower levels.

- Level 0   The default rules defined in /etc/make.cfg are used at the lowest level. These rules and macros will define the standard list of suffixes recognized by `make` and the default rules used by `make` when processing files with these suffixes.
- Level 1   make examines the AIX environment in which it is running and will redefine certain macros depending on this environment. The three main environment variables used by `make` are listed below.

*Environment variable*        *Functionality*

MAKEFLAGS and MFLAGS
> These two variables may be used to specify command line options that will be used by `make`. Most command line options may be specified in this way, with the exception of the -p, -f and -d command line options. See command line options in Section 17.5.

MAKERULES
> This variable if set will redefine which file is used for the default rule set used by `make`. The standard file is /etc/make.cfg, but setting the value of this variable will cause the filename specified to become the default rule file.

MAKESHELL and SHELL
> This environment variable defines the AIX shell that will be used to process the `make` rules. The default value is /bin/sh.

- Level 2   At this level macros and rules will be read from the makefile source. These rules will be used to process the files specified with this source file.
- Level 3   This final level is the command line of the `make` utility itself. This will allow macros to be redefined as described above.

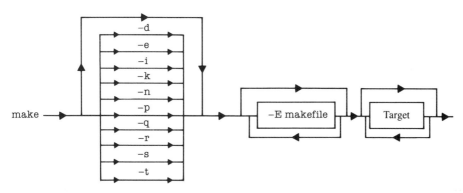

Figure 17.3. Make utility command line options syntax.

## 17.5   make: command line options

Under AIX 3.x the make utility may have the command line structure shown in Fig. 17.3. The flags in Fig. 17.3 may be specified on the command line of the make utility. Their meaning is described below.

*Flag*                                          *Meaning*

-d

Causes make to display additional information about the target and dependency file which it is using to re-generate targets. This information will be in the form of filename and modification times. This option is used to debug makefile source definitions.

-e

Causes make to allow definitions made in the AIX environment to redefine definitions made within the makefile source. This is contrary to the normal behaviour when environmental definitions are redefined by definitions with the makefile source.

-f makefile

Allows the definition of the makefile source name makefile that will be used to make the targets specificd within it. This option may be repeated several times on the command line, and in such cases each file is processed separately. If this option is not present then the current directory is searched for any file called makefile, Makefile, s.makefile or s.Makefile, and these are used as default files for the creation of targets.

-i

Causes make to continue to process the makefile source, even if a command rule returns a non-zero result. This non-zero result will normally cause make to abort the current makefile source with an error message. This flag is used to globally disable error processing within the makefile source, but for any single command rule line whose first

| *Flag* | *Meaning* |
|---|---|
| | character is a -, any error status returned from that single command will also be ignored by make. Thus there are two levels of error avoidance, the global level with the above option, or a rule level with the - character. |
| -k | Causes make to abort the processing to the current target file if an error occurs, but will continue to process all other targets that do not depend on the target that was aborted. |
| -n | Causes make to display but not execute all command rules that will be executed during the processing of the current makefile source. This is very useful for debugging makefile source files. Within any makefile source a pre-defined macro $(MAKE) may be used to recursively call a new copy of the make utility, so a makefile may contain another reference to the make utility and yet another makefile. Under these conditions the -n is also placed on the command line of the new copy of make so it will only execute the $(MAKE) macro as did its parent process. |
| -p | Causes make to display the complete set of target descriptions and macros defined before executing and command rules. This option is also very useful for debugging makefile sources. |
| -q | Causes make to return a value of zero if the target is up to date, and non-zero if the target is not up to date. This may be useful if the make utility is executed from a shell script. |
| -r | Causes make to ignore all the default rules and macros defined in /etc/make.cfg. In the file defined by MAKERULES it will use only macros and rules defined within the current makefile source. |
| -s | Causes make not to write any command rules to the STDOUT file before executing them. This is the same as the .SILENT fake target described above. This option again is a global option, and will cause all command rules to be effected. However, if a single command rule has a first character of @ then this rule will not be echoed to the STDOUT file before processing. This is similar to the way the -i and the - character options work as described above. At the command rule level the - and the @ may be combined using the character sequence @- which will force errors to be ignored and no echo of the command rule. |
| -t | Changes the modification date on all of the targets defined within the current makefile source. This is similar to the utility touch which also changes the modification dates of files. The command rules are not executed when this option is present. |

# Appendix: Exercises and questions

## A.1 The shell

### A.1.1 Exercises

1. Write a shell function for the Bourne shell or Korn shell which takes one or no parameters and changes directory to the directory specified or to the user $HOME directory if no parameter is specified. This function should also cause the shell prompt PS1 to become equal to the current directory, so that the shell prints the current working directory as a prompt. (Why can't this function be called cd? Why can't it be used in shell scripts that run in sub-shells?)

2. Write a shell script for all shells that allow the user to return to the current working directory at previous logout upon login.

3. Write a shell script to determine which shell you are running under and print its results to STDOUT.

4. Write a new shell in C using only the system calls fork(), wait() and exec(). This shell should allow commands to be executed in foreground and background. It should use the metacharacters % and ! in the same way as the * and ? within the Bourne shell, and should allow only DOS-style metacharacter expansion, with limited use of the % and ! metacharacters.

5. Write a shell script that will execute commands given on the command line but make a log of all output sent to the STDOUT file by any commands executed in a file call log.out. This script should also have a command line option -l filename; this option if present should specify the filename used by the log file, overriding the default log.out.

### A.1.2 Questions

1. Show how you would remove the following files using the rm command in the Korn shell, Bourne shell and C shell:

- `*?>aaa`
- `[gh]*<`
- `-rf *`

2. Explain the difference in the meaning of the character sequence |& in the Korn shell and C shell.

3. What is the effect on the user's current working directory of executing the following commands in the Bourne or Korn shells:

- `(cd \bin ; ls -1)`
- `cd \bin ; ls -1`

4. What is the difference between the -f options in the Bourne shell, Korn shell and C shells?

5. What is the effect of the command line option -e on the Bourne, Korn and C shells? What effect does executing the command `false` have, and why?

6. What are the differences between the command invocations $ ./script and $ ../script? Explain these differences in terms of the shell environment and processes involved.

7. What is wrong with the following Korn shell script ? (The script should accept a filename from the user.) A filename of * will cause the script to terminate, and to print for each filename the result of executing the command `ls -1 filename`. Explain all the mistakes found within the shell script, and rewrite it so that it functions correctly.

```
echo **********************
echo *                    *
echo *                    *
echo * Korn shell         *
echo * Example            *
echo **********************
while ( true )
  do
    echo "Enter Filename >> "
    read filename
    if [ $filename == * ]
      then
          break
    fi
    fileinf='ls -1 filename'
    echo $fileinf;
  done
```

## A.2    The system call interface

### A.2.1  Exercises

1. Write a library for binary tree management using the memory management system calls found in AIX 3.x. This library should allow any data type to be

stored within the nodes of the tree, and provide all of the functions required to define, add data, remove data, and search for data within the tree structure.
2. Extend the memory management functions described in Chapter 9 to include the following functionality:

(a) Extended error processing to allow identification of the function in which the error occurred. (Clue: additional parameters will be required of the command line for `malloc()`, `free()` etc.)

(b) Extend the `malloc()` and `free()` functions to allow memory block allocations to be allocated and freed by a group identifier, instead of the `FREE_ALL` or `FREE_THIS` directives. (Clue: this may require additional functions to define what the current allocation group is.)

3. Write a C program that will allow the library support to be bound to it at run-time to be defined. Show how this could be used to allow the implementation of library code to be changed at run-time for debug purposes. (Clue: use `load()` and `loadbind()` system calls.)
4. Using the memory allocation library defined in Part Two write the export files required to allow this library to be used as a shared library. Show what differences, if any, there would be in using the shared module types 1L, RE and RO in the construction of the shared library. Show the commands required to construct the shared library, and define an import file so that the functions may be used within a program.

## A2.2 Questions

1. Explain why the system calls `brk()` and `sbrk()` set and extend memory in fixed units which are often greater than the size of the memory block requested. Explain the significance of this for the memory management functions.
2. Explain why memory freed by the library function `free()` by one process may not always be available for use by another process.
3. Explain the significance of pointer alignment with respect to memory allocation. Using C examples, explain the use of the `sizeof()` function to define the size requirement of data types during dynamic memory allocations.
4. Explain how the library `libc.a` is implemented under AIX 3.x, given that it is a shared library which imports objects exported from the kernel.
5. AIX 3.x has a dynamically linked kernel, in that the kernel is linked at load-time. Discuss how this facility allows for kernel extension and sub-systems to be configured after system startup. Also discuss how this mechanism could be used to facilitate the construction of a 'pageable kernel' such as that found in AIX 3.x.
6. Discuss the advantages and disadvantages of load-time and run-time linking of objects. The discussion should compare and contrast the implementation

of other UNIX variants and AIX 3.x. What implications, if any, does this have for system resource requirements?

## A.3 Processes and communications

### A.3.1 Exercises

1. Write in C a generic interprocess message library with the functions, `m_init()`, `m_create()`, `m_open()`, `m_send()`, `m_receive()`, `m_close()` and `m_destroy()`, which provide the user interface for the library. These functions should initialize, create a message channel, open a message channel, send and receive messages, and close and destroy a message channel. These generic functions should be coded so that the library implementation can be defined as either shared memory, message queues or FIFO pipes. Write the code for the implementation of this library for each of the three interprocess communication primitives defined above. The definition of these functions should be the same for all three implementations.

2. Write a record-locking library using semaphores which will enable records in one or more files to be locked and unlocked as a single atomic operation. This library should allow the definition of exclusive locks and read locks. The exclusive lock excludes any other type of lock from being obtained while this lock is present. Read lock allows other read locks to be obtained, but not an exclusive lock. This library should have the functions `set_lock()`, `remove_lock()`, `test_lock()` which will respectively set, remove and return the type of lock currently in place. Discuss the problems this library may have with dead-locks, and discuss ways in which dead-locks may be avoided.

3. Show using code examples the use of signals within AIX 3.x, and explain why the `SIGKILL` signal may be ignored by certain system calls under certain circumstances.

### A.3.2 Questions

1. Explain the differences between a process and a program.
2. Explain in terms of memory management how shared memory segments are implemented under UNIX. Discuss the limitations of the use of shared memory for an interprocess communication mechanism.
3. Explain the difference between a named pipe and a regular pipe. Discuss relationships of device special files, device drivers and pipes.
4. Explain why the signal `SIGKILL` may seem to be ignored by a process under certain conditions. Explain what these conditions may be, and the significance of atomic system calls.

# Index